B E Y O N D
COUNTERFEIT
LEADERSHIP

HOW YOU CAN BECOME A MORE AUTHENTIC LEADER

Ken Shelton

Executive
Excellence
Publishing

Executive Excellence Publishing
1344 East 1120 South
Provo, UT 84606
phone: (801) 375-4060
fax: (801) 377-5960
web: http://www.eep.com

Ordering Information:
Individual Sales: Executive Excellence Publishing products are available through most bookstores. They can also be ordered direct from Executive Excellence at the address above.

Quantity sales: Executive Excellence Publishing products are available at special quantity discounts when purchased in bulk by corporations, associations, libraries, and others, or for college textbook/course adoptions. Please write to the address above or call Executive Excellence at 1-800-304-9782, ext. 104.

Orders for U.S. and Canadian trade bookstores and wholesalers: Executive Excellence Publishing books and audio tapes are available to the trade through LPC Group/Login Trade. Please contact LPC at 644 South Clark Street, Suite 2000; Chicago, IL 60605, or call 1-800-626-4330.

Also available on audio from Executive Excellence Publishing: ISBN 1-890009-21-0.

Library of Congress Cataloging-in-Publication Data

Shelton, Ken, 1947–
        Beyond counterfeit leadership: how you can become a more authentic leader
/ Ken Shelton.
                        p. cm.
            ISBN 1-890009-20-2: $22.95
            1. Leadership. 2. Performance. I. Title.
HD57.7.S48 1997   92-23472
658.4'097—dc20

First edition
First printing 1997
Printed in the United States of America
10 9 8 7 6 5 4 3 2 1   02   01   00   99   98   97

Cover design by Joe McGovern
Printed by Publishers Press

Praise for. . .

Beyond Counterfeit Leadership:
How You Can Become a More Authentic Leader

"Bravo! I'm convinced that *Beyond Counterfeit Leadership* will hit the bestseller lists."

> —Warren Bennis, author of
> *On Becoming a Leader*

"This insightful book will help you to be more effective in your work, life, and leadership."

> —Stephen R. Covey, author of
> *The Seven Habits of Highly*
> *Effective People*

"*Beyond Counterfeit Leadership* is wise, lively, and important. Reading Ken Shelton's memorable metaphors will save you from many mistakes. Most important, you will find a path to greater authenticity."

> —Gifford Pinchot, president of
> Pinchot & Company; author of
> *Intrepreneuring* and *The*
> *Intelligent Organization*

"*Beyond Counterfeit Leadership* is a prescription for world-class leadership. Shelton provides a brilliant and insightful view of the way organizations are run. He shows us that excellence isn't something you do. It's something you are. It's a state of mind."

> —Frank Sonnenberg, author of
> *Marketing with a Conscience*

"Ken Shelton makes perfect sense: You can't maintain success over time if you are counterfeit at the core. This book will help you get your leadership act together and become an original—and in that sense, second to none."

> —Charles Garfield, author of
> *Second to None* and *Peak Performers*

"In the 21st-century organization, we need, above all else, authentic leadership at all levels. *Beyond Counterfeit Leadership* addresses this challenge and provides a realistic road map for personal and organizational growth."

—Buck Rodgers, author of
Getting the Best Out of
Yourself and Others

"In a world of tabloid heroes and skin-deep virtues, Ken Shelton gives us laser-accurate core values and the absolute essence of authentic leadership. He gives us substance in place of style, fact in place of fallacy, and timeless wisdom instead of faddish notions. This is a guidebook for personal and professional integrity, the most significant issues of the decade."

—Denis Waitley, author of
The Psychology of Winning

"Counterfeit leaders are experts at waste. *Beyond Counterfeit Leadership* will help you reduce waste in your organization—the waste of time, resources, talent, and human lives. It will teach you and your people how to be creators instead of consumers, originals instead of copies."

—Hyrum W. Smith, chairman of
Franklin Covey Co., and
author of *10 Natural Laws of*
Successful Time and Life Management

"Basic and solid, yet creative and inspiring, *Beyond Counterfeit Leadership* strikes at the very heart of many of the needs in our society today. It identifies problems and offers solutions. Read it. Study it. You'll be glad you did.

—Zig Ziglar, chairman of The
Zig Ziglar Corporation; author of
See You at the Top

Acknowledgments

I am grateful to many authentic folks for their inspiring examples of superb stewardship and leadership.

In particular, I am grateful to the following:

To the contributing editors and writers of *Executive Excellence* magazine, who for the past twelve years have filled my mind with cogent ideas on management and leadership.

To Stephen R. Covey, a professor, client, friend, and mentor.

To my friends and former associates at Brigham Young University and the Marriott School of Management, two of our best hopes for needed reform in leadership development.

To European and American satirists and novelists—DeFoe, Dickens, Thackeray, Fielding, Poe, Cervantes, Menken, Twain.

To my colleagues, Richard Elton, Dan Bolz, Ginger M^CGovern, and Trent Price, for their generous gift of time and talent in producing the book.

To my friends at Executive Excellence Publishing for their encouragement and patience.

To my wife, Pam, and sons Andy, Adam, and Chris for allowing me to share time and life with them.

To all men and women who are thought to be "common" and yet do quality work and get worthy results in spite of counterfeit leadership. And to the authentic leaders who reform counterfeit systems and processes to improve the quality of life, and the quality of products and services, for millions of other people.

Contents

Foreword: Where Have All the Real Leaders Gone?
by Warren Bennis ....*ix*

Introduction: Close Encounters of the Counterfeit Kind 1

Step One: Emancipation: Free at Last 15
Chapter 1: Plantation Management: The Not-So-Civil War 17
Chapter 2: Shocks and Fresh Starts: The Scrooge Experience 27
Chapter 3: Real Freedom, True Identity: No More Tokens 37

Step Two: Emulation: Beauty and the Beast 45
Chapter 4: Imperfect Models: In Madonna We Lust..........................47
Chapter 5: Improved Models: Winning by Association 59
Chapter 6: Character Growth: From Night to Morning Light............73

Step Three: Enlightenment: Beyond Grades and Degrees......89
Chapter 7: Secular Education and Situational Ethics:
            In Fraud We Trust 91
Chapter 8: Moral Education and Absolute Values:
            Growing Leaders from Seed 101
Chapter 9: Authentic Wisdom: Solomon Brothers and Sisters 113

Step Four: Enterprise: The Entrepreneurial Spirit 123
Chapter 10: False Starts, Bad Habits: The Demise of Enterprise.......125
Chapter 11: More Work, Less Waste: Just Do It 135
Chapter 12: Abundant Wealth and Power:
            Free of Debt and Illicit Desires..149

Step Five: Empowerment: Power to Be and Do........................161
Chapter 13: False Followership: Pushing Power Up 163
Chapter 14: Life and Body Balance: On Beam, With Team 173
Chapter 15: Triple Crown: Quality, Relationships, and Results........187

Step Six: Environment: Creating Your Own Space 197
Chapter 16: Hierarchy and Bureaucracy: The Political Maze 199
Chapter 17: Cultural Alignment: Correcting System Errors..............211
Chapter 18: New Environments: Beauty, Safety, and Security 221

Postscript: 20-20 Hindsight: Who's the Leader of the Band? 239

Foreword
by Warren Bennis

Where Have All the Real Leaders Gone?

Over 200 years ago, when the nation's founders gathered in Philadelphia to write the Constitution, the United States had a population of only three million people, and yet six world-class leaders contributed to the making of that extraordinary document. Today, there are more than 240 million of us, and yet we would be hard pressed to find a dozen leaders in the same league as the founders. What happened?

One good answer can be found in this remarkable book: *Beyond Counterfeit Leadership*. As 18th century America was notable for its free-wheeling (but authentic) adventurers and entrepreneurs, and early 20th century America for its scientists and inventors, on the eve of the 21st century, America has become famous for its (counterfeit) bureaucrats, business managers, and celebrities.

What those Philadelphia geniuses created, and their rowdy successors built, counterfeit organization men in both government and business have remade, or unmade. Unlike either our nation's founders or industrial titans, the managers of America's giant corporations and the bureaucrats, elected and appointed, have no gut stake in the enterprise and no vision. More often than not, they're just hired guns, following the money. This new breed are as cool as their predecessors were hot, analytical rather than intuitive, and careful rather than careless. More often than not, these hired guns have no vision beyond the quarterly report.

America continues to bypass democracy in favor of government of, by, and for special interests. As bureaucrats and managers trade favors, a kind of stalemate develops. Nothing much grows in a stalemate, of course, but managers and bureaucrats are less gardeners than mechanics, fonder of tinkering with machinery than making things grow.

Meanwhile, the United States has lost its edge because, however skillful managers and bureaucrats are at holding actions, they have no talent at all for advancing. Thus, today, America no longer leads the world, and is itself leaderless.

What Is Leadership?

Leadership is all about innovating and initiating. Management is about copying and managing the status quo. Leadership is creative, adaptive, and agile. Leadership looks at the horizon, not just at the bottom line. A good manager does things right. A leader does the right things. Doing the right things implies a goal, a direction, an objective, a vision, a dream, a path, a reach. Managing is about efficiency. Leading is about effectiveness. Managing is about how. Leading is about what and why. Management is about systems, controls, procedures, policies, structure. Leadership is about trust and about people.

Joseph Campbell notes that a lot of people spend their lives climbing a ladder—and then they get to the top of the wrong wall. Most losing organizations are over-managed and under-led. Their managers accomplish the wrong things beautifully and efficiently. They climb the wrong wall.

Many of our citizens have come to see the United States as the biggest, most mindless, and clumsiest corporation of all. They can't find either its head or its heart. But, ignoring all the signals, along with their responsibilities, the managers and bureaucrats continue to flex their considerable muscle. White House underlings run covert actions in violation of the law, while corporate honchos gather their wagons in a circle in paranoid preparation for the ultimate shootout.

For all their brass, these new business kingpins are not leaders but merely bosses. Like the dinosaurs, though they may tower over their surroundings, they are not necessarily equipped for survival. These bosses confuse quantity with quality and substitute ambition for imagination. Much like Washington's tin soldiers and sunshine patriots, they do not understand the world as it is.

Like the big old American car, America seems too big and too awkward to work very well, much less respond quickly and wisely to events. Like its big corporations, the nation seems devoted to outmoded methods and ideas that were not very good to start with and seems unwilling or unable to change direction, or even to recognize that its foreign and domestic policies are not only outdated but dangerously insufficient.

Once upon a time, we all wanted to be Lindbergh or DiMaggio or Astaire, because they were the best at what they did; now we just want to be rich and powerful. Far too often now, our idols are all smoke and mirrors, sound and fury, signifying nothing. But these "phantoms" do not rise unassisted—our need, as much as their greed, catapults them into the spotlight's golden glare.

The longer I study effective leaders, the more I am persuaded of the under-appreciated importance of followers. What makes a good follower? The single most important characteristic may well be a willingness to tell the truth. In a world of growing complexity, leaders are increasingly dependent on their subordinates for good information, whether the leaders want to hear it or not. Followers who tell the truth, and leaders who listen to it, are an unbeatable combination. It is the good follower's obligation to share his or her best counsel with the person in charge. Silence, not dissent, is the one answer that leaders should refuse to accept. The follower who is willing to speak out shows precisely the kind of initiative that leadership is made of.

CorpKings and McHeroes

Our need for true leaders goes unspoken, but it manifests itself in pathetic ways as—in our idolatry of show business stars, our admiration for corporate kings, our instant elevation of McHeroes, and the popularity of instant leadership courses.

The courses demonstrate our confusion about what constitutes leadership. Some claim it derives automatically from power. Others say it's mere mechanics. Some say that leaders are born, while others argue that they can be made, instantly. Pop in Mr. or Ms. Average, and out pops another McLeader in 60 seconds.

Billions of dollars are spent annually by and on would-be leaders, yet we have no leaders, and though many corporations now offer leadership courses to their more promising employees, corporate America has lost its lead in the world market. In fact, more leaders have been made by accident, circumstances, and sheer will than have been made by all the leadership courses. What makes a person a leader? Some would say it's charisma, and you either have it or you don't. Many leaders, however, couldn't be described as particularly charismatic but nevertheless manage to inspire an enviable trust and loyalty among their followers. Through their abilities to get people on their side, they make changes in the culture of their organization and make their visions of the future real. When I ask them how do they do it, they talk to me about human values: empathy, trust, mutual respect—and courage.

The founding fathers based the Constitution on the assumption that there was such a thing as public virtue. At the moment, not only do we not agree on what the public good is, we show no inclination to pursue it. Instead, people are retreating into their electronic castles, working at home and communicating with the world via computers; screening their calls on answering machines, ordering in movies for their VCRs, food for their microwave ovens, and trainers for their bodies; and keeping the world at bay with advanced security systems. Trend spotters call this phenomenon "cocooning," but it might more accurately be described as terminal egocentricity.

For the moment, anyway, we don't seem to want leaders. In these mean, greedy times, we seem to prefer co-conspirators, and that is exactly what we have in the White House, the boardrooms, even the classrooms. There is, then, no doubt that we could do better but considerable doubt as to whether we want to, and so we are destined to drift on dreamlessly, secure in our cocoons of self-interest.

Why have we not had any true leaders in the White House in a generation? Why are there no potential presidents who inspire or even excite us? Where have all the leaders gone?

In the last two decades, there has been a high turnover, an appalling mortality both occupational and actuarial among leaders. The shelf life of college presidents and CEOs has been markedly reduced. Corporate chieftains' days at the top seem to be numbered from the moment they take office. The great business leaders of the past—Ford, Edison, Rockefeller, Morgan, Schwab, Sloan, Kettering — are long gone. Our corporate heads are either organization men who have risen to the level of their incompetence, or one-man bands who devote at least as much time and energy to blowing their own horns as to business. The most celebrated businessmen now are those who spend their days demolishing rather than creating companies.

One reason why many executives *seem* so out of touch with the real world is that they *are* out of touch—insulated by position, money, and circumstance from what really goes on inside the organization. Our leaders must reacquaint themselves with the world, must explore in the presence of others, must reach out and touch the people they presume to lead, and must, occasionally at least, risk making a mistake rather than doing nothing. In the meantime, they will continue to sound as if they were talking through a plate-glass window—distant, isolated, removed from the complex lives of living people.

In this very material world, the prevailing ethic is at best pragmatic and at worst downright cannibalistic, as corporations eat each other's flesh and sell off the muscle and bones. There's no such thing as the common good or the public interest. There's only self-interest.

The Rise of Counterfeit Leadership

As Shelton points out in this book, many would-be authentic leaders are out there pleading, trotting, temporizing, putting out fires, trying to avoid too much heat. They're peering at a landscape of bottom lines. They're money changers lost in a narrow orbit. They resign. They burn out. They decide not to run or serve. They're organizational Houdinis, surrounded by sharks or shackled in a water cage, always managing to escape, miraculously, to make more money via their escape clauses than they made in several years of work. They motivate people through fear, by following trends or by posing as advocates of "reality," which they cynically make up as they go along. They are leading characters in the dreamless society, given now almost exclusively to solo turns.

Thus, precisely at the time when the trust and credibility of our alleged leaders are at an all-time low and when potential leaders feel most inhibited in exercising their gifts, we need authentic leaders—because, of course, as the quality of leaders declines, the quantity of problems escalates. As a person cannot function without a brain, a society cannot function without leaders. And so the decline goes on.

Nevertheless, I am an optimist. Otherwise, I would not have spent my life striving to find ways for us to use ourselves better and more fully. Each of us is, in a sense, a miser who has vast resources that he or she hoards rather than spends. Our best qualities are integrity, dedication, magnanimity, humility, openness and creativity. As Ken Shelton shows in this book, these are the basic ingredients of leadership, and if we are willing to tap these qualities in ourselves, we may put a dent in the shortage of authentic leaders.

Introduction

Close Encounters of the Counterfeit Kind

Have you ever encountered a counterfeit? No doubt you have in such mediums as art, money, photography, antiques, gems, jewelry, fashion, fabrics, metals, etc. Originals are rare; copies everywhere.

In this book, I apply the word "counterfeit" to matters of character and culture. And I take a broad view of "leadership," believing that while segmentation of roles and styles may be helpful, fragmentation hurts both leaders and followers. Leaders tend to think of their lives in terms of discrete compartments, and followers tend to get only bit parts and sound bites. Where context and perspective end, fanaticism begins.

Using this metaphor of counterfeit leadership, I hope to help you see more clearly what might be considered counterfeit about your own life and your leadership of others—and then to suggest some ways to move along the continuum toward more authentic styles of living and leading. Please understand my bias: that authentic leadership of self, of personal relationships, and of family units is as important as leadership of business and government organizations—and that those domains are not mutually exclusive.

I try to avoid finger-pointing and name-calling; in fact, in the final draft, I deleted many names. In recent years, we have all read and seen enough documentaries depicting the follies and failures of leaders. My objective here is rugged introspection on both a personal and corporate level, followed by transformation—a conversion from counterfeit ways of thinking and behaving that inevitably waste and alienate to authentic ways of living and working that build and beautify.

Painful Personal Encounters

Beyond reading news stories about people in leadership positions who are "found out" for some covert activity, have you ever experienced pain and loss first-hand from encounters with counterfeit leaders? Have

1

you, for example, ever met an impersonator, impressionist, or impostor? A fraud, fake, or forger? One who is more caricature than character? Have you ever invested in such a person and felt cheated, victimized, or disillusioned?

The tales are all too common. Even in polite society, the "who's who" has become synonymous with "most wanted," in some cases, dead or alive. Find a list of the "best and worst" in any community and you find a spectrum, a continuum of counterfeit, ranging from rather innocent imitation to pathologic and criminal action. Perhaps you can relate to one or more of the following cases.

• *Boss.* You apply for employment with a company and are interviewed by a recruiter who presents a very positive picture. You fly in to meet the boss and see for yourself. You want to be open and positive. You accept an offer, even though you have mixed feelings. You believe the business to be above-board. You believe the products and services to be worthwhile and valuable. But once inside the organization, you find a Mr. Hyde in Dr. Jekyll: You find much that is objectionable about your boss and the company. You may even learn that you've been fed a few lies.

• *Teacher.* You enroll in a reputable university and pay expensive tuition and board, only to register for classes taught by absentee professors, graduate assistants, and dead-wood faculty. Even the more popular teachers are often providers of entertainment and easy grades, more actors than academicians. You wonder about the worth of your education and diploma. You become cynical and seek the fastest way out, willingly sacrificing learning for marketable grades and degrees.

• *Politician.* You vote for a man who says all the right things, hits all your political hot buttons, looks good, and seems to have the support of many high-profile people in the community. After the honeymoon year in office, you find him to be out of touch with the constituency, enmeshed in the political world, writing bad checks, cavorting with patrons, and looking ahead to his next step.

• *Minister.* You enjoy his Sunday sermons, but with each passing week, you become more and more disillusioned with your pastor because he doesn't walk his talk or look after the flock. He's passive and distant, removed from reality, pontificating platitudes and telling sentimental stories for emotional effect. You stop confiding in him, and start to see him as a curious sort of welfare recipient.

• *Musician.* You enjoy her love songs and dance tunes and seek to emulate her life. But over time, you find that her private life leaves much to be desired. At first, you dismiss the bad news as tabloid nonsense, but the evidence adds up. The image is shattered. You look for a new star to follow.

• *Actor.* The television roles and movie scripts make this popular leading man out to be a macho hero, but up close and personal, you find him shallow and insecure. You wonder if there are any "real men" anymore. You learn that few "leading men" are manly leaders; many, in fact, are manic followers.

• *Business executive.* From a distance, you perceive him to be all powerful. For years, you are fed a steady diet of propaganda about your corporate leadership, as public relations pumps out reams of press releases, white papers, speeches, and positioning statements. Over time, you learn that much of the material that appears under his signature he never sees, let alone says; his speeches are products of hired talent; and the closer you get, the more you find major discrepancies between policy or principle and practice.

• *Friend.* You're close in proximity and personality. You confide in each other, sharing openly the most intimate and confidential matters of your life with trust and love. But then you discover that your precious words are now being played against you and spoken in derision by others who hear them second hand out of context. You feel betrayed.

As we deal in real time with real people, we are influenced by the externals—personality, voice, face, figure, gesture, clothing, and speech. Counterfeit leaders can be very persuasive. Many pass themselves off as real leaders worthy of followers because they are on the screen, on the field, in print, or on the platform. Because they have visibility, we often imbue them with credibility—but those are very different concepts.

The Detection Dilemma

Whenever something is highly prized, whether it be gold coin or genuine leadership, we can expect to see masterful counterfeits. Real leadership is often hard to detect, even harder to reward once recognized, because of rules and biases built into social, academic and professional systems. Hence, we are short on leadership, long on counterfeits. Our coffers are filled with fool's gold (pyrite), and our offices filled with gilded fools (pirates).

Professional counterfeit is an art, and the artful imitation has the look and feel of the original. To the eye, even the educated eye, it may even appear to be identical. And to the child or the uninitiated, the cheap imitation not only has the same look but the same worth as the genuine article. In fact, to the child, the cheap imitation may be even more valuable because it is affordable, available, and accessible. But alas, children soon learn what is and what is not legal tender, what trades over the candy counter.

Buyer, Beware. Part of the maturation process is to pass through close encounters with the counterfeit kind, judging for ourselves who is who and what is what, and then associating with the kind and sort we're most comfortable with. But from cradle to grave, it's "buyer beware."

Indeed, along the newly paved "information highway," we see fewer familiar warning signs and symbols. Where visibility means credibility, hitchhikers have the same status as licensed drivers. And anyone with a late-model personal computer—with fax, modem, CD-ROM, and a data base—can speed into the market or into a "low barrier to entry" profession and capture share within minutes.

The merchant's old trick is to put the best fruit on display at the top, the bruised at the bottom. The new tricks take on sordid new twists. And the new targets—children.

We sing anew to children, "Beware: If you go out in the woods today, you better not go alone." Many classic children's songs and stories try to teach children, even warn them, that appearances can be deceiving and that people and things are not always what they seem. The worst villains are those who try to deceive the innocent for their own gain.

- The grandmother (wolf) in *Little Red Riding Hood*
- The wicked queen in *Snow White and the Seven Dwarfs*
- The selfish stepmother and sisters in *Cinderella*
- The puppeteer and his cronies in *Pinocchio*

None of us makes it through childhood unscathed. We are deceived, disillusioned, wounded, and perhaps even abused. No wonder that several authors and lecturers are finding such a big audience for their message about reclaiming and nurturing the "inner child" in adults.

Missing in all this, however, is the idea of the "inner adult" in children—of being wise beyond our years, not only from reading the classic "wisdom literature" but also from following the wisdom of the heart and the whispers of the conscience.

What's Real and Right?

Since media depictions of "real life," both at work and at home, revel in the sordid, and since the "new morality" has all the relativity of the market, many are left wondering what's real, what's right, and where's the truth.

The discontinuity between the real and the ideal, between who we are and how we act at one point in time and who we are and how we act at another point in time, is confusing, both to ourselves and to others. The real (the here and the now) loses all extended meaning, and the ideal (what may be) becomes an impossible dream.

We are all enticed to exchange genuine articles for cheap substitutes, or to trade what's real for what's not. In fact, *not* has become the favorite cryptic comeback of today's young people—a one-word sum, a catch-all criticism. The questions of the day are, "Who and what is genuine, original, and authentic? Who and what is worth believing in? And who is not?"

Often, *not* wins over anything affirmative because it's easier to berate than create. Denial is easier than belief. But as Cervantes' character Don Quixote says, facing his hostile jurors in *Man of La Mancha*, "I never had the courage to believe in nothing." Wanting to believe in someone or something, we sometimes grasp at straws. At grocery counters, we may throw out a good head of lettuce to afford the tabloid nonsense about the rich and famous. What do we see nonstop in tabloids and on TV? Ads and episodes on the "good life" of sun, fun, and fashion. Many models and mentors flash before our eyes.

For example, on one episode of *Lifestyles of the Rich and Famous*, a certain TV game show host was featured. The man had been an actor early in his career, and although now in his forties he was still a bachelor, living alone in his Hollywood mansion with his toys and pets, well-insulated in his self-made cocoon. One scene showed him at his wardrobe with an array of hats, and in rapid sequence, he put on and took off different hats.

For me, this was a poignant picture of a man who could wear any hat and play any role. Shakespeare's Hamlet covets the ability of the actor who could read a couple of lines of script and then, on cue, go and cry his eyes out, or laugh, or assume any emotion or face. In his comedies, Shakespeare often deals with being taken by appearances. He uses game playing and mistaken identity to titillate audiences and to comment on the masquerading he saw in Elizabethan England. Masks, actual facial coverings, were common: Ladies rarely went to social events with their faces exposed. Masks became a way of life.

Of course, we see the same masquerading in today's society, from the stage to the executive suite. On the streets and in offices, we see many masks of arrogance, conceit, and aloofness. People who hide behind screens, roles, and pretenses—hiding honest feelings and trying to make things go along smoothly—risk losing themselves behind a curtain of social politeness. And yet, the person is always more impressive, likable, and interesting than the mask. When we drop the mask and respond as we honestly think and feel, we experience greater personal health and improved interaction with others. In several of his plays, Shakespeare's central message is this: Behind masks, we make mistakes—and only when we are honest and open are we redeemed from our follies. When we remove the disguise, all ends well.

Substitutes are not the real thing, and yet we often buy them, exchanging girls and boys for goodies and toys; family, fidelity, and fulfillment for fashion, fame, and fornication. As "freshmen" in the college of life, we may succumb to the sweet seductions of appearance and imitation. We may bed with some strange fellows out of naivete. We may go like lambs to certain slaughters.

But after an encounter or two, we ought to spot a trend, have the eyes to see certain signs, certain things coming, before we experience them. However, our very goodness, at times, makes us open and trusting, vulnerable to deceit and treachery. So even as adults in the business world of buy and sell, we may mistake coins and currency, credentials and character; we may fail to reward the legitimate and then learn to live with sham, fraud, forgery, deceit; with fakes, impostors, impressionists, impersonators, and third-generation copies of genuine and original folks and works.

The great literature of the world teaches us the value of being true to self from an early age. In Aesop's fable, *The Man, the Boy and the Donkey,* we see what can happen when we try too hard to do what other people think we should, rather than what we think is right for us: we walk while the donkey rides.

We are all susceptible to the donkey syndrome. When one area or aspect of our lives or of our organizations is more or less legitimate, all other areas then borrow credibility from the *Bank of Strength* (our strong points). So, on the counterfeit continuum, we may be highly legitimate in one area, highly counterfeit in another. For example, our research and development may be above reproach, and yet our marketing and administration may border on make-believe. But on the whole, we pass for legitimate on the strength of one shining department, division, or individual talent.

When we borrow from our *Bank of Strength*, we often do so to imbue the counterfeit areas with legitimacy and to try to pass for authentic in all areas. In certain aspects of our lives or business, however, we may be very counterfeit. And when our faults, failures, weaknesses or incompetencies are found and ferreted out, we tend to be defensive. If we are ever exposed as a fraud, fake, imposter, pretender, or criminal, our loved ones are typically "stunned" or "shocked," and quick to come to our defense because they know us to be legitimate and lovable in other roles.

If in some areas of our lives and leadership we are very legitimate, we tend to think all aspects and activities of our lives are legitimate—and resent any feedback to the contrary.

And yet, we may be based on a solid foundation in a profession only because it imposes a certain discipline on us, meaning we must abide by certain rules and regulations, checks and balances within the system. But once outside that system or specialty, we may register counterfeit to a high degree.

High costs. Even on a personal level, when we make mistakes in judgment, the costs can be incredibly high. On a corporate level, the costs of counterfeit leadership simply boggle the mind; worse, they ruin lives. Maybe you know what I mean. Several notable news stories document the costs every day.

• *In industry,* a captain who is a problem drinker spills thousands of gallons of oil into a pristine bay, causing billions of dollars in damages. The clean up, both in public relations and the natural environment, can't erase the black mark.

• *In the military,* defense secrets are passed out by agents and others who betray national trusts in return for personal favors.

• *In business,* executives are caught lying, cheating, and stealing in white-collar crimes that impact an entire department, division, or corporation and waste billions of dollars.

• *In religion,* we read of leaders who are exposed for fraud, embezzlement, and quackery. The costs, counted either in lost contributions or in lost faith, are enormous.

• *In education,* we not only hear of violations and sordid crimes in athletic departments, too numerous to count, but also in presidents' offices. Imagine the total cost in terms of lost credibility and revenue to those universities.

• *In government,* deceit, waste, and double-dealing cost taxpayers millions of dollars a day—the sums in every branch are staggering.

• *In small and family-owned business,* examples are legend of partners (even spouses) cheating each other and becoming bitter enemies over a piece of the action.

• *In families,* when parents or teens tip into counterfeit ways, the incredibly high costs are usually borne by women and children who are left in a disadvantaged position.

One reason counterfeiting is so popular is because it can be very rewarding in the short term, especially with a catch-and-release "justice" system. The near-term costs of honest behavior are well documented, making the ethical choice very tough, especially when the long-term payoff or advantage seems remote at best.

Counterfeit Continuum

Counterfeiting is most often about subtleties, gray areas, whispers, shadows, nuances, and noise. And because of duality in people, differences can be hard to detect. We are all composites, not 100 percent counterfeit or authentic. We are both originals and copies—nurtured from seed and made from scratch in some areas, and influenced by imitation, comparison, or competition in others.

Having elements of both counterfeit and authentic, we are somewhere on the continuum—from saint to serial killer. We each have strengths and access to truth, but we also have weaknesses and blind spots. And so difficult judgments and choices must be made daily—not between obvious good and evil, but between people, policies, products, and processes—all reputable to some degree.

There are at least two sides to every person. Seen from different perspectives, we are all polygons. In any given person, one might see pride, arrogance, indifference, aloofness, doubt. And in the same person, others might see just the opposite: humility, compassion, charity, civility, belief.

One reason is that we see counterfeit by degree—a continuum of counterfeit. One of the greatest obstacles to progress is the thought that we have already arrived. Objective assessment will show that much refining work remains to be done—that many degrees lie beyond the Ph.D. And yet we tend to talk only in extremes and dichotomies—of hell and heaven or of black and white, forgetting that life is color, and an entire scale of gray.

For example, I see six degrees of counterfeit along a continuum, reading from right to left.

Incapacitation	Imitation	Ignorance	Indolence	Irresponsibility	Insecurity

• *Insecurity.* At the root of counterfeit leadership is a core insecurity. Many a sin starts with insecurity, resulting from a lack of self-identity and unconditional love.

• *Irresponsibility.* Insecurity leads to inconsistency and irresponsibility: inflated expectations and promises fizzle into deflated delivery and performance.

• *Indolence.* Bad habits take over the body and affect judgment and initiative. Without movement and challenge, the body and mind become obese, damaging self-esteem.

• *Ignorance.* Our graduations, rather than being commencements of learning and inquisitive living, may signal the end of an intelligence era and the beginning of an ignorance era in life.

• *Imitation.* As counterfeit leadership takes hold, we see less innovation and more imitation—more attempts to be like something or somebody else.

• *Incapacitation.* A tragic consequence of counterfeit leadership is the incapacitation of people and organizations. People may actually lose capacities once considered strengths.

As we regress along the counterfeit continuum, we may try to cover up tell-tale signs—the nicotine stain on the index finger, as the Music Man, Harold Hill, himself a huckster, was telling the town of River City. Soon, as he said, we'll be trying out "tailor-mades like nicotine fiends and bragging all about how we're going to cover up a tell-tale breath with sen-sen." And that spells trouble in any home, business, or community.

Authentic Continuum

The following six "steps" toward authenticity typically represent stages—not short hops, skips, and jumps through hoops.

Emancipation	Emulation	Enlightenment	Enterprise	Empowerment	Environment

- *Emancipation.* We can't make much progress when we are hobbled by controlling, limiting, and addicting forces, habits, or relationships. And so the first step toward authentic leadership is emancipation from the "plantation," the proverbial time and place of enslavement, entrapment, dependency, or addiction.
- *Emulation.* Following authentic models and mentors leads to character growth. Following flawed models leads to the development of manipulative personality traits and tactics.
- *Enlightenment.* Enlightenment, learning that leads to wisdom and life balance, is possible at any age, even in youth. But an education short on absolute values and long on moral relativity may darken the desired outcome.
- *Enterprise.* Honest and wise enterprise leads to real earning power and potential, whereas work-avoidance and false followership result in an enormous waste of resources.
- *Empowerment.* Becoming ever-more empowered and effective in our work leads to the triple-crown outcome of quality, results, and relationships.
- *Environment.* Creating or enhancing our immediate environment leads to greater safety and security.

When the two continuums are juxtaposed, we more clearly see the sharp contrasts between the regress of counterfeit and the progress of authentic leadership.

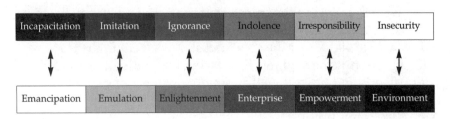

Leadership Cycle

Each of the six sections in this book represents one progressive step in the *cycle* toward more authentic leadership.

Each section begins with an introduction, followed by chapters discussing a cause, cure, and desired outcome. I suggest that the root *causes* of counterfeit leadership lie mostly within ourselves, although we can also pin plenty of blame on bad systems.

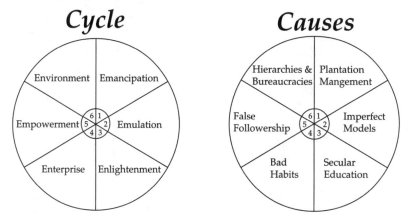

Because the causes of counterfeit may be well entrenched in our lives and systems, the *cures* for counterfeit require deep personal commitment—and may require professional treatment. The target *outcomes* of authentic leaders represent the core desires of all of us. They are the delicious fruits that grow naturally from the character and culture roots of authentic leadership.

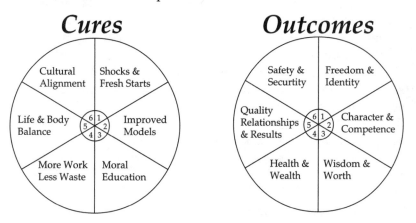

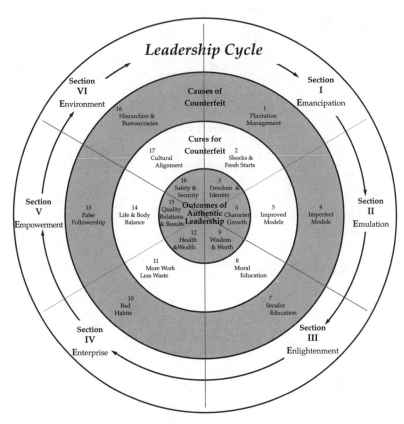

The leadership *cycle* can start at any step and go in either direction, toward a greater degree of counterfeit or toward a greater degree of authentic behavior. The direction affects both individual character and organizational culture.

Unless we consciously reject all forms of counterfeit leadership, we will likely embrace counterfeit to some degree. And beyond rejecting counterfeit behaviors through abstinence or passive resistance, to be authentic leaders we must wage war on the bogus elements in ourselves, our organizations, and our societies.

I like the C.S. Lewis line: "*It is a serious thing to live in a society of possible gods and goddesses, to remember that the dullest and most uninteresting person you talk to may one day be a creature which you would be strongly tempted to worship, or else a horror and a corruption such as you now meet, if at all, only in a nightmare. All day long we are, in some degree, helping each other to one or the other of these destinations. It is in the light of these overwhelming possibilities, it is with the awe and circumspection proper to them, that we should conduct all our dealings with one another. There are no ordinary people. You have never talked to a mere mortal. Nations, cultures, arts, civilizations—these are mortal, and their life is to ours as the life of a gnat. But it is immortals whom we joke with, work with, marry, snub and exploit—immortal horrors or everlasting splendors."*

The two ends of the continuum, and all points in between, are intimated in this paragraph. Long ago, I committed it to memory. I recite it to myself periodically in remembrance of the potential of those whom I am tempted to condemn.

Authentic leadership is worth following—and believing in—if and when we find it. It is something nurtured from within, from research and development, from seed and soil, mind and muscle, vision and action. It is made from scratch, from the mixing of elements. It is an act of creativity, an extension of the best self into form and function.

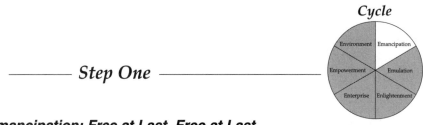

——————— *Step One* ———————

Emancipation: Free at Last, Free at Last

The curse of counterfeit leadership is the subtle, and not-so-subtle, subjugation of people and human rights. In Chapter 1, I explore a primary cause, plantation management; in Chapter 2, the cure, shocks and fresh starts; and in Chapter 3, the outcome, new freedom and true identity.

These are very basic elements of the counterfeit equation. Consider this:

1) If we are stuck on some plantation—no matter what our position might be—we can't make much progress toward becoming an authentic leader. We may not even enjoy the "rights" and "freedoms" of convicts in prison. The plantation, incidentally, may be a condition, place, or mindset of our own design and making.

2) Unless we receive a few shocks, we may never get a fresh start. We may forever be "locked in" to a self-defeating relationship, lifestyle, job, or a way of thinking and acting. And what defeats us as individuals ultimately works against the people, organizations, and causes we associate with.

3) Without finding real freedom and true identity, we will flounder in new ventures. We may be set free from "prison" only to commit the same mistakes and crimes and be sent again to some other jail (a familiar pattern in the penal system).

Emancipation, then, is the first step toward authentic leadership— emancipation not only from the plantation-like organizations of our lives, but also from our own self-made cells and self-defeating behaviors.

I place heavy emphasis on starting with self. Otherwise, once off one plantation, we will likely just join another. To "make ends meet," some people will justify any and all means. But a repeated pattern of "rational lies" makes a sad life story for any person, family, or corporation.

——— *Chapter 1* ———

Plantation Management: The Not-So-Civil War

"When those cotton balls get rotten, you can't pick very much cotton . . . down in those old cotton fields back home."

—Song Lyric

Counterfeit leadership—of self and of organizations—makes slaves of us all. In a sense, whenever we lose our freedoms or become addicted, controlled, or abused, we move back to the "plantation," a time of servitude or place of entrapment.

Of course, counterfeit leaders would want it no other way. Counterfeit leadership breeds plantation management, meaning the employment of people and the management of assets solely for the economic benefit of the owners. Authentic leaders liberate people from various forms of exploitation and ignorance. And enlightened self-leadership seeks emancipation from self-defeating habits, relationships, contracts, and controls.

Many leaders unwittingly inherit or help create and sustain plantation systems. On corporate plantations, life can be sweet for those on the right side of the invisible white-picket fence. Even in the heat of the day, the agenda for white-collar executives may call for sipping lemonade on the veranda, while blue-collar workers are kept in the cotton fields and held to quotas.

Emancipation is both one of the first steps toward and sweetest fruits of authentic leadership. Perhaps only those who have once been confined to a plantation can fully appreciate what many folks in the organization take for granted: physical mobility, rewarding visibility, mainstream credibility, meaningful participation, real involvement, and basic social freedoms.

Historical Perspective

For the first 100 years of American history, plantations were one of the primary forms of corporations, mostly located in the southern states and commonly associated with slavery.

The Civil War and the Emancipation Proclamation ended slavery and virtually ended the plantation era, although for many Americans, plantation management has continued uninterrupted.

The premise of plantation management is that the owner's office, plant, estate, factory, farm, or field needs low-cost labor to produce goods, deliver services, and harvest crops at acceptable profit margins. The plantation needs loyal, enlightened, or endowed management to keep labor in line, at work. The modern organization typically operates as a plantation when ownership is either located off-site (absentee) or seen as a privileged class (aristocracy). The plantation manager may be a dominant sort who hails from a more "progressive" area, or may be a benevolent owner who has a long list of personal and family needs that must be satisfied before any other individual employee is liberated.

Plantation managers tend to see local workers as indentured servants—natives who are born to pick their cotton. These folks are basically seen as expendable, exploitable, anonymous. They have no full name, no family identity, because they are not real people. Therefore, the logic goes, management can rightfully treat them unfairly and claim most monetary returns on their work.

While plantation style management may draft noble mission statements for public view, their real "constitution" and "bill of rights" are rarly set in type or spoken aloud—rather these are set in minds and whispered behind closed doors.

Constitution of the Counterfeit Corporation

Preamble

We, the principals of the Corporation, in order to form a more perfect organization for ourselves, to establish a form of frontier justice, to ensure our own tranquility, to provide for our common defense lawyers, to promote the welfare of a few privileged junior executives, and to secure the blessings of liberty from poverty, mess, and manual labor for favored family members and tenured faculty, do establish this constitution.

Bill of Ten Rights (or Wrongs)

1. Freedom from religion, beliefs, values, ethics, and principles. We, the principals, become the law, the great society, and the ultimate authority.

2. *Freedom from creative thinking and constructive writing. We can hire writers, editors, agents, and lawyers to do that for us. We will deliver the orations and "author" the books, claiming all materials as original to us.*

3. *Freedom from meaningful free and open assembly. We want senseless meetings and mindless, faceless, nameless crowds, so that people easily lose their individual identity and become more tractable and excitable.*

4. *Right to bear arms for self-protection and self-promotion. In fact, covert arms deals are permissible to promote our private causes and interests. Arms shall also refer to any and all psychological artillery and social and political weaponry.*

5. *Right to search desks without reason, to arrest initiative without warrant, to silence whistle-blowers, to censor critics and free thinkers, and to kill all messengers of bad news.*

6. *Right to a "fair" trial or performance appraisal. Of course, "fair" will be defined by management, and the good old boys will conduct rubber-stamp appraisals of each others' performance and biased assessments of the performance of all others.*

7. *Right to misrepresent our internal opponents and external enemies in pertinent meetings. We hereby condone dog-piling on rabbits and rebels who are not in attendance.*

8. *Right to share all rewards, spoils, compensations, monies, and goodies simply by virtue of being a member of the management fraternity.*

9. *Right to take pride in the work of others, also the right to claim it as our own, even put our name on it.*

10. *Right to retain outside interests, special agents, and covert relationships, including private counselors, secret admirers, expensive habits, and illicit affairs.*

Management-Labor Disputes

Of course such "constitutions" and "rights" cause a few management-labor disputes. Typically, plantation workers are the talent—the hands, arms, backs, and feet—of the organization. They sweat and toil in the "labor" of their profession, producing the product or service that management then markets.

Modern plantation management involves the subjugation of people through more subtle means than slavery, but the end result is about the same. People *feel* like slaves: they feel trapped, owned, victimized, and enslaved. Creativity and innovation wilt with prolonged exposure to plantation management. The net effect of plantation management, aside from possible high profits, is low morale, with all the attendant management-labor disputes.

These age-old disputes arise from two different perspectives. Management sees itself as benevolent providers of jobs and wages for workers who, without management, would be adrift and penniless. Therefore, all that labor is, has, or hopes to be belongs to enlightened management. Any gain or progress, any comfort or convenience, is due to management.

For the most part, plantation management views labor, including professional labor, as dispensable, disposable, tradable commodities. While plantation managers may become attached to a particular worker because of the worker's unusual strength, talent, beauty, or yield, they don't allow these personal attachments to get in the way of business (money) decisions. Even highly paid professional athletes, endowed with free agency, may not be real "free agents."

In worst cases, laborers are seen as so many cotton pickers, as commodities or assets, as things, not people. Labor has but one-syllable first names; and rather than bother to learn these, owners often refer to labor collectively by one common name. Labor, even highly educated professionals who occupy key performance positions in the organization, have little right to exercise individual judgment even within the narrow confines of their job descriptions. They are to follow orders, or at least prescribed methods.

Plantation managers religiously keep certain things from the people they employ: travel (mobility), visibility, professional credibility, money, resources, possessions, property, sacrosanct business relationships, human rights, freedom, knowledge, opportunity, education—except as these rights and "privileges" relate directly to their specific tasks or jobs (and even then, they are administered or controlled by management). When labor receives any such "perks," they are expected to pay homage to management.

Plantation managers keep these things from labor out of fear of losing control. These managers fear that some among labor, if endowed with any of these advantages, might prove contrary, start a revolution, oppose the party line, or, heaven forbid, become accepted, upwardly mobile, and move into mainstream society.

Fear drives all counterfeit systems, and counterfeit leaders fear independent talent most because they can't control or predict it. At best, they can only contract with it and hope it works for them.

Many a promising talent has been taken aside by an immediate supervisor and told: "If you will just do your thing well for us and go with the management flow, we will reward you richly. We dispense all special favors and privileges—and you might as well get your fair share." The between-the-lines implication, of course, is "shape up or ship out."

Today, plantation management is practiced widely throughout the world, not confined, as it once was, to any one geographic area or to any one race, minority, or ethnic group. The modern "slave" may be not only white-collar and white-faced but found working at any level of the corporation or company, including the executive ranks. Still, corporate cotton picking is primarily the work of women, minorities, youth, local- and third-world labor.

Plantations come in various sizes, ranging from entire corporations to small, privately held, family-owned companies. Plantations may exist within otherwise progressive organizations. They may be found in government, business, industry, religion—and in divisions, departments, or groups within organizations.

Plantation Conditions

How does plantation management get hold? The creation of the corporation along plantation lines fosters capitalist expansion by putting the money in the hands of a few owners while freeing its users from personal guilt about the consequences. New technology, for example, makes it possible for plantation managers to consume massive amounts of natural resources, spurring further expansion.

Political and economic institutions of immense power exploit people on an unprecedented scale by promising them money, by using the coercive force of government, and by using the military to anchor their power. They may swing deals where outsiders can't prevail at reasonable cost. Anyone who has worked several years for a major corporation in a position of strategic importance knows something of political "power plays."

The dangerous idea that some people are born or educated to lead creates conditions ripe for plantations. When we assume that some folks are born to lead and others are born to follow, we encourage the plantation syndrome. Who are these "born-to-lead" people who have leadership in their genes and who are endowed as if by birthright with all rights, privileges, power, and authority? Some are third-generation elitists who marry and breed according to social etiquette and calendars. Who conferred upon them these magical powers? Was it done by common consent or self-appointment?

Self-appointed leaders become dangerous as they develop planta- tions, often in third-world or economically depressed areas, where there are abundant pools of cheap labor and natural resources. They probably won't call their laborers "cotton pickers," but whether these workers are free or enslaved, they typically are slaves to the plantation owner- ship and management. The exploitation of local talent is commonly disguised by a lofty mission statement or noble quest. And often it is a fairly thinly disguised, self-aggrandizing mission of the landowner. In other words, "People, if you continue to labor and sacrifice, someday all of this will be. . . mine" (as if that were a motivating mission for the folks who work the hot fields and dark mines of the plantation).

Plantations will continue as long as people are willing to sell themselves too cheaply or surrender themselves too quickly and com- pletely to management's causes and objectives. Local workers rarely have a global perspective on the value of their work—they only know what it sells for that day in the local market. And so they fail to see the real worth and potential of their talent and enterprise.

Other conditions leading to the practice of plantation management and counterfeit leadership include: management-labor dichotomies and clear divisions between workers and managers, performers and super- visors; the absence of a career track for talented laborers and working professionals; command-and-control management practices; power centered in a few people at the top who operate without strong checks and balances; the poverty, ignorance, dependence, low self-esteem and pressing needs of workers; charismatic managers who thirst for publicity, notoriety, fame, glory, and wealth; supporting cast members and taskmasters who covet a piece of the action; and governments, regimes, constitutions, and missions that operate on false values, principles, and assumptions.

Crossing Lines

Plantation management invites the drawing of lines and, eventually, the crossing of lines. For the most part, in an advanced society, these lines are invisible; nevertheless, they can be impenetrable. These lines draw subtle distinctions among people and territories. Like the River Jordan, the lines can separate the wilderness from the promised land. Many a hard-working Moses has been stopped short of ever seeing a land of milk and honey.

In attempts to abolish or abate plantation management, organized labor typically tries one of the following tactics: unionizing, collective bargaining, passive resistance, tacit obedience, mass demonstrations, revolutionary factions, or subversive actions—typically with little success.

Well-intentioned management may start some type of profit-sharing plan, restructuring, stock distribution, shared ownership, or other combination of motivations and incentives. These may work as long as the motives of managers are aligned with their methods.

Still, something is missing. I will never forget sitting in a meeting with the dean and department chairmen of a major school of management. To a person, all believed and expressed the *Doctrine of Demarcation*. That is, in today's organizations, a man or woman can rise no higher than first-level management or front-line supervision without an MBA degree. Without such entitlement, he or she "will never cross the threshold." With it, they will hire in above the threshold, and be welcomed into the fraternity of mainstream management, given the keys to the executive washroom, lunchroom, and social calendar.

How perverse! The mindset and heartbeat of a privileged, enlightened, entitled, endowed, educated management will ensure the continuation of plantation management. If the conditions aren't right or ripe, they will create them.

What's missing is a change of mind and heart—from a position of power and preference to one of empowerment and deference from entitlement to stewardship. The body is the metaphor of the perfect, interdependent organization. The head without the feet is nothing. Every part is important. Each has its function.

But such a mindset and heartbeat are uncommon on the plantation. Those values come from reflecting on life experience, accompanied with some pain or remorse for the suffering we cause others; from playing on the field of labor for a few seasons under various management styles

and systems; from working our way through school and up the
organization, as opposed to jockeying and lobbying for entitled executive
placement; and from listening and gaining empathy and real understanding for the position and plight of plantation workers.

An eternal flame burns at the grave of the unknown soldier in
remembrance of the sacrifice of some mother's son. Abraham Lincoln
suggested in his Gettysburg address that we will all die in vain—we
are all destined to anonymity in unmarked graves—unless someone
cares enough to remember us, by name, and to carry on, to give new
birth to the work and mission we lived and died for. Why are the parks
and plazas of the world pocked with shrines, monuments, statues,
plaques, and memorials? Because caring people keep a vigil in memory
of their leaders. Authentic leadership lives forever in the hearts of a
grateful few. For the handful of great leaders that the world has
known—and for all unknown soldiers—there burns an eternal flame.

Address of Redress

*Four score and seven years ago, our founders brought forth in this com-
munity a new corporation, conceived in free-market liberty, and dedicated to
the far-fetched proposition that all men are created equal, even if they aren't
all shareholders.*

*Now we are engaged in a great turf war—coping with the MADness of
mergers, acquisitions, and downsizings—testing whether this corporation, or
any organization so conceived and so dedicated, can long avoid a leveraged
buyout or hostile takeover.*

*We are met in the boardroom, a great battlefield of that war. We have come
to dedicate a portion of this office as an interim resting place for those who here
give their lives that this company might be competitive and profitable.*

*While the ethics committee deems it proper for us to do this, we sense
that we cannot hallow our corporate headquarters. The brave men and
women, living and dead, who have managed here, have compromised it far
beyond our poor power to add or detract.*

*We hope that the media will little note nor long remember what we say and
do here, but we can never forget what has been done to us by our critics and
competitors. It is for us, the currently employed, therefore, to be dedicated to the
unfinished work which they who labor here have thus far so boldly advanced. It
is for us to be here dedicated to the great reengineering task remaining before
us—that from these honored workers, we take increased profits from that very*

cause to which they give their best efforts and some measure of devotion — that we here highly resolve that these people shall not commute in vain — that this corporation shall have a new bottom-line, and that mismanagement of the people, by the people, for the people shall not perish from this business or industry.

Employee Emancipation Proclamation

Ordered against all corporations — and parts thereof — run as plantations.

On this date, all persons esteemed or held as cotton pickers within this organization shall be, henceforth and forever, set free. The executive office will recognize and maintain the freedom of such persons and will do nothing to repress such persons in any efforts they may make for their actual freedom.

Any division, department, or branch that refuses to recognize the freedom of all employees will be considered in rebellion against the corporation.

As the chief executive officer, I do order and declare that all persons held as slaves within said designated divisions and departments shall be free, and that the executive office, including marketing and accounting, shall recognize and maintain the freedom of said persons.

And upon this act, sincerely believed to be an act of justice, warranted by the corporate constitution, I invoke the judgment of our employees and the gracious favor of the Board of Trustees.

Write Your Own Emancipation Proclamation and Plan

If you feel a need to be free of someone or something in your life, I invite you to write your own emancapation proclamation. In writing your proclamation, consider the following four steps.

• Ask: *From what (or whom) do I wish to be liberated?* Think of your own bad habits and self-defeating behaviors first; otherwise, you will likely think that the whole problem is "out there" with other people and things. And with that attitude, you will likely either fight or flee to escape personal responsibility for results.

• Write a first-person statement of liberation:

I, (your name), proclaim myself to be free from illicit, unfair, unwise, secretive, possessive, and abusive relationships, including those in my private and professional life.

• Create your liberation plan. How will you liberate yourself, and possibly other people? Consider these questions:

What opposition will I face? How will I overcome it? Who might assist me (allies)? What resources can I gather and rally? How, when, and where will I start the campaign? How will I see it through to a successful conclusion?

• Imagine yourself going through these steps. See yourself in a new condition, a new environment of your own choosing and making.

Enlightened leaders do all they can to abolish plantation management. In its place, they try to establish participative management, self-directed teams, employee involvement, and work force empowerment.

Abolishing plantation management in our time will cap the tremendous gains in civil and human rights made by pioneers and martyrs in many countries in recent decades and days.

Only then can people sing, as did Martin Luther King, Jr., "Free at last, free at last. God Almighty, we are free at last."

Cures

Cultural Alignment / Shocks & Fresh Starts / Life & Body Balance / Improved Models / More Work Less Waste / Moral Education

Chapter 2

Shocks and Fresh Starts:
The Scrooge Experience

"Men's courses will foreshadow certain ends, to which, if persevered in, they must lead. But if the courses be departed from, the ends will change."

—The Ghost of Christmas Yet to Come
Charles Dickens: *A Christmas Carol*

The cure for plantation management and counterfeit leadership often starts with an overdose of the drug, a nose rub, a tough loss, a slap in the face, a cold-water shower, a citation, a summons, a shock—or with objective feedback, accurate assessment, or an early morning call for improved performance.

The laws of motion apply to leadership: A body at rest, or a low level of motion or achievement, tends to remain at rest unless acted upon by some outside force; conversely, a body with motion and momentum tends to remain in that state unless blocked and stopped. To progress from one state to the next, we sometimes need a wake-up call.

In organizations, these wake-up calls can take many forms: we lose a valued contract, customer, or client; we suffer a huge financial loss; a key executive quits; labor goes on strike; a product is recalled; we receive notice of an ethics violation. On a personal level, the wake-up call may come as a death in the family, a divorce, disease, heart attack, disabling injury, accident, or being passed over for promotion or fired.

Like most people, I have had many wake-up calls in life; in a sense, I have one every morning. You see, my body has a built-in alarm. On most mornings, I wake up at the time I "set" in my mind the night before. But when I check into a hotel late after flying across a few time zones, I usually ask for a wake-up call to guard against sleeping past my first appointment.

Often, our wake-up calls come all too soon, before we are ready. Our bodies may cry for more sleep before facing the work of the day.

27

Our minds may cry for more preparation before taking the test of the day. Our spirits may cry for nourishment before being subjected to the toughness of the street. But cry as we might, when the cock crows and the whistle blows, the games and tests begin, ready or not.

Before the start of my senior year of high school, I was elected co-captain of the football team. During the summer, I enjoyed the status of the position. But as drills began, I felt the weight of the responsibility. Hours before the first game, against a top rival, I was nervous, almost sick.

Fortunately, on the run back of the opening kickoff, I received my first big hit. That was my wake-up call. It's what I needed. From that point, I was totally in the game. On every play, I tried to make a difference. And on the first play of every game thereafter, I tried to give or take a good hit to get myself more fully in the game.

For two years, while serving as a missionary in the vast grassy plains, the Pampas, of Argentina, I started each day by taking an early morning, cold-water shower, as part of what I called "daily initiatory activities." These were simple start-up practices—a sequence that took about 90 minutes but fully prepared me to face the day: awakening and rising at a set time (6:30 a.m.); doing aerobic and flexibility exercises; taking a cold-water shower; dressing in clean clothes; reviewing my commitments; planning my day; eating the best possible breakfast; reading the scriptures; and praying for guidance and wisdom.

To be cured of counterfeit, we may need a daily initiation and conditioning program that works for us. Beyond that, from 8 to 5, we need to face the tough competition or opposition in the ring. For example, when I failed to make the high school basketball team as a sophomore, my coach put me in a conditioning and weight-lifting program for the winter. After about a month in the program, the wrestling coach recruited me because he needed someone of my weight. Four days later, after beating the only other wrestler in my weight class, I suddenly found myself on the varsity team, wrestling against seniors with three years of experience.

Lacking experience, I lost my first 10 matches, all by pin, and suffered the humiliation at home and around the region of hearing the referee slap the mat after counting to three. I then resolved never to be pinned again. I lost six more matches (none by pin) before I resolved never to lose again. After that, I lost only three close matches in two years, finishing fifth in the state.

The Scrooge Experience

To kick off our conversion from counterfeit to authentic leadership, we may need to have some version of the supreme wake-up call, the Scrooge experience. In the classic story *A Christmas Carol* by Charles Dickens, Scrooge undergoes a dramatic transformation, engineered one Christmas Eve by ghosts who show and tell Scrooge what will happen if he doesn't change his ways. Perhaps for the first time in his life, Scrooge sees that he is not in total control of his own fate, that there are natural cause-and-effect consequences of his actions, and that observance of timeless laws and principles ultimately governs outcomes. Clearly, he understands that to change the outcomes, he must change his attitudes and behaviors. The acid test of his change of heart comes in his social and professional interactions—in the way he sees other people, feels about them, and exchanges with them.

Before most people will change, they must have some sort of Scrooge experience—a visit from a "ghost" of the past, present, or future. They must have a perspective expansion—an "out of body" experience, either at night as they sleep, during the day as they contemplate and meditate, or in nature as they reflect on their lives. These "ghosts," these apparitions, may take us on a tour of our lives, just as they escorted Ebeneezer Scrooge when he was visited by the ghosts of Christmas past, present and future. Only then do we see ourselves clearly.

In the case of Scrooge, his life was largely centered in his possessions. One of the great lines comes when Scrooge attempts to console his former business partner, Jacob Marley, who appears to him in chains as an apparition: "But Jacob, you were always a good man of business." And Marley exclaims, "Business? Mankind was my business!" In other words, "Don't bother me with your petty, narrow definition of business: All of mankind is and was my business!" He still feels cheated by the pettiness and miserly nature of his former partner in the accounting firm of Scrooge and Marley.

What ultimately changes Scrooge is not the condition of Tiny Tim and the prospect of seeing that boy dead in the future if Scrooge doesn't act. Certainly, that preview is a motivating factor, but what really changes Scrooge is the insight and perspective he gains on his own life. He sees the dramatic difference between what he is and what he can be—and the dramatic difference that change will make, not only in his own life but in the lives of many other people.

Six Ways to Simulate the Scrooge Experience

Every one of us—so suggests Tiny Tim—can have a transforming Scrooge experience if we seek it. It may not come as a dream in the night, or not without a fight, but we can change our course and thus change the outcomes. Here are six ways to simulate the Scrooge experience.

• *First, recognize the supreme importance of little things and little people.* Scrooge sees what small matters these life-changing things are! When he visits the party, for example, he is amazed to see that the "small things" done by Fezziwig, his former boss, make all the difference in the world to people. And he sees that the satisfactions and joys of life are in these little things and that it doesn't cost so much to do them. Scrooge also sees that he is capable of doing such things, and not just because he has money and means. His money helps finance some favors, but what capacitates him is his change of heart and his new vision of things. When he wakes up on that Christmas morning and discovers that it isn't too late, he is filled with the joy of having a fresh start, a new lease on life.

"The greatest things ever done on earth," says Thomas Guthrie, "have been done little by little—little agents, little persons, little things, by every one doing his own work, filling his own sphere, and holding his own post."

Some things only the blind see well. Helen Keller observed: "We are free to use or abuse the million little things that drop into our hands, the small opportunities each day brings." And Russell Conwell writes: "The power of little things to give instruction and happiness should be the first lesson in life."

Scrooge finally learns the lesson that life is made up of little things and that smiles, kindnesses, and small favors are what win and preserve the heart and secure peace and joy.

That is the same joy felt by hostage Terry Anderson, who after five years in captivity, announced that he was not bitter but that he wanted only to look ahead to his new life. One prisoner of war who was held captive in Japanese prison camps during World War II likewise said that every morning now is a glorious day because it is part of his new life.

This is the joy of the transformed life, the joy of seeing life as if for the first time and saying, "What a golden morning," and "What a delightful boy," and "What a prize turkey." It's seeing things—and people—with new eyes and a new heart.

Significantly, the first person the reformed Scrooge encounters on Christmas morning is the small boy who happens to walk by when Scrooge opens the window. Most assuredly, just the day before, the boy would have been treated with contempt. Now, Scrooge finds him "delightful" and useful and worthy of hire. This once counterfeit leader has discovered the great value of so-called little people.

• *Second, expand perspective.* To start and sustain such an inside-out reformation in your life, you will need the perspective Scrooge gained through his ghostly visits—and those can be hard to come by. However, the Scrooge experience can be staged. One vicarious way to gain that valuable perspective on your own is to imagine your own funeral, to see yourself in attendance, listening to the talks that are given by spouse, family members, business associates, friends, and neighbors, and hearing those people, just as Scrooge had to do, as they talk about you. Remember, Scrooge had to see what people did and hear what they said and sense what they felt about him upon his death. He also had to revisit a few decisive moments in his life.

Having a similar experience will give us that "out of body" perspective on our own lives. Without such vicarious experiences, we may never know the deeper joys of life, nor gain inner peace.

I once knew a young man who was a master of disguises. He used them to win the affection and complete the seduction of many young women. He participated in student government and in high school and college fraternities. He gladly played the role of comic and clown, the life of the party, the toast of the town. I last saw him at a gas station after he had been drinking a few too many beers. He was then about 29 years old, divorced and rather dissipated. He talked moodily about his life. "I really don't have any friends, just contacts and acquaintances," he said. "Nobody stands by me. I'm a college graduate and I've been in the Army, but I really don't have any marketable skills." He felt betrayed by all the individuals and institutions of his life. Within a year, having no long-term perspective on his life, he committed suicide.

Counterfeit leaders often lose perspective by hiding behind a facade, a mask. They are magicians who can make black appear white, white appear black; they can make day seem as night, or night seem as day. They are cunning and crafty, masters of deceit, camouflage, imitation, and illusion. In the closing scene of the movie *Dangerous Liaisons,* when the madam removes her makeup, we clearly see what a crass, counterfeit woman she is and how ugly she is without her "mask-era." When she looks at herself plainly in the mirror, she, too, sees how ugly she has become as a natural consequence of the game playing, deceit, seductions, and liaisons that she had engaged in. Without those "mirror" experiences, we can't see with clarity and alacrity who and what we are. With them, we gain the courage and self-honesty to see ourselves with 20/20 vision in the context of our past, present, and future.

• *Third, legally cross new borders and old boundaries.* As we enter a new job, or any organization for the first time, we often have an unsettling encounter with the new culture. We sense that we have crossed a border into a new and different territory with different language and customs. We are amazed that such an artificial barrier, such as a border line, could create such change.

When we pass from the United States into Mexico, for example, we encounter different customs, languages, and traditions. Likewise, when we move from one company or place to another, even among divisions within companies, we find significant differences in how people do things, how they think, whom they admire, whom they model, what passes for coin of the realm, what trades over the counter, what is considered legitimate, and who has credibility.

When we take a new job with a company, we also join a society. At first, we may not notice what we later see as counterfeit in the culture, either because we don't care to see it or because our vision is a bit blurred. It takes time to see things as they are. At first, we tend to see things in extremes. We get sharp sensory perceptions of the differences and experience very acute, visceral reactions. As we settle in, we tend to see less but feel more; some things become less clear, others more clear. We begin to see as natives, not as tourists, and begin to understand why things are done a certain way. We then have the choice—to be part of the solution or part of the problem.

In the age of information, often these borders are more psychological than physical, more electronic that geographic, more invisible than visible. The alarming increase in white-collar crime is one indication that without physical restraints or speed bumps, we tend to race right over borders and trespass at will. We regress along the continuum toward the counterfeit whenever we trespass, step over those boundaries, limits and borders that define who we are, without regard to the rights and properties of other people.

Illegal intrusions and trespassing become a way of life for counterfeit leaders who fail to recognize the sanctity of borders or to respect the sovereign rights of other nations and people. They may profess to do so, however, even as they plan their next invasion. Of course, now, with satellite dishes and cable TV, no home security system can keep out unwanted intrusions of counterfeits, as they leap from the tube into our hot tubs, our living rooms, and, alas, even into our beds and heads.

• *Fourth, seek objective assessment and feedback.* Unless we are getting feedback from a variety of objective sources—feedback that is not filtered through self-protective agents who are either looking out for themselves or telling the boss what he wants to hear—we can easily be duped into believing that we have a genuine article, a quality product, or leading-edge technology. With a little self-deception, we might believe that we are number one when in fact we're not even on the charts.

If our research, surveys, assessments, and counselors have no more validity and objectivity than Star Wars (the movie or the defense plan), we will only hear lies in stereo. We will hire Ph.D.s to feed us the statistics and "market research" we need to defend our biases. We will swear on a stack of Bibles that our results are accurate and valid and represent truth when, in fact, we know that the final report is 100 percent pure, unadulterated trash because the premise was all wrong, or the questions were leading, or the instrument lacked integrity to begin with.

Many individuals and corporations get into that self-defeating, self-deceiving cycle where, even as their capabilities and products deteriorate, they believe that they are improving, getting better and stronger with each passing day. But positive attitudes tend to wilt under the light and heat of day, unless quality is designed and built into products and services from the beginning and from the inside-out.

To detect what is counterfeit in our corporate culture, we may need to look at origins, to the founders, and to the products and services; weigh them against global, best-of-class standards; and recognize that since success in business is relative to the competition, we can find some degree of waste, obsolescence, defect, and counterfeit in every product. As "zero defects" becomes the universal standard, we need to apply the standard to our people and products, and ask, "How do we stack up against the best in the world?" If our market is regional or local, we will still want to ask, "How do we stack up against the best in our league?"

In every business, we need to take stock periodically by asking ourselves a few questions: "Are we clear about our purpose?" Do we have a favorable market image and position? Do we have adequate resources? Are we effective in our work? Do we put out quality products and services? Do we work well with all our customers, suppliers, and stakeholders?"

Under scrutiny, we will likely discover, as did Scrooge, that we need to make some fundamental changes, even redesign some business processes. Some defects slap us in the face—they are painfully obvious to all, except in some sad cases, to those who live with them. Only people who live in the forest can't see the trees. Only the fish don't know they are in water, even hot water. Executives may be flooded with information and still lack the vital information they need. They are dying of thirst in the middle of the ocean because, while there is water everywhere, there's not a drop to drink. And so, they don't know if they are counterfeit or genuine. They don't know who or where they are. Of course, some may not want to know.

• *Fifth, learn from your shocking encounters with counterfeits.* Many who have been jolted, jilted, and bilked by counterfeits learn some valuable, albeit painful, lessons from these encounters. Some even seek to share their experience in therapeutic associations known as "encounter groups." Here's but a random sample taken in California.

• On the first night of a week-long family vacation in Southern California, my wife, three sons and I enter a family restaurant in Newport Beach. We are seated in a non-smoking section between two "encounter groups." We can't help but overhear sordid tales of infidelity, divorce, love triangles, and assorted woes that seemed to come right out of the scripts of soap operas. Undaunted, the fearless discussion leaders (self-confessed graduates of the encounter group system) fan the flames by saying, "Some of you are holding back. Let's be open. We need each other." My family and I don't need it; we move to another table.

• Along the sandy beaches of Southern California, we see a different sort of encounter group comprised mostly of young people whose chief occupation day in, day out is riding the waves of the ocean. Equipped with wet suits and advanced technology surf boards, these addicts of mother motion search for swells, trying to capture natural momentum, and ride the wave to shore.

Their counterparts can be found several miles inland in a wide variety of occupations: stock analysts, investment bankers, financial advisors, management consultants, political candidates. They prefer dry suits and dry martinis, but they too surf the waves of the market, seeking the fleeting thrill of a fast ride atop a powerful monetary wave. It's an illusion of progress. It's power and momentum they neither create nor maintain—it's all there for syncopation and dissipation. But since these high tech exchanges often produce more highs than lows, many people make a livelihood of sorts. For a series of stock exchanges, many are willing to sacrifice marriage, family, health, and personal honor.

• In Los Angeles, I encounter a company that deals in gold, silver and other precious metals. The general manager tells me, modestly, that they make many millions of dollars, but all they do is transfer paper. He came into that company with a high degree of self-respect. Within 18 months, he lost much of that and began to feel counterfeit himself, compromised in an industry where one makes money by moving paper representing coins, bars, and bricks. The actual gold and silver bars stay in the same spot—it's just a paper (or electronic) transfer from one owner to another. Meanwhile, he tells me, several hundred silver bars are "leaded" by counterfeiters who replace 40 ounces of silver with 40 ounces of lead. Altered bars often turn up on the secondary markets (the primary markets are too well scrutinized).

This slice of life by no means suggests that California has a corner on the market. Rich veins of counterfeit can be found in every state and country, nook and cranny. Throughout history, people have sold their souls, and their friends, for 40 ounces of silver on the open market. The good news is that men and women, boys and girls, can learn and turn from counterfeit to more authentic behaviors.

When we experience a set back, we may be starting a painful transformation that leaves us, like Pippin in the Broadway play, with a simpler but much happier existence.

We all need a knock on the noggin or a slap in the face once in a while. "Thanks, I needed that" is a phrase uttered in sober retrospect of the benefits of one's come-uppance. But we don't always need to learn by sad experience. We can learn to better detect and reject counterfeits before we buy into them.

• *Sixth, go to a church that challenges you to change.* Once a certain young woman who lived and worked in Texas went about seeking "true religion." She encountered various preachers. She entered their churches and sat among their congregations. She told me that as she educated her senses, she could shortly detect whether the church and preacher were counterfeit by the degree of flattery and entertainment built into the service. "If the preacher said that it was okay to lie and cheat a little as long as you confessed and donated on Sunday, I got worried. Salvation by grace too often sounded like salvation by dona-tion. It was like a warm jacuzzi bath every Sunday morning instead of a wake-up call."

She then attended a conference and heard a man whom she described as "prickly," meaning "my conscience was constantly pricked and called to repentance. Listening was not comfortable; in fact, it was prickly like a cactus. But I felt deeply moved to change and be a better person." Such is the power of an authentic leader.

One such leader, J. Irwin Miller, chairman of Cummins Engine Company and former president of the National Council of Churches, says, "Churches must be risk-taking and prophetic—and they should direct their moral witness against me and the rest of society. The role of a prophet is active, often disruptive, and always painful—it is thor-oughly unpleasant to those on the receiving end of the preaching."

Once we are awake to what is counterfeit in our nature or cul-ture, we then must take the cold-water shower and look into that objective bathroom mirror, checking for signs of cancer in all parts of the body. If we hope to be cured of counterfeit, we must see who and what we are, what is naturally and rightfully ours—and who and what we might expect to become. The natural eyes may not be that helpful in assessing potential. We may be too close, or may not have the angle, to see either warts or worth.

With a Scrooge experience and perspective, we are in a better position to assess the relative worth of things. We then might choose to care for our own, to tend our gardens, to grow something organic (from chives to children), and to stop stealing and trespassing—to be content with what we know, who we are, what we can do. Hopefully, after a shocking experience, we will seek a fresh start and make a strong bid for new freedom and identity.

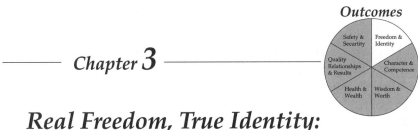
Outcomes

Safety & Security | Freedom & Identity
Quality Relationships & Results | Character & Competence
Health & Wealth | Wisdom & Worth

Chapter *3*

Real Freedom, True Identity: No More Tokens

"No man is free who is not master of himself."

—Epictetus

Once on a trip to the island of Jamaica in the Caribbean, I found myself waiting for a ride back to the hotel after playing a round of golf. I then met four bus and taxi drivers who were waiting there for other people to finish their rounds. We struck up a conversation.

I sensed from three of the men a high degree of resignation with their current status. They felt that they were just one step removed from the old sugar plantations, driving busses for owners who paid them low wages and would never cut them in on the action.

But the fourth man was different. He owned his own car (a 10-year-old Chevrolet in immaculate condition) and had his own taxi business. He had been driving the roads of Jamaica for many years, and seemed to know half the people on the island. If they didn't know him personally, they at least knew his car. After listening to his colleagues gripe and moan about their "hopeless" condition, he spoke to them: "You never want to give in and give up," he said. "If you have faith and work toward the modest goal of owning your own car, you can do it. This is no miracle. I did it. You can do it. We are not slaves. We are free men, and we—you and I—can own and manage our own business."

He said this emphatically, in a deep, "James Earl Jones" voice. It was as if God Himself had spoken. Even so, the other three men were so deeply resigned to their fate that they were more amused than motivated by his remarks. With their minds on the plantation, they couldn't imagine a new freedom and identity.

Now What?

Elephant trainers say that once a young elephant accepts the limitations imposed by a heavy chain on its leg, it will not try to break away later even when the chain is replaced with a light rope. In its mind, it is still in captivity or, at least, confinement.

Many people, too, are reluctant to leave the "plantation"—a demeaning job, a fraudulent company, a confining condition, an abusive relationship, a violent neighborhood—even when their "chains" (physical, emotional, social, or legal restraints) are removed. At least, there on the plantation, they have some measure of security and identity.

Once on a business trip to Hilton Head Island, just off the coast of South Carolina, I observed with interest that developers had elected to keep the old "plantation" designation in creating their new estate properties, as well as in developing recreation and commercial real estate. "So what?" one might ask. "What's in a name?" Well, some of the new "plantations" bear a strong resemblance to the old. Behaviors and attitudes haven't changed all that much. We still see sharp divisions between rich and poor, haves and have nots, service providers and those being served.

But what's most curious is that no one seems to mind: the modern plantation still works, at least as a money-making unit.

I believe that it works, financially, not because it's the best possible organization but rather because people at least have a sense of place—a roof, a role, a routine, a goal, and even some reward for good behavior. Of course, even convicted criminals have all that. But mental ruts and physical routines are as good as prison bars and gates. No need for chains when habits will do.

Once you leave the planation, it's hard to know what to do. You're on our own. You may be good, but good for what? When your whole life has been spent in servitude on a plantation—taking orders, responding to crises, doing a simple repetitive task—you naturally feel a bit unsettled when you gain new-found freedom or identity.

A new identity, or true identity, is often the first fruit coming from a personal "roots" experience. That's when you learn that you are not your job; you are not your present condition; you are not your past experience. Nor do you need to be a victim of your conditions and conditioning. You see that your roots sink deep into human history and family genealogy and connect with divine creation. It often takes true self-identity to preserve, protect, and expand personal freedoms.

Token Image and Identity
We all want a new image, a fresh start, or a second chance. We

hope to sell the romance of our dreams and visions, but often we are weighed down by the messy realities of our current world.

Every culture has its tokens and signs, passwords and buzzwords. Access to the top, typically, is limited to those who display their tokens at the right place and right time. Symbolism is the name of the game, and maintaining integrity in the system is the challenge.

Once I visited the offices of New York Transit Authority, managers of the subway system in New York City. To their credit, management was trying to change from a counterfeit system of smoke and mirrors to one of spit and polish. But they carried some baggage in the form of a bad reputation.

As my colleagues and I met with the two senior managers of the massive rail system, they explained their goals and objectives and reviewed their current operating realties. They then wondered openly, "How might we get from here to there?"

The problem was how to get the people who had stopped riding the subway back in the cars. The Authority had made a considerable investment in upgrading cars, cleaning stations, training operators and scheduling trains. They wanted more return on investment.

I happened to have a token in my pocket. I held it up and spoke of the symbolism. "One side of the token is like a mirror," I said. "What does it reflect?" I answered my own question: "To many people, it reflects danger, darkness, detachment, filth, and stink."

I introduced a key word—*perception*—the perception of the paying public, their customers. "A subway token costs one dollar, and it's good for one ride," I continued, suggesting that for many, the ride implies risk, an assault on the senses, if not on the body. I asked, "What *should* this token symbolize?" And we came up with some words like "security, confidence, convenience, efficiency, economy, cleanliness, safety." We then talked about ways to get from one side of the coin, or token, to the other.

They got the message, but unfortunately opted for a flawed solution: They hired a high-powered PR firm to upgrade their image.

Following our meeting with the managers of the subway, we had to return to Manhattan for our next appointment. The managers were so proud of their recent improvements that they insisted we take the subway. They escorted us to the station and showed us their new, computerized access and ticketing system. But, as fate would have it, as we approached the Manhattan tunnel, the train came to a halt, and everyone was ordered out because there was smoke in the tunnel.

We emerged from the dark, smoky tunnel into blinding sunlight in a tough area of town where there were no taxi cabs. After walking several blocks, we finally flagged down a cab, but we arrived late and out of sorts for our next appointment.

One night on the *Tonight Show*, Jay Leno said, "Yes, the NYC Transit Authority has done a great job getting the graffiti off the outside of their subway cars. Now if they can just get the blood off the inside." In fact, not long after that experience, a young man from my community was murdered in the New York City subway when a gang attacked his family to get a little dance money. Unfortunately, it took that event to drive meaningful change, beyond cosmetics.

Conversion from talk to walk is tough. Once you have a system that is physically dilapidated, once people get used to writing on your walls, once graffiti becomes the primary language, once your tiled entry becomes a urinal, your station a camp for the homeless and a trading post for drugs and delinquents—at that point, only those with no other option will ride the rails. And your precious tokens will symbolize the opposite of what you intend.

Indeed, a man or woman who feels like a "token" after being admitted to a school or hired for a job typically opposes the well-intentioned quotas that got him or her through the door.

From Talk to Walk

After explaining the difference between counterfeit and authentic leadership to a group from a major electronics firm, I was asked by one man, a senior executive in the company, "Your description of counterfeit leaders and cultures fits us perfectly. How can we change to authentic leadership?"

He wanted the authentic models installed immediately, as if one could change leaders and cultures like light bulbs. I asked him, "Do you believe that the problem is all with your leaders? Are you asking me how you can fix *them?*"

He told me how the corporate office had released an effective but "soft" people pleaser and replaced him with a bulldog who was all bark and bite. Since that time, the culture had deteriorated into a confederation of "crooks and cannibals." The company was losing its competitive edge. Product and service quality had dropped, and he was sick and tired of it, considering a career change even though he had about 25 years with the company. He really felt that resignation was the only answer.

I told him the story of the Manville Corporation, and suggested he follow the path taken by CEO Tom Stephens to turn the company around. In an article published in *Executive Excellence* magazine, Stephens spoke of steps Manville had taken to gain a new image, market identity, and freedom from creditors. These six steps apply equally to the New York Transit, the Jamaican taxi drivers, and the electronics firm.

1. Make a commitment. Change starts with an attitude and belief about the human capability of making commitments and being account-able. Only with strong commitment can dramatic transformations in culture take place. At Manville, Stephens faced billions of dollars in potential liabilities from asbestos products. When he became CEO, the company was in Chapter 11; employee morale was down; confidence and the company's image were low. "At one point, we led the list of least respected companies in the United States," said Stephens. "But the chal-lenge excited me." Stephens managed to unite the people and financial resources necessary to redesign Manville for the future.

Commitment is key to development. Every oath of office begins with a pledge or promise. And every culture has its ceremonies to sanction these commitments and to make it tough to break them sim-ply because of whim or convenience.

2. Accept responsibility and risk. In the Manville case, a trust was created as part of the reorganization to pay personal injury claims to those injured by exposure to their asbestos products. The year Manville exited Chapter 11, the company booked a $1.3 billion dollar loss in net income. "That was the cost to put our asbestos obligations behind us," said Stephens. "It sounds like a tremendous price to pay. But, we kept the promises we made as we entered Chapter 11. Our commercial creditors got paid in full, plus interest. Our shareholders were hit hard, but retained some value in their securities."

Stephens also started a "pay for performance" program for the majority of Manville's work force: "Manville's people share in the rewards when the company reaches or exceeds planned results; they share the risk as well if we lag behind our potential."

3. Choose the right way out. CEO Stephens had a clear choice between the right way and the easy way out. "In seeking an equitable solution, we recognized our responsibility to those injured by our asbestos products. We knew it could take years for many injuries to show. Liquidation may have provided enough cash to settle current liabilities. It would have been the easy way out, but it would not have provided a fair solution to future claimants. Preserving a profitable company was the only way to assure we could meet our responsibilities. It wasn't the easy way; but, it was the right way."

Bailing out in bankruptcy may look good on paper, but when the pilot starts parachuting out of the plane, the crew and passengers tend to get worried. And yet that is what's happening in many companies. And they do this as if there are no consequences; as if desertion is okay because "it's good for me, and so why shouldn't it be okay for the creditors and employees who are still on board?"

Contrast that stance with the heroic stories about pilots who miraculously land their planes in spite of damaged engines and fuselages. They fight to compensate for the damages to bring the plane down with little or no loss of life. They even try to compensate passengers for the trauma and losses they incur.

4. Go for the long-term solution. At Manville, Stephens said, "We are focusing more on long-term, rather than quarter-to-quarter results. We intend to continue to take a longer view. Buzz words like *reposition, turn-around, reengineering,* or *transition* are often used when people talk about the changes at Manville. What really occurred was a transformation from one company to another. When a company relies heavily on a single raw material, as we did with asbestos for a century, and then within the span of a decade finds itself completely out of that business, that is dramatic transformation!"

Manville is no longer in the asbestos business, "yet we are stronger today than at any time in our history," Stephens continued. "We intend to grow the company by identifying and seizing opportunities for growth around and within the products and technologies we know. We dumped our procedure manuals. We stopped making posters of our organization charts. And, we put together dozens of teams of employees, involving them in helping to resolve problems and recommend solutions."

5. Restore confidence and credibility. Stephens saw only one way to restore confidence in the company: "Let all concerned stake-holders, including the public, know what we were doing and why. Truth is the best antidote to rumors. I reassured our customers on a personal basis that Manville remained determined to be their best supplier. We trained our salespeople for this role. They not only sold goods, they sold the idea that Manville is around to stay. We established an aggressive public information program to let the public, our employees, suppliers, customers, and lending institutions know what we were doing, and why."

Another way to restore credibility is with strategic hiring and firing and the symbolism and celebrations around those actions. Nothing turns a culture faster than to kill a couple of wicked witches of the west, east, north or south. As people see some of these wicked witches being killed, they then feel liberated. If the wicked witches are replaced by good fairies, the Munchkins become liberated, transformed and empowered.

When Stephens saw the need for reorganization at Manville, he moved forward decisively: "Even before the plans were final, we started refocusing, reorganizing, and restructuring around businesses rather than functions. We sold our old headquarters and moved to take a lot of the starch and formality out of the culture. We pushed decision making down, waged war on expenses, and invested $800 million to improve production and upgrade facilities."

6. Encourage new growth. Stephens and Manville learned a lot of lessons in Chapter 11. "Growth is the key-word of the transition, and the new mission is shareholder value," he said. "We work around strategic business plans that evaluate the competitive environment and compare and contrast our strengths with those of our major competitors. I'm teaching others what we learned with the hope that other businesses can learn something from Manville about corporate responsibilities."

As anyone in drama knows, dynamic or developing characters undergo a transformation during the couse of the play. Type-cast characters are more stagnant, or stationary—they don't change. They stay in character, they have a certain personality, and their lines are consistent throughout the play. That's true enough in life. We see developing and dynamic characters, and then we see people who are static. Developing characters are often teaching others, because the very act of teaching expands their knowledge and reinforces their commitment. The teacher learns more than her students because she learns from so many sources, including her students. What she gives her students is a mere fraction of her total preparation.

In entrepreneurial and creative organizations, mistakes are encouraged as part of a cycle of learning. The spirit of innovation and entrepreneurism is fueled by the understanding that people make mistakes as they get into new areas, new growth, and new learning. Mistakes are seen as part of the developmental cycle.

The cures for counterfeit come in cycles of learning and growth. Teaching others is a healthy part of the curing process. Your example should teach others what corporate responsibility is all about. This teaching can be done in different formats: writing articles for publication, being interviewed for publication, making speeches and presentations, one-on-one interactions, personal visits, modeling, mentoring, participatory management, employee involvement, continuous improvement techniques.

Cures won't come in closed-door climates. Autocratic and dictatorial styles don't work well over time, as they cheat constituents of growth. Dictatorship is a powerful form of counterfeit leadership because it takes power from the people for the purpose of control. It's not power *of*, *by* and *for* the people; it's power *from* the people to the leader. Those aren't just different prepositions; they are different propositions altogether.

Authentic leaders understand the ecology of relationships. They know that trust can't be violated with impunity. They are sensitive to the small infractions, not just to hardened criminal activity, because they know that these, too, will have disruptive consequences. They sense, intuitively, that we can rise to great heights if we are true not only to natural laws and correct principles, but also to the buoyancy in our own nature. If our conscience stays vibrant, then things we had never supposed come into view; routines turn resplendent; ordinary people become extraordinary; and the static humdrum gives way to symphonic strains. We can then trade our old tokens for a real ticket to freedom.

Cycle

Environment | Emancipation
Empowerment | Emulation
Enterprise | Enlightenment

——————— *Step Two* ———————

Emulation: Beauty and the Beast

Every leader is a model of sorts. By virtue of their position, power, platform, and visibility, leaders are introduced as people worthy of audience and emulation, whether they like it or not or whether they're ready or not.

In this section, I look at imperfect models as another cause of counterfeit leadership, see improved models as a cure, and imagine growth in character and competence as an outcome.

• Once emancipated from the plantation, we need new role models. If we pick as a model the first person to come along, then we gamble with our very lives. In the high stakes game of life and death, we ought to give careful thought to our choices of models and heros. Random selection may lead to many regrets.

• We can expect to find "improved models" in improved places, in places such as reputable schools, churches, businesses, health and wellness centers, libraries, and the professions. There are no guarantees, of course. No one is perfect. But the better models and mentors have much to teach us, by precept and example.

• The traits and characteristics of our leaders tend to rub off on us. The better the company we keep, the more authentic the leaders we follow, and the more we apply the lessons of our best teachers, the more we grow in character and competence.

Not all leaders are worthy of whole-life emulation, but we can learn something from each of them, even the worst of them. And the more we learn from the best of them, the more we grow and develop, the more trustworthy we become, and the more we appear to others to be a beauty, not a beast.

Causes

Hierarchies & Bureaucracies | Plantation Mangement
False Followership | Imperfect Models
Bad Habits | Secular Education

——— *Chapter 4* ———

Imperfect Models: In Madonna We Lust

"Insist on yourself; never imitate. Using your own gifts you can face every moment with the cumulative force of a whole life's cultivation; but of the adopted talent of another, you have only an extemporaneous half-possession."

—Ralph Waldo Emerson

Another major cause of counterfeit leadership is emulating or cloning flawed models. Genetic imprinting, parental encoding, and cultural conditioning greatly influence us, but our adult choices of leadership models also contribute greatly to the degree of authentic or counterfeit leadership we build into our personal and corporate characters. In fact, it is in and through these choices that we move along the continuum, in one direction or another.

When we choose our models, we ought to check them against "standard weights" and authentic measures—or at least read their lips. Do we know, for example, in what and whom they trust? Do we know to what degree they trust us? Do we know to what degree we can trust them? The practical value of counterfeits is that they make things accessible and affordable. Synthetics and composites are usually cheaper. Pyrite, plastic, and polyester have their place. Not everybody can afford gold and diamond—the precious gems, genuine articles, and natural fibers like cotton and wool. Without the synthetics, many people could not afford to be housed, dressed, and fed.

While counterfeit leadership often defrauds, defames, misguides, maligns or simply mismanages people, it rarely starts with sinister intent; in fact, much of it is manufactured in traditional forms, models, molds, casts, and dies—in the most reputable of academic, business, and social institutions—and with good intentions and with noble missions and motives.

And it's all done in accordance with the law of supply and demand. We have a need for models and heroes, and certain studios and factories are only too happy to supply them.

47

Seven Categories of Models

Many attractive models of leadership pass before our eyes each day. If we change cable TV channels with a remote (channel surf), we will see more than a model a minute—and on MTV, a model a second. Models, good and bad, come from various sources: homes, neighborhoods, churches, schools, professions, and organizations, and athletic teams. We typically assess these; accept and adopt some; and begin to integrate or implement them.

1. *Media celebrities.* From birth to death, we are imprinted with images and ideas from media, especially movies. We borrow a bit from each flick; each model impresses itself on the tender emulsion of memory, the very film of our recorded lives.

As children and adults, we may be deeply impressed by a particular movie, scene, or actor. And for days or decades afterward, we play the part of the hero or heroine in the movie: we become Indiana Jones, Robin Hood, or Maid Marian. Just two hours of film can so powerfully impress us that we may attempt to be or do whatever we see the hero do in the movie. We imitate them—talking, dressing and acting like them—and that goes on in the lives of boys and girls, Kens and Barbies, G.I. Joes and Annes of Green Gables. Kids imitate their heroes skillfully. They are quick studies of models and ready impressionists, imitating their models to a "T" (or T-shirt). They imitate to acquire the attributes of that person—the look, the voice, and the mannerisms of the hero.

Media sell moguls, masters, mentors, actors, anchors, and expert commentators. We rely on these models to keep us informed and entertained. Hence, newsman Peter Jennings becomes "the most trusted man" in America. One month, we criticize him for being superficial, "just another pretty face," and the next we rate him the most trusted. "People who do my kind of job have a major impact," says Jennings. "But frankly, I don't want that much impact." No wonder! He's only reporting the news! But these newscasters and sportscasters soon *become* the news—stars of their own shows.

If Vanna White can become a national model by turning letters on *Wheel of Fortune* or Karen Valentine and John Davidson on *Hollywood Squares,* or Jerry Brown on *Presidential Race 1992,* then maybe we don't know the difference between white and brown, love and lust, humility and vanity, round and square, son and daughter, fortune and wealth, numbers and letters, president and performer. Ignoring the lessons of history, we reinvent the wheel, canonize our own saints, and go Hollywood. A game show or talk show then becomes as good a platform for presidential politics as anything else—what matters is name and face recognition. Using that criteria, anybody on the tube, anyone with money, can become a national model, hero, or celebrity—even if they have an inane act. At least they make good fodder for mediated "cock fights"—those extreme point-counterpoint frays between people on talk shows and some news programs.

As the media impose certain models upon us, we dutifully give them celebrity status, whether they want it or not, merit it or not. Who is a leader, anyway? Any celebrity, anyone whose name or face is recognized in public? The few times I've encountered "celebrities" in public, I've had the feeling that not only are these people terribly ordinary, but in some cases extremely hollow, even boring. The persona is not the person. Few celebrities hold up well under close scrutiny. They get it anyway, of course, as their private and "secret" lives are exposed and broadcast into our living rooms. We get all the sordid details, loud and clear, through antennas and satellite dishes, morning and night.

During my teenage years, I traveled twice a year to Palm Springs, California, to escape winter and to visit my grandparents. When they first moved to the desert, they took us grandkids in the back seat of their Cadillac through the elite neighborhoods, pointing out the homes and estates of Bob Hope, Bing Crosby, Phil Harris, Liberace, and Lucy, but we would have rather been in the swimming pool or on the golf course. Whether we live in Holland or Brazil, Hollywood or the Bronx, we still have a bed, bath, toilet, closet—and it matters not the size and the shape of those things, or how many people know our name, face, and voice. What matters is how well we use and maintain what we have.

2. Peak performers. Fashion models, athletes, and performing artists are among the many individual peak performers. We see the latest styles paraded in shows and featured in dozens of magazines. Tragically, as we succumb to an emphasis on externals, we are easily taken by the appearance of things—the wearing of expensive apparel or experimenting with garish fads. In a counterfeit culture, we succumb more easily to the folly of judging others on the basis of fashion and appearance. In an authentic culture or community, we are obliged to downplay appearances, without resorting to negative snobbery or antisocial behavior—or to the second form of hypocracy, appearing to be less than we are.

Surely, clothing should not rate on the same scale with competence and character. But in the fashion-conscious world, apparel may count even more. Fashion takes itself very seriously, even when carried to obvious extremes. The notion that clothing should be but neat and simple, clean and proper, is considered outmoded. The ideal of the "lilies of the field"—unadorned and inexpensive, but pleasant and naturally becoming—doesn't seem to sell either. In a counterfeit culture or fashion-conscious community, appearances are everything—city hall, campus, court, and theater are simply places to show off the latest style and fashion.

The sports world promotes models who contribute performance, talent, charisma, personality, style, and points. Sports is a major factory of heroes and models: the underdogs and the champions, the come-from-behinders and front-runners. While some athletes and coaches may be, to a great degree, good role models, others fall far short as models of authentic leadership. They tend to be transitory and event-oriented, here today and gone tomorrow, subject to injury and penalty, faults and fouls. We all know how fickle even the most faithful fans are and how fast sports heroes can fall from good graces. In baseball, once you stop hitting .300, or in basketball once you stop scoring 20 points a game, or in football once you throw an interception or fumble the ball, you quickly go from hero to goat. All of these stats are recorded religiously and remembered by fans. Blow the big game or violate their trust, and they may make you a scapegoat in a minute, quickly forgetting all the great things you did on the diamond or in the ring, as Pete Rose and Mike Tyson could testify.

Moreover, since many athletes are not as disciplined and decisive off the field as they appear to be on the field or court, the best bet is to imitate only the best of their on-field behaviors.

3. Business executives and consultants. Straight out of business school, before they even have their first real job, many young professionals turn to consulting. As members of firms large and small, they start making jigsaw models of management and leadership that feature jargon and jerry-rigged constructs. Others start watching trends and forecasting the future. Of course, since much of their "vision" comes from mentors or magazines, they sometimes make about as much sense as the stewardess who, while still in the air on a late-arriving plane, dutifully announces the connecting flights, even as those flights are taking off on the ground (that's happened to me more than once).

It isn't all sorcery, of course. Many consultants make respectable models and forecasts. They do a great service if only they help in-the-trenches executives to see more clearly the here and now. Once in Minneapolis, I had dinner with a CEO and a trusted consultant to a Fortune 500 firm. The consultant kept saying, "There are signs of troubled times right now inside the company, if you have eyes to see and ears to hear them. These things are happening now, and in two years, based on present trends, this is what I predict will happen."

With well documented evidence before him, the CEO could see that he had to start redeploying some people and resources and taking some preventative measures to avoid certain catastrophes—such as experiencing a downturn, downfall, or bankruptcy or being leveraged out, bought out, forced out, blackballed, backbitten, or snake bitten. He could see that any one of several nasty things could happen without preventative action. But most counterfeit leaders ignore those signs and keep driving people and pushing machinery harder and harder, over the edge.

Corporation derives from *corpus*, a body. That's all the natural eyes see—what's visible, material, evident and tangible about the company. But much of what executives must find and foster inside companies isn't even listed on the charts. The whole of the corporation is more than the sum of its parts. The more we probe inside, the more likely we'll discover *esprit de corps*, the spirit of the body. Invariably, we find what we're looking for, what we have eyes to see. Executives need bifocal vision: one part adjusted for close focus on the corporeal parts of the corporate body, and the other adjusted for distance, for vision, especially of the intangibles. They need to see beyond the obvious, having eyes for inner qualities and outer opportunities. Otherwise, their organizations become corpulent, if not a corpse, a dead body, a defunct corporation.

Every industry has its own models, the captains of industry, that spotlight lore, legend, myth, tales, and larger-than-life wizards. Any CEO might identify with the Wizard of Oz, an old circus man whose balloon was blown off course and landed in Oz, where, by using technology and a few tricks, he became the local wizard. Even though he lived in a castle in Emerald City, he still had to contend with the wicked witch and his own illusions and anxieties over being all-powerful. Sometimes, it takes a Toto to reveal the wizard for who and what he is.

Few corporate public relations czars are willing to risk their turf and kingdom by letting the public see too much of their clients, until they are fully clothed and briefed for staged press conferences. But all institutions and organizations are only too happy to provide, free of charge, models of both authentic and counterfeit leadership—people, patterns, systems, and processes that reflect best-and-worst examples.

The ethics of financial barons and wizards are often situational, as depicted in the movie *Wall Street*. People who never pierce the imposing facades of banks, investment firms, and other financial institutions and who never suspect the superficiality of their strategies nor the innate artificiality of money, markets, stocks, and bonds will never understand the nature of crashes. They don't understand the real value of anything. They simply ride the roller coaster of buy and sell, low and high—and the centrifugal force of it all keeps them pinned inside their cars, cabs, cells, and work stations.

At times, brokers recommend stocks with the full understanding that the value is artificially inflated—too much money chasing too few stocks. They just pray the market inflates even higher, even if by their own hot air. When it all comes crashing down around their ears, they hope to be out of the market themselves, their money safe in some Swiss bank. The voices of the few who say, "We are in danger" are drowned by the din around them. The few who cry warnings are cast out. Their voices are rarely heard, even in the most responsible financial media.

4. *Professional models.* Doctors, dentists, accountants, and lawyers provide their own models. Whether the subject is Anwar Kashoggi or some hometown personality, the story line is the same: People of wealth, power, and position become laws unto themselves—thinking they can intimidate, litigate, negotiate, purchase or power their way through any deal.

• *Lawyers.* Besides making lawyers the butts of many jokes, the adversarial, win-lose mindset has mired us in litigation. We have more lawyers per capita in America than in any other country—no other country is even close. Of course, we need more lawyers: ours is a litigious society. We expect to sue and be sued. We refer to "the justice system," as if that were the by-product of the legal system. We have little hope of justice in "trial by jury," as Mark Twain suggested and several highly publicized trials proved. The degree of counterfeit within the system is alarming, and the loss of faith in our courts dangerous.

• *Service agents.* Court games and corporate service games, once played with certain protocol, are now commonly pursued with ego and alcohol. Intent players, hoping to win applause or purse, often snub time-honored traditions, throw tantrums and lash out at line judges, even (alas) on the hallowed lawns of Wimbledon and the halls of Harvard. Junior executives learn to think more in terms of *me* than *we*, ace than deuce, as they master top spins, rifle serves, self-service, underhanded jabs, backhand returns, offensive strategies, defensive lobs, and overhead slams. There's no such thing as "love" for the 30- and 40-somethings—only advantage or disadvantage.

Indeed, service games, as played in the public courts, are in a sorry state: Sloppy amateurs, professing some knowledge or experience, seek to lower or do away with the nets, design their own rackets, and erase the lines, or at least appoint permissive judges. Great service companies are managed differently, and those differences add up to service break-throughs—and break points—in service encounters when the customer comes in contact with a service provider and the supporting cast.

• *Craftsmen.* Traditionally, the standards of craftsmanship— quality, excellence and performance—have varied from one culture to another. Even in the global market, we still tend to use measurements that are very self-oriented, not calibrated to universal standards. They are cultur- ally or internally defined. Every person, in effect, has his or her own counter, compass, or system. And people get in the habit of judging what quality is too quickly, based on their cultural conditioning and prejudices.

Some cultural allowances need to be made, but if we are open- minded about what works for other people, we will progress from one league to the next—from primary to secondary, from an internship to a professorship, from apprenticeship to profession. We learn that what is considered real achievement on one level doesn't pass inspection at the next level, and that if we expect to compete at the new level we have to improve every time out. We must gain more maturity, quality, a higher degree of excellence, craftsmanship, and leadership.

• *Marketing and sales people.* Marketing and sales models are more oriented to hunting and fishing, golfing and gaming. Not much farm- ing here; in fact, in my days in marketing, I didn't plant many seeds because I was too busy swinging the sickle. But few strokes result in sales. Sadly, much of marketing and advertising is a misuse or outright abuse of the physical, human, and monetary resources of the company.

When I stepped away from marketing communications, I apologized to trees for what I had put on paper—on all those rolls and reams of paper that went into playing a numbers game—with worse odds than what the house gives you in Las Vegas. What I have since learned, thanks to Regis McKenna and others, is that marketing is all about relationships. The best models in marketing and sales teach us about building and maintaining quality human relationships over time.

5. *Entrepreneur models.* The *Inc.* magazine models are winsome folks we can all identify with. These are people next door, not all gamesmen and gamblers, who start businesses from scratch and make them grow. Americans, en masse, are exiting large companies. After bad experiences in corporate America, many quickly get into a "second marriage" with entrepreneurial models, without taking a close look at counterfeit elements. The model, for example, may be all talk, no do; all show, no go; all ideas, no dough; all proposal, no marriage; all activity, no results.

• *Maverick models.* Personalities who overcome natural obstacles and social barriers have been rewarded throughout history, especially in America. The frontiersman, gunfighter, athlete, inventor, go-getter and robber-baron all sought success, sometimes at any cost. Our admiration for maverick heroes shows that this ideal is still alive and well. We salute or envy John D. Rockefeller but also John Wayne and John Dillinger, Henry Ford as well as Henry Thoreau, Billy the Kid only a little less than Billy Graham. We turn our admiration for achievement into justification for the concentration of massive wealth and power in a few hands. We tolerate, even enjoy, ostentatious displays of wealth and privilege out of respect for what we consider a mainstream desire to "get ahead."

When I was visiting an editor at *Fortune* magazine, we talked about CEO compensation. "No one at Disney seems to care how much money Michael Eisner makes as long as the company is dong well," he said. And if it's true at Disney with Michael and Mickey, it's true at other companies with other mates and mavericks.

We tend to promote flash-in-the-pan managers—people who come in and get fast results—even if they are ruthless with people and wasteful with other resources.

6. *Public servant models.* Political parties reward the compromiser, the facilitator, the diplomat, and the speech, law, and policy

maker—models made for platforms and parades. The best models seek a creative balance between the interests of individuals and the needs of the community in formulating public policy. The framers of the Constitution knew that our system of government could not work if it were driven solely by self-interest. Effective public leaders spur people to new heights and arouse in them a willingness to transcend their self-imposed limitations. This requires treating them fairly and trusting them. Public officials who put their own self-aggrandizement first betray others to gain their own ends. But to openly acknowledge their tendency is to give them license to undercut others deliberately. Trust begets trust, and even those who aren't totally trustworthy find it hard to betray a trust placed in them.

• *Academic models.* Schools from first grade to post graduate market various academic or conceptual models of leadership that celebrate intellectual, cerebral, compartmental, statistical, financial, analytical, theoretical, functional, and measurable elements with an explicit trust in credentials and accreditation.

One of the top professors at a leading university once told me: "If my students knew my vulnerabilities, knowledge gaps, and personal struggles, they'd be disillusioned. We all need models—they are more powerful than medals. But discipleship is dangerous if you don't see beyond it. That's why all great teachers are transparent, so that their students can see beyond them to the true source of all wisdom."

Teenagers will find and identify with a model—good or bad. Since they have instinct for imitation, they need models worth imitating—models who understand that greater freedom comes from being in harmony, not at odds, with the laws of nature and of man. Students can't choose to violate the law and still reach their potential. If they want what their mentor has, they must duplicate the discipline and become models themselves.

• *Religious models.* When my oldest son was restricted from dating the daughter of a community leader, I told my son, "Welcome to the world of prejudice, discrimination, and dominion—or what some call *the real world.*" I told him to take comfort in knowing that nothing much has changed in the world since the Montagues and the Capulets (*Romeo and Juliet*). Image-conscious parents have long used labels to dismiss or discredit suitors whom they deem unworthy. I reminded him that the dark ages—along with their tried but untrue methodologies—are still with us. Agency, trust, and stewardship struggle to advance against such sick substitutes as control, coercion, and official edict. Such "small matters" are the things that try people's faith. Infractions ranging from subtle discriminations to double standards to forms of spiritual abuse create divisions in the congregation. Instead of unity, we then find mutiny or apostasy.

   7. *Family models.* As good as our family members are and our ancestors were, they still have their faults, flaws, foibles, and human frailties, suggesting again how dangerous it is to model one's life after another imperfect human being or to become satellites of those people, whether they are living or deceased.

   We all need good family role models: real men and fathers, real women and mothers. No one gets into life without, at least, a mother and a father. I know that *families* are being redefined, but it still takes a man and a woman to produce offspring. Yes, marvelous things are happening in medicine; many women who were once unable to conceive or give birth are now having babies. But we are still working with the sperm and egg, bird and bee, male and female.

   In counterfeit corporate and family cultures, older citizens are considered relatively useless and therefore expendable. Once retired, workers sometimes die within days because they have no other role, identity, or purpose. Sorely needed are more models of productive retirees, like my own grandfather, who at 98 years of age was still dating women, going on field trips, attending university functions, teaching and speaking in church, and playing with his great-great-grandchildren.

   The retired workers of an aerospace company in San Diego, California, helped create and care for Missile Park, a multi-acre recreational site, complete with a model railroad. Every retired worker needs his own "mini-park" for family and friends.

No Perfect Model

   Modeling is not all bad. We need heroes. And good models abound; in fact, something worth modeling can be found in every person and every enterprise. Every company provides a model or two, a president or precedent to follow.

   When there is a change of leadership at the top, we search for cues that tell us what the new leader prefers—what he or she wears, drinks, and eats—and we cater to those preferences by adjusting our behavior. When we are immersed in a counterfeit culture, we may fail to see clearly what models are counterfeit because they are regarded as genuine within that culture.

Our leadership models, like our fruit trees, need pruning. Fruit trees that are never pruned have small fruit, if any; many are barren. Likewise, many leaders are barren and hollow, "full of sound and fury, signifying nothing." They are wizards of their own Oz, scarecrows and strawmen who under scrutiny don't hold up as models of authentic leadership. The more imperfect our models, the more counterfeit we are likely to be.

Cures

——— *Chapter 5* ———

Improved Models: Winning by Association

"Be cautious with whom you associate, and never give your company or your confidence to those whose principles you question."

—William Coleridge

Shortly after our third son, Christopher, was born, my wife and I decided that we needed a bigger car. And so on an unseasonably warm December afternoon, I drove my trusty Honda Accord to the local Lincoln dealer and debated whether to trade it for a one-year-old Continental. Admittedly, I liked the idea of leather seats, full power and the luxury of leg room. I drove the car only briefly, as I was pressed for time, and left that day undecided.

Bright and early the next morning, the dealer put the car through the wash and wax and drove it to my office, leaving it parked right outside my window, sparkling like a diamond in the sun. Admittedly, I liked how it looked in front of my office. An associate said to me, sincerely (without wax), as we both gazed at the car, "You deserve it— why not buy it today?" On my lunch break, I returned to the dealer and made the trade.

As the deal was being done, I noted that the weather was changing for the worse, as a fast-moving cold front was bringing in the first winter storm. Within a couple of hours, my new car was covered with snow. By the time I left work that evening, it was dark; the air temperature fell below freezing; and the roads were very slick. Suddenly, appearances and luxuries meant nothing.

My old Honda, equipped with a fairly new set of all-season radials, had been very sure-footed in snow and ice. I immediately noticed a big difference as the Lincoln, equipped with a worn set of fair-weather tires, tended to slip and slide. At the first red light, I slid into the intersection and had to back up to avoid being hit. I lowered the front power windows to remove snow from the rear-view mirrors. Neither

59

front window would come back up. One was binding in its track, and the other seemed to have a short in the electrical circuit.

I pulled my suit coat around my neck and drove slowly home. Early next morning, windows still not working and the outside temperature at 10 degrees Fahrenheit, I drove 50 miles on the freeway to Salt Lake City. It was the first time I had driven the car faster than 45 miles an hour. I noticed at 65 mph a slight play in the steering. I learned much later that the car had been damaged and repainted. The electrical connections and the alignment were never right; consequently, my love for the car wore down faster than the tires.

I learned that shiny new models of cars, like slick leaders, aren't necessarily better. They may be "sunshine patriots" and "summertime soldiers," not very sure-footed in winter seasons, uncertain and inconsistent in using power, and the cause of rapid wear and tear because their lives are out of balance and their priorities misaligned. And so with them, rather than bask in love and security, you get the big chill, as their plans get short-circuited and bound up in bureaucracy. The cosmetics and surface features you thought so fine when struck by love at first sight turn ugly over time—from sugar to salt, from accord to discord—as the environment changes and the costs for maintaining relations escalate out of sight.

Put Them to a Test

Before we buy any leadership models, we would be wise to put them to one or more of five tests: 1) alignments; 2) templates; 3) competencies; 4) relationships; and 5) roots/fruits. Any combination of these tests makes it easier to detect counterfeit.

First, a caution: *No one instrument or individual is infallible.* We all must confess limitations in intelligence and wisdom. We are often intimidated by irresponsible claims of scientists and scholars, duped by false claims of advertisers, taken by the sex appeal of actors and actresses, and impressed by images created by public relations, in part because we generally operate on the basis of trust and openness. However, by being aware of the basics of any discipline, we can assess fairly accurately the strength of certain claims and characters.

But alas, even as educated and experienced professionals, we may be hard-pressed to tell the difference between counterfeit and genuine articles, especially when the cultures we live in (and help create) have a high degree of counterfeit built into them. We can't always compare the bogus bill with an original in the quick exchange of business. But over time, we can hope to improve on the leadership models we choose to emulate.

The tools used to detect counterfeit leadership range from hard to soft, from various standard weights and measures to intuition and discernment. Certain situations serve as "litmus tests" for counterfeit leadership. Like those tests in chemistry where the paper turns pink or blue depending on the solution, the litmus tests of counterfeit show an ink or hue depending on character and culture.

Test 1: Alignment of Mission, Motives, and Means

To test for alignment among mission, motives, and means, we simply ask the questions: "With what mission are we operating? With what motives? And with what means? And are these three elements in alignment?" The premise, of course, is that a noble mission, worthy motives, and commendable methods and means yield good things. The inverse is equally illustrative: foul mission, motives and means bring an even higher degree of counterfeit, and what appears to be progress will ultimately prove to be regress.

A basic cause of counterfeit is misalignment of mission, motives and means. When the leadership is so misaligned, many odd problems develop, and these spread like cancer into other healthy parts of the organization. Soon the mission begins to justify the means; the means gain momentum and override the mission; the motives become polluted; good intentions masquerade for real reasons. We then begin to substitute expediency for priority, imitation for innovation, cosmetics for character, style for substance, pretense for competence, rationalization for research, and public relations for on-going development of people and improvement of products.

• *Mission.* The mission of leadership may be to create market or margin; to provide for basic needs; to supply incentives and reward hard work, resourcefulness, efficiency, and effectiveness; to benefit all stakeholders in win-win ways; to enrich and refine the soul; to supply light, leaven, and salt.

Inevitably, even in the most mundane, militaristic, or malevolent of organizations, the mission is articulated in artistic, if not altruistic, words. People want to believe that what they do makes a difference;

that the company or the cause they work for is constructive; that the products and services they provide are needed and valued. Hence, looking at the mission statement alone won't reveal much.

Moreover, mission-centered, cause-driven organizations are rather easily counterfeited by con artists who learn the right buzzwords and passwords, gain entry and corrupt the systems. Self-deception and egocentricity set in, often accompanied by feelings of euphoria or invincibility.

Why is leadership characterized by high missions and holy crusades often counterfeit? Because motives and means are rarely aligned with the stated mission. Time may be the best test of the validity of a professed mission. But who can afford to wait for 20-20 hindsight to determine if the mission is self-serving or selfless? This leads us to an examination of motives.

• *Motives.* Trust is the tender of trade, and if the motives are pure, there is sanctity and trust in relationships, an openness in style, a simplicity in systems, a candor in communications. The motives of genuine leaders engender trust and encourage the growth and development of people. They are tempered by a long-term view, disciplined by systems with memory, and checked by counselors.

Counterfeit leaders may profess to have noble motives, missions, and means—even clean hands and pure hearts—which is why so many heinous crimes are committed in the name of religion, patriotism, and nationalism. It's a distortion of a good that creates a false god, an unhealthy adoration that creates an aberration, a selfish or possessive love that creates a hate.

The motives of counterfeit leaders are tainted by pride, ambition, lust, desire, passion for power, wealth, fame, publicity, or sensuality. Their motives often shift during the course of events; secrecy becomes mandatory to counterfeiting. Such leaders begin wearing two or more faces and many hats. Few followers dare question or challenge their motives. Even with foul motives, a person's behavior may be very believable, even commendable. Examining motives takes X-ray discernment, since motives are internal organs. Counterfeits are adept at disguising such nasty motives as blind ambition, vanity, lust, greed, selfishness, and possessiveness as something more socially acceptable. Since the root source of sin is often a form of selfishness, foul or covert motives must be discerned, ferreted out, and dealt with before they wreak havoc in harmful public behaviors.

In authentic leaders, we find relatively pure motives, even sanctity, nobility, and integrity. Their motives are to bless, not impress; to empower, not seize power; to promote innovation and learning, not keep people in subservience and ignorance. Their motives relate to three metaphors—light, leaven, and salt: light in the sense of wanting to do the right and bright thing; leaven in the sense of wanting to uplift, enrich, raise standards, and improve quality; salt in the sense of adding color, spice, and laughter to life.

Counterfeit leaders lose sight of the twin principles of service and sacrifice, placing emphasis on meeting their own wants and needs, which become greeds. They become servants, even gods, unto themselves. Their "public service" is poorly disguised "serve-us." And when motives shift, we see some massive behavioral shifts—quakes measuring at least 7.5 on the Hypocrite scale. Over time, people pick up on the real motives of their leaders, and if they find their motives to be tainted with selfish interests, it's every man (and woman) for himself. Soon, sabotage and subversion spread like wildfire in a strong wind.

Motives are hard to detect and correct without the benefit of time or the perspective of history. Master counterfeiters hone the skill of hiding their motives by putting on masks and acting out scripts. Given the capability of men and women to masquerade, we simply can't detect motives without keen discernment. Seasons of experience and enlightenment may be needed to discern foul motives and to decide not to deal with the person or to buy his products and services.

• *Means.* To counterfeit leaders, the means are ever justified, even such messy means as killing, spying, stealing, cheating, lying, fighting, and deceiving. Notable leaders have, throughout history, done such things to achieve a worthy mission. While some exceptional circumstance may justify such extremes, these certainly must be rare. Rape, pillage, and plunder are not the everyday means of authentic leaders.

Counterfeit leaders often justify their means because they tend to judge others by actions, themselves by intentions, always giving themselves the benefit of the doubt. They fully justify embezzlement, theft, fraud, and forgery; indeed, they would bend all the rules to achieve a "worthy" mission. Even prophets and kings have done horrible things to win some "holy war." And in the grand scale of the global economy, it may well be better that a dozen people perish than a million live in ignorance. Of course, an autocratic leader will judge for himself what means are justified, and if that leader considers the ends to be right, then any and all means are justified.

And thus into overtime goes the game of self-deception, a game where all are justified in their aggression. All players justify their means by their lofty mission, initial motive, or the final results. Soon, no one knows the end from the beginning, right from wrong, what anything means, the real worth of things. This much is certain: If the motive is wrong, the follow-through won't be right; and if the means are foul, the ends are suspect. The means—how work is done, what systems are used, what style prevails—easily break down when foul motives work against them from the top and when urgent cries for more resources and results sound from the bottom.

Test 2: Templates: Standard Weights and Measures

The second test is to evaluate leadership according to universal standards, including best of class, best in industry, the pertinent models, and the top awards. Hopefully, these benchmarks create new levels of performance and ever-higher standards.

• *Global standards.* Culture was once the ultimate cop-out. The old question was, "How can there be international standards if all countries, companies, and cultures are different?" The new question is, "What does culture have to do with it?" Sure, those timeless standards and principles must be culturally defined and translated—but the language, norms, and values of the culture should not define what constitutes authentic leadership. Leaders considered "legitimate" in an illegitimate culture are still counterfeit!

One implication of "going global" is that international standards of quality take precedent over internal, local, regional, or national standards. International markets and trade missions demand that there be universal, global standards for quality. If you're in the airline industry, for example, you must abide, roughly, by the same standards and principles whether you're operating in Bolivia or Boston. What constitutes safe air travel does not differ much from country to country.

Do certain standards also apply to effective leadership? Can we talk about an airship in one breath and leadership in another and deny that timeless, universal standards apply? I think it's a cop-out for a culture to say, "We have our own ways, thank you." That simply doesn't wash! When flying in international air, sailing in international waters, and trading on the international exchange, we simply can't opt out or cop out that easily.

As the United Nations has suggested, no society can say, "We play the game by different rules here. If we want to be terrorists and capture people and hang hostages, we have every right—this is simply the way we do business and the way we define leadership."

If your brand of leadership is based on folklore, mysticism, isolationism, or communism, count on a counterfeit culture—and deficit spending. Time and nature are working against you.

• *Professional standards.* Every profession has its standards, and these may be used to detect counterfeits. If a candidate or company is way out of line, you need not be Sherlock Holmes to pick up on the clues—all you need are some standard weights and measures for assessing performance. If one does not measure up to those standards, one is suspect.

In a natural environment, where you are only paid for performance, it's fairly easy to detect counterfeit. But in an artificial social or political environment, it's much harder to detect counterfeit because there are few reliable measurements. There are no real standards; and so counterfeits can float, coast, hide, and get away with murder for years. They can be career assassins who are promoted in the name of management into positions where they can do even more harm. Leaders and followers need to pick up on little clues and cues, and put pieces together. They need the eyes to read trends and patterns and to project outcomes if things continue as they are. In some cases, they may need to put a stop to a course of action, put some people behind bars, reform them, or fire them.

Every industry and company must read and respect its bible, its universal standards or principles of leadership. Benefits and blessings are predicated on observance to natural laws and standards. Standard works or sacred histories, such as the Bible, are great guides for detecting authentic or counterfeit leadership. The purpose of these books is to expose what is false and forged and to highlight what is not—to contrast constantly, almost on every page, the difference between a Cain and an Abel, a Counterfeit and an Authentic.

• *Personal standards.* Great leaders are willing to risk much because they feel that they can recover what they lose because the real value is in their resourcefulness—not in their assets. They can always fall back on native talent and initiative. Even when they get down, they manifest buoyancy.

The unsinkable Molly Brown of our day is the unflappable Dolly Parton. In *Parade* magazine, she said, "I can't stay down long. When I get up in the morning, I want to go to work. If I found myself locked out of heaven, I would pound on the door until they let me in. I would shout, 'Isn't there a song I can sing, a choir I can join, some work I can do?' I would make myself useful and find a way in. People who know me know that beneath these big boobs is a big heart, and beneath this big hair is a big brain. Over time, people see me as a real person and stop staring at the anatomy."

Authentic leaders, while attending to outward appearances, give more attention to the interior. They set their own goals and keep their commitments.

Once at LaGuardia airport in New York City, I was checking my luggage when a captain walked by. The woman behind me said, "Look at that man. He's the prototype captain, as if cast into the role by a movie director. He has the airs of confidence, the stripes of command, the look of experience, the face of constancy."

Midway through that scheduled non-stop flight across the country, the captain proved worthy of this assessment. One passenger in the first-class section of the big Boeing 757 had a heart attack. The captain was notified and asked any medical doctor on board to assist the stewardesses. He then made the immediate decision that one life on the line was more important than the schedule and convenience of all the other passengers. He received clearance to land in Omaha, Nebraska, and brought the big jet out of the sky fast. Once on the runway, he raced to meet the waiting ambulance.

While many people were greatly inconvenienced by this act, possibly even missing international flight connections, my bet is that no one complained, because if it had been any one of us, we would have wanted the captain to do exactly what he did for the one who had the heart attack.

Leaders inspire men and women, whether it is in war or in business, to respect the value of human life and put their lives on the line for a cause. It's not that they have a "devil may care" attitude; but rather, they have an "I care" attitude, and they are willing to make the ultimate sacrifice for a cause.

Ambling through a maritime museum one day, I was struck by a note: "The captain is the character of the ship, and if he has flaws, those are translated to the crew and endanger the voyage." These ships went out to sea in the last century very much at the mercy of the elements. The character-based leadership of the captain was needed to make that mission successful. As I stood with my hands on the wheel, I could sense the responsibility of the ship's captain. Like the captains of today's jet-liners, they are perched high above ground level and put in charge of a massive vessel, the crew, and all passengers. They may have a co-pilot and navigator, but the ship, essentially, is in their hands.

Developing authentic leadership means leading real ships, and managing real-life relationships in concert with personal and professional standards. As leaders in the making, we may find ourselves at some point in time behind the wheel—responsible for lives, missions, and cargo. We feel the weight of responsibility in our bones. We toss and turn those first few nights, concerned about our ability to measure up, make it work, and finish well. But over time, we gain experience and confidence and earn our stripes. Leaders are made by being put in command of air, sea, and land ships. And their high personal standards guard against leading with the narrow perspective of "here and now" and doing only what's best for "me and mine."

Test 3: Competence: Your Ship Has to Float

The poet John Holmes tells of his boyhood experiences with an old, deaf New England shipbuilder who taught him without speaking. In the presence of this craftsman, it suddenly came to him with the force of a voice shouting in his ear that, "No matter how you build it, your ship has to float: You can't fool the ocean."

Authentic leaders are practical idealists, craftsmen who realize that their ship has to float. Some things, like ineffective leadership, just can't be explained to an unforgiving ocean of discontented stakeholders. So authentic leaders are growing all the time, improving their performance and products by being open to feedback and by exploring, experimenting, evaluating, and revising. A person who is serious about quality must first be an example of what's desired in terms of honesty, integrity, scholarship, and industry.

Tragically, because of advanced technology and education divorced from reality, craftsmanship is endangered. In many vocations, it takes 20 years to develop true craftsmanship. But processes change so fast in industry that after a few years, some skills become obsolete.

Real craftsmen remain good at what they do, refusing to sacrifice quality to technology, to expediency, to unions or other attempts to make work uniform at a level of mediocrity.

Competent performers are often bridled by managers because they make others look bad. Management may inhibit craftsmanship by taking responsibility from individual workers. In some businesses, production workers seldom see the results of their work and are typically never held accountable for it. As far as the customer is concerned, automobiles are made by anonymous people—defects are neither attributed nor traced to individual workers. They are divorced from the consumer and even from internal quality control people. Often their pay is unrelated to performance, and since they never know if they are doing good or bad work, soon they don't care.

Real craftsmen work with risk on projects that require a great deal of personal judgment. To them, every job is different, and every project requires that skills and abilities be brought together in a different relationship. Craftsmen deal directly with customers; they have good tools, and they take care of them, knowing that if their tools are not well maintained, they can't do superior work. They understand that people don't develop pride in processes, only in products, and that you have to accept raw material for what it is—imperfect—and realize that not all "defects" are to be cut out, filled in or stained over. Gradually, leaders transfer the ideals of simple beauty, sturdiness, and usefulness from projects to people.

Craftsmen shape raw material into something more useful, strong, and beautiful—without violating the integrity of the material. Leaders likewise shape people. Without violating the agency of the person, they observe what is not obvious to everybody else. But seeing the potential of the piece, they make something classic out of material that others might reject and throw away. They develop an ability to see diamonds in the rough and then to produce skillfully the finished product.

Competence and craftsmanship will always be in demand. If you need a job done right, who do you go to? Someone who gets paid the same whether he or she works or not? Somebody whose main concern is job security? No, you go to an independent producer, a craftsman, a peak performer.

Test 4: Relationships: Do They Hold Over Time?

Examining intimate relationships is one of the most conclusive, fool-proof tests of leadership. As we magnify these relationships many times, we might ask, "How well do they hold up under close scrutiny?"

Authentic and counterfeit leaders manage relationships different-ly—especially in challenging times of disaster, chaos, confusion, conflict, opposition, and competition. By examining intimate family relationships, close professional relationships, and other stakeholder relationships, we begin to see true colors. Authentic and counterfeit leaders differ also in how they treat children, minorities, and people who many might con-sider poor, dumb, ugly, or plain.

Intimate and family relationships are especially telling. People who are committed to long-term relationships with one another tend to behave responsibly and equitably. When people anticipate a lifetime of living or working together, they can't afford to let deep rifts develop. People on the move, however, not only may be indifferent to rifts, but they may be incapable of establishing close bonds.

For example, suppose we find a young couple living in California. They have no kin or childhood friends nearby, belong to no church or clubs, and reside in an apartment complex that turns over at the rate of 20 percent per month. At the end of the day, both husband and wife put their entire emotional burden on their spouse for the simple reason that they have no one else to share it with. Marriage was never intended to carry that much freight single-handedly. The only alternative to abusing the primary bond is to sever it, to divorce, leaving both the husband and the wife alone.

Authentic leaders, realizing that their family relationships are their most important states of readiness, make regular deposits in the emotional bank accounts of spouses, children, and colleagues—the people they spend the most time with. They may retire from the heat of the battle for a week to regroup and have a bonding experience with the family or a one-on-one experience with a spouse, particularly when a relationship has been strained.

Authentic leaders are sensitive to these primary relationships and try to maintain healthy communication and interaction. Of course, at times, every leader has to make tough judgment calls that cause people to second-guess their motives. Even the leader's own spouse and chil-dren may not understand why he or she does some things.

For example, in the play *A Man for All Seasons*, the wife and daughter of Sir Thomas More didn't understand why he couldn't take the oath, get out of jail, and go home. He responded to his bewildered daughter, Margaret: "When a man takes an oath, he's holding his own self in his own hands like water. And if he opens his fingers then, he needn't hope to find himself again. And since we see that avarice, anger, envy, pride, sloth, lust and stupidity commonly profit far beyond humility, chastity, fortitude, justice, and thought, why then perhaps we must stand fast a little—even at the risk of being heroes."

Some decisions and actions are misunderstood and misread. These result in withdrawals, misunderstandings, stress, or strain on the relationship. Divorce is the common result, especially when people are centered on careers. Authentic leaders have a sense of mission and perspective and balance and base their behavior on principles that transcend petty, immediate, or transitory concerns.

Test 5: Roots and Fruits

To detect counterfeits, we may have to examine the roots and fruits, doing our due diligence before entering into relationships, negotiating deals, and signing the bottom line.

• *Roots.* When looking at origins, ask yourself, "Who is behind this? What is at the bottom of this? What is the history of this person or enterprise?" Author Alex Haley heightened awareness that all people have genealogical roots and a genuine heritage and that by honoring our roots we move closer to authentic personal and family leadership. As we identify our ancestors, remember their lives through research and reading, and honor them by doing things they could not do for themselves, we gain appreciation for who we are and for what has come before us. If we fail to cultivate a sense of identity, history, and legacy, we are more easily drawn to counterfeit models and more easily enticed to accept other scripting.

Returning to roots also suggests that we return to nature and to the soil. What matters is not the size of our garden plot—be it an apartment window box or a 100-acre ranch—what matters is growing something from seed, having something organic to water, nurture, cultivate and care for (preferably something we intend to eat). Having a garden reminds us of our very real dependency on the harvest of field and flock.

Nature has many lessons for us. Unfortunately, few take the time to learn them. Having worked in four National Parks—Zion, Yellowstone, Grand Canyon, and Glacier—I can attest that 90 percent of park visitors never get off the main road. They see the parks through car windows and brochures when the real beauty and serenity is to be found hiking the trails. Those who find their roots, whether in nature or nuture, discover a certain peace that has nothing to do with possessions or titles.

• *Fruits.* Ultimately, by their fruits shall we know authentic leaders. But we can't always wait for the fruits to ripen. Fruit takes a season to mature, and in the early stages we don't have much evidence of the eventual harvest. At first, the subtle differences between wheat and tares are extremely hard to detect—until they slowly become manifest in visual or consequential ways.

Experienced leaders need not see the fruit on the vine or branch to believe in the process; they understand natural growth cycles and seasons. They can detect, even predict, what products (and people) are no more substantive than cotton candy, mere tastes on the tip of the tongue, mere shadows and fleeting images. Real leaders seek to build a product line more substantive than pizza, popcorn, and videos.

When culture deteriorates, people lose their sense of what constitutes quality. In the store, they pass up the juicy apple, orange, and pear to purchase artificially flavored candy like gummy bears. And in business, they pass over creative, innovative, and fruitful workers to promote sterile managers who kill more talent in a day than God can grow in a decade.

Winning by Association
To cultivate authentic character and culture, we need to associate with authentic leaders. When hatchlings are exposed to the songs of their parents, they learn to sing with the same sparkle and luster. But when given no model, they only learn to sing a dull approximation of the song of the species. Most people are never exposed to the entire song, the full melody, of the human species. They only hear parts or approximations of the song. But they think they know the full melody because what they hear is beautiful compared with the vulgar and raucous noise around them. Authentic leaders sing the song of the species.

From a study of geology, we can learn a lesson from the geode: being ordinary on the surface safely conceals the dazzling display of crystals inside. Even if our figures and features do not fit the social definition of handsome or beautiful, our countenances can still beam a precious commodity, such as joy, peace, self-respect or optimism. We need not be jaded; we can maintain an adolescent enthusiasm for life.

But chances are we won't maintain enthusiasm if we don't associate with others who have it. And they won't have it for long unless they, too, sing the song of the species periodically. Teaching people universal melodies and principles first is not only a palatable way of influencing them, it may be the only way.

In paying tribute to an authentic leader who was leaving office after eight years of service, his close associates said:

There is little selfishness in him. Although humble and unassuming, he is a tower of strength, a man of great initiative and foresight, a doer in every sense. His struggles have given him knowledge, understanding, and great insight into the human condition, and ultimately have motivated him to care for others with acts of love and tenderness. Here is one man who is honored by those of his household. We not only love him as a person, we sustain him as a leader. He has made that easy for us by having so few weaknesses. In this man there is great virtue. It is too much to say that he is perfect, but he comes wondrously close. There is in him devotion, consistency, and power. He shows remarkable strength and great personal courage in meeting issues on principle, not pressure, even when he knows his decisions will not be popular or completely understood.

Such is the legacy of authentic leaders.

In addition to associating with great leaders, we need to associate with great companies—companies with products and services that are world-competitive, not companies living on the legacies of the past . We need to work for companies that are concerned about quality, customer service, equity, ethics, and integrity; that are getting feedback from their stakeholders, and that are motivated to keep improving, day by day. Other companies likely won't last long.

——— *Chapter 6* ———

Character Growth: From Music of the Night to Morning Light

"Let your darker side give in to the power of the music that I write—the power of the music of the night."

—Phantom of the Opera

Once in Manhattan, I stood in a long line, hoping to see a sold-out performance of *Phantom of the Opera* on Broadway. One ticket, a standing-room only, became available. Although I was well back in the line, all others in front of me were either in groups or didn't want to stand, and so I got the ticket.

I stood next to the control panel, where the electric magic on stage was engineered by a young man. Seated on a stool by his side was a young woman, who by all appearances was a friend he was trying to impress. During the performance, I watched both shows—the one on stage, and the one behind the scenes at the control center. The lighting engineer had done the show often enough that his moves were automatic, and he could flirt with and court his "Christine," the companion at his side.

Like this phantom at the controls at the opera, some chief executives become phantoms who manipulate controls at the office to impress a vast captive audience of employees, investors, spectators, and a few intimate admirers.

The Phantom pleads: "Sing once again with me our strange duet, my power over you grows stronger yet...in this labyrinth, where night is blind, the Phantom of the Opera is there—inside your mind." And indeed, these phantoms get inside our minds, and thereby gain power over us—our thoughts, emotions and actions.

In his lair, the Phantom sings seductively: "Let your mind start a journey through a strange, new world! Leave all thoughts of the world you knew before! Let your soul take you where you long to be! Only then can you belong to me...Floating, falling, sweet intoxication! Touch me, trust me, savor each sensation! Let the dream begin, let your darker side give in to the power of the music that I write—the power of the music of the night."

Such a possessive, controlling "love" is really a lust, a selfish indulgence, a false promise, a seduction to satiate appetite and passion. To dominate, we resort to tricks of the trade. We become phantoms, stationed at our own control centers, keeping up appearances and orchestrating actions on stage. We become victims of our own inventions and illusions, thinking we can win in Oz or Opera or Office by intimidation—a popular notion with counterfeit leaders who see the world in terms of managers, musicians and Munchkins.

10 Counterfeit Traits

From observation and assessment, I have come to believe that the following 10 traits characterize counterfeit leaders.

1. They do much of their work in the dark. Counterfeiting creates pockets of secrecy and darkness wherein we withdraw, keeping things from our closest loved ones and colleagues, preferring to work in a "darkroom," developing film that we shoot in our minds and imaginations. We work in closets, behind curtains and walls, behind and titles and positions, behind closed doors or in remote retreats. We think we can hide, as some two-year-olds do, merely by covering our eyes or by throwing a blanket over affairs.

The cover of darkness is the canopy of counterfeit. Night provides the camouflage, cloud, or smoke for covert activities. Counterfeiting requires a degree of secrecy and reduced visibility. It takes advantage of confusion and poor vision; thus, it is usually a night game, often played with drugs and alcohol in bars and cars, bedrooms and boardrooms.

Counterfeits dabble in various forms of babble, deception, stealing, lying, thieving. They falsify, forge, and change the facts to satisfy their own designs and desires. They may fool their loved ones—even other people with high degrees of discernment—into believing that they are legitimate when, in fact, they are forging, defrauding, hoodwinking, and creating counterfeit deeds and documents. Like the fictional character Walter Mitty, counterfeit leaders revel in make-believe daydreams and confuse fantasy and reverie with quality and productivity.

2. They believe themselves to be above the law, laughing at the very idea of judgment. For many counterfeit leaders, the very idea of judgment, of ever having to answer to anyone for anything—let alone for every thought and deed—is ludicrous. They believe themselves to be the law, the constitution of the land. They may acknowledge a supreme court, possibly even a god, but they see themselves always in good graces, in the right, worthy of merit and mercy. No judge would dare slap a sentence on them.

Even if we don't believe in a final judgment, we must admit, upon sober reflection, that the judgment is happening here and now, day by day, and that it's a consequence of inviolate laws and principles that always operate in both human and natural systems and ultimately govern.

Eventually, we must all fall to our knees and make our petitions, naked. We come as we are to judgment—as we do every day to the doors of restaurants and banks and businesses. To the very gates we come, seeking entry. What a wonder! To see that we are all beggars, "drunken sailors on horseback," as novelist Thomas Wolfe said, who must all plea for a degree of mercy to temper true and uncompromising justice; otherwise, we have no chance, not even "standing room only" to enter into celestial theaters.

3. They breed false emotion (sentimentality). As a freshman in college, I had an English teacher who tested and graded very tough. In the margin of our papers, he would often write a brief criticism: "unearned emotion." It was his way of telling us, "You haven't made the point, won the argument, or earned the emotion you want the reader to experience. Instead, you are taking the shortcut of sentimentalism."

That same year, I had a wrestling coach who pushed us to the point of throwing up in every workout. He summed up his philosophy in three words: "Win before pin." It was his way of telling us: "I don't want you to go for a quick pin. If it's there, take it; but be prepared to go the distance and win on points. Against the best competition, you often must."

Counterfeit leaders relish false emotion and rely on "pin before win." Emotion is central to leadership because it ties to motivation. Counterfeit leaders opt for false forms of motivation: sentimentality over spirituality, fear over care, revenge over forgiveness, lust over love, pleasure over joy, vulgarity over humor. The distortion of legitimate emotion leads to affectation, one of the primary traits of counterfeit leaders.

As their speech and mannerisms become more and more affected, counterfeit leaders become masters of ambiguity. All is subject to interpretation, because their livelihoods are gotten in the gulf between what is plain and what is uncertain. And so they speak and write to be politically correct or ambiguous. In the corporate world, no one in his right mind would ever write a memo in plain English—candor and truth telling are strictly taboo. The preferred practice is to write expressly to be misunderstood. That is job security. Memos written in plain English, very to the point, will be tacked on managers' walls—as Martin Luther's 13 theses were tacked to the door of the Sistine Chapel—and remain there for months. Eventually, such memos become "bills of sale," as their authors are sold down river into slavery.

4. They create uniformity and conformity. Counterfeit leaders may admire creativity, but in reality they try to control speech, curb expression, and bring about uniformity and sameness, as opposed to unity and oneness. They may covet the fruits of creativity and diversity, but they can't quite trust people enough to allow the freedom that leads to innovation. The former Soviet Union proved conclusively that Communism, in concept and practice, is a counterfeit form of government, and yet the holdout Communist countries never tire of proving the same point: Uniform systems don't yield much fruit, or produce.

Many leaders resort to regimentation: everybody is put in uniform. But put in uniform, people put on a persona and a mindset, and start marching in lockstep. Military regimes, sports teams, and all-male academies discovered long ago that uniforms lead to instant uniformity. But without authentic leadership, such uniformity won't have half the tensile strength of unity, especially under fire. If the troop marches only to the beat of uniformity, conformity, and nationality, it may win a battle but lose the war.

Counterfeit leaders are uncomfortable in situations that call for creativity, flexibility, adaptability, or originality. Why? Because they don't work well from scratch; they are imitators, impressionists, modifiers, forgers. They require something to rebel against, campaign for, or play off of.

Most counterfeits leaders, like chameleons, change their colors to match the environment. They can be very hard to detect in their native habitat, but once out in the open, they are easily spotted and detected. Their great fear is to be caught with their pants down, out of their element, stripped of their camouflage. Uncomfortable alone, they like to run with a certain crowd and be seen in places where their colors blend in.

5. They waste resources. Counterfeit leaders enjoy the expansive and the expensive; they waste and exploit people and other precious resources. Their style is to use and abuse, consume, and create dependencies. They view the public masses as asses. Their appetites and passions are either socially and systemically checked or out of control. They both want and need much money, and to get it, they will do whatever is necessary, including start their own printing press or inflate the currency. They put their own image or imprint on the coin of the realm, and then decide what it is worth on the market. They try to tell people, even Father Time and Mother Nature, what the best time is to buy and sell; little wonder, then, that they waste and consume rather than conserve or create resources.

Counterfeits don't value resources because they don't know the real worth of things. Wasting food, for example, is of little import to them when they are also wasting human life. If they see little wrong with killing, they won't worry about spilling.

6. They are addicted to the artificial. Counterfeit leaders are often addicted to artificial highs, not only through alcohol and drugs but also through artificial emotions and political motions. Their humor borders on pornography and vulgarity. They resort to ribald jokes or humor at the expense of others. Delivered with a twist of cynicism and sarcasm, their barbs put down instead of build up. Their wit is often taken out of the papers—playing on headlines, news events, and newsmakers and taking a cheap shot, a low blow, often with sexual innuendo.

What attracts many people to counterfeit leadership is the leader's ability to have a "good time," often defined as losing all inhibitions and letting it all hang out. Because the counterfeit can appear so genuine in this party mode, the difference is best detected in the aftertaste, the "morning after" come-uppance.

The counterfeit leader is often a pied-piper who plays a song that people can dance or march to. These musicians are often winsome, popular people who know how to please and appease. Smooth socially, they know how to drink and drive, date and dance—how to oil and ooze their way around the floor, doing the tango, foxtrot, and other seductive steps, including some "dirty dancing." They subscribe to magazines that help them perfect the art of seduction. They believe in the *Playboy* version of virtue—contributing to a "save the rain forest" fund—even if they waste entire forests to print and spread bane all over the planet. Few healthy and happy children result from all this prescribed copulation, as fertilization is to be avoided, and fetuses aborted. And so, rather than experience joy in their posterity, they experience some pleasure in their prosperity, thinking it to be a good trade—until the forties fill them with pain and panic.

7. *They exploit people and opportunities.* In situations of chaos and confusion, counterfeit leaders see opportunity to gain control. If they don't appoint themselves to be in charge, they quickly build constituency for election or revolution. When chaos and confusion are the orders of the day, opportunities to exercise leadership abound whether you are the pilot or co-pilot, stewardess or passenger. Counterfeit leaders seek control of situations rich in opportunity. Having eyes for opportunity, they see a chance to achieve high position or to seize power using just their voices (no votes needed). Blessed with great voices and with some acting ability, they then enter the stage and sing, "Follow me; I will lead you to better times; I will get you out of this mess."

Even in distress or disaster, where there is fire and confusion, we are better served to follow our own instincts than to follow the voice of a counterfeit leader. But how can we know? Should we blindly follow anybody who moves, who says, "Follow me—I know the way." True and false leaders may both use the same words, and so the difference is hard to detect in the heat of the moment. But counterfeit leaders will create internal conflict, opposition, and comparison for the sake of competition—situations where you are fighting internally to get things done. Some of your biggest and toughest competition may then be within your own organization. And who needs that when the competition outside is gaining market share?

8. *They are cool actors and hot reactors.* They relish politics, theatrics, dramatics, short-term flashes, and short-cut finishes. Masters of make-up, they often judge on appearances. And as followers, so judged, we all become actors, often after the order of the movie or soap opera of the day.

Once in Argentina, I went to a see a movie, *Cool Hand Luke,* and was so impressed that I was scripted for a month. I entered the theater with one identity and came out with another. If we so bounce from show to show, we then go from cool to hot, as the mood or the movie dictates. Our hands and feet become those of puppets, as we take on the lines—and very lives—of our mediated models (many of them mere figments of imagination to begin with). We gradually fall prey to escapism. As

James Thurber wrote, reverie and rationalization replace real thinking. And as James Harvey Robinson said in his classic essay, "Four Kinds of Thinking," we are so controlled by reverie and rationalization that "most of our so-called reasoning consists in finding arguments for going on believing as we already do."

Becoming impressionists, imitators, or impersonators leads to pretention. After a season of such acting and reacting, we may forget who we are and sell out, seeking positions and possessions, creating dissension and division, and chasing the elusive "good life" of comfort and ease.

Counterfeits are often students of symbolism as applied to the visual arts. In effect, their life becomes a parody of things and scenes played out on stage. Yes, we are all players on the stage of life, but some play it straight, and some don't. Counterfeits merely memorize and act out scripts written by others for them. Their lives, like their films, are produced and directed by others. And yet many people look to them for cues on what to wear, what to think, what to believe, what to say and do.

9. They harbor deep hates, biases, and prejudices. Counterfeit leaders vent their anger, hating their loves and loving their hates. Full of bias and prejudice, many, inevitably, become elitists, believing in race supremacy or segregation. They want to wall off their territory and turf, in spite of giving lip service to improving the plight of the poor. They are often soaking the working class for a greater degree of comfort and security for themselves.

Thanks in part to counterfeit community leaders, we can be in danger within the walls of our own homes—or "the woods" just outside the door. One woman stepped outside her back door and was shot to death on the patio by a trigger-happy deer hunter. Like that tragic story, there are many who are shot, berated, belittled, abused, and fired by crazed leaders who desperately seek quick solutions and profits. In reduced daylight and at night, "the woods" are no place for man or beast, let alone woman or child, as dangerous predators practice blindside attacks.

10. They succumb to vanity and pride. Counterfeit leaders tend to be proud, vain, and self-promotional. More than most folks, they love flattery. With an emphasis on externals, they care deeply about the size, slant, and shape of bodily features, opting for cosmetic surgery to fix what doesn't fit the prevailing idea of what's beautiful, stylish, sexy, or fashionable.

In seeking the ultimate floor plan and home, the counterfeit become homeless. They are always on the move, buying and selling, attending home shows and open houses, and using their real estate to make symbolic statements regarding their wealth and status. But in truth, they often become so financially burdened that they have neither disposable income nor recreational options.

When we get caught up in image, fashion, and cosmetics, we take one giant step toward chronic vanity. We begin to subscribe to magazines like *GQ, Vogue, Esquire, Mademoiselle* or *Cosmopolitan,* and to the attendant editorial philosophies. Once proud and vain, we discover many new ways of counterfeiting, as pride and vanity are springboards to all sorts of chicanery. Armed with perspective on civilizations and cultures, historians have long documented that "pride comes before the fall."

Pride creates barriers by imposing definitions and descriptions of what's in and what's out, what's right and what's wrong, what's fashionable and what's fun. Pride becomes discriminatory, possessive, and exclusive. Where once all were welcome, now there are barriers to entry. Leaders of the campus fraternity or sorority may plead innocent, but their strong social castigation of the "poor and plain" speaks for itself.

Morning Light: Traits of Authentic Leaders

What passes for masquerade at night is usually exposed in the morning light. The chorus in *Phantom of the Opera* sing: "Masquerade! Paper faces on parade. Hide your face so the world will never find you! Every face a different shade...flash of mauve, splash of puce, fool and king, ghoul and goose. Take your turn on the merry-go-round in an inhuman race. Seething shadows, breathing lies...You can fool any friend who ever knew you."

Yes, but the morning will come, the day will break, the rooster will crow, all will awake! And then, in the piercing light, where now will you hide your face? It may well appear on a million television screens as the world awakes to its news. Can you then fool your friends? No, says Raoul, "No more talk of darkness. Forget these wide-eyed fears. Let daylight dry your tears. Let me be your shelter, let me be your light."

Many of us have spent long nights of worry and pain, fear and doubt, hoping and praying for relief and light. Much of our travail is the work of phantoms, real and imagined, who play their music upon our minds, our emotions, perhaps our bodies. And our transformation, if it comes, will likely be the work of an authentic leader—perhaps a woman who, like the moon, lights the night; or a man who, like the sun, brightens the day.

Once out of high school, I found work in a state institution for the mentally deficient, where I tended to the needs of "worst case" human beings—all mentally disabled to the maximum degree. I often worked the night shift, spending from 11 p.m. to 7 a.m. alone with 60 inmates in a drab, depressing building. Some nights, especially in the dead of winter, were dreadfully long.

The one real leader in this institution—and the one person who kept me going—was a woman who worked the morning shift. She clocked in promptly at 6 a.m. every morning, always bright and cheerful, singing songs and barking out crisp commands like a Marine drill sergeant. Although petite in size, she handled these "monster" men as babies and boys, showing boundless energy and gymnastic mobility. She had the perfect touch of tough love.

How did she do it? I'll never know. But she did it every morning for decades, in spite of the counterfeit leadership of the institution. "I'm not going to let incompetent administrators and a few retarded men determine how I feel about life," she once said. All who worked there took inspiration from her.

10 Authentic Traits

From a wellspring of love and trust, great leaders perform anonymous acts of service, even sacrifice. They are responsible stewards over time and talent. They discipline appetites and passions, budget time and money, even after acquiring an abundance. They also do real work and maintain close ties to nature or to natural processes. Their speech is unaffected and unpretentious—natural, efficient, effective. And they are appropriately meek, humble, contrite, submissive, and obedient to proper authority.

1. They continue to do real work throughout their lives. Authentic leaders try to achieve a balance between mental and physical labor. If their primary labor is intellectual, they will often have hobbies where they work with their hands or help people with their hands. If their primary work is manual, they will enrich themselves with reading and study and mental activity to achieve a balance. They discipline their appetites and passions and keep them within limits and bounds. Even if they have an abundance, they continue to budget both time and money, not wasting resources. Knowing that there are people in need, they seek to help fill those needs in meaningful ways. They attempt to keep fit and healthy.

In the scheme of things, they would rather make a significant contribution and a real difference on a small scale and on a small plot than to constantly seek advancement and titles and kingdoms and salaries that may impress others. They would rather raise real kids and crops on a small farm than to operate in the "Big Apple" and do something more or less meaningless.

2. They respect the law, roots, and heritage. Authentic leaders respect the law, their roots, and their history, and yet focus on the future, living more out of imagination than memory, which is why they are always progressing. They love truth and virtue—defining progress in terms of further light and knowledge. They realize what is transitory and what is lasting. They have the wisdom and character to seek treasures that may not be worth much here and now, but will be worth a lot later. They are grounded, rooted, anchored. They realize that common cement makes a better foundation to build on than fanciful long-range forecasts.

If they were cheated out of strong footings and faith in childhood, they seek to establish these in their teens, twenties, or thirties—or whenever they begin to be converted to agricultural principles and processes. I have seen men and women in their forties and fifties who finally realize that they are being blown about by every wind of opinion and change, and they say, "I've had enough; I know now who I am; I am going to become more grounded, rooted, anchored." And they make some amazing transformations. One man had "done it all," but when he came home drunk one night and frightened his son, he quit drinking and started asking himself the right questions. He is now engaged in worthy projects.

3. They tell it like it is. Authentic leaders are clear about their position on an issue. They don't make people guess what they are about or what they believe. They take a stand, clearly communicating their position. They love simplicity, brevity, economy, plainness. Their speech is more natural, efficient, and effective. They don't waste or mince words. They believe in the economy of truth—that it's not only the best policy, but the best buy. It is real, earned emotion, springing from a love and a joy in life. In contrast, counterfeit leaders have long used the Big Lie to create a sense of nirvana or utopia and to lead their followers to some promised land. Little "white lies" are also used to lead people down the primrose path.

4. They are home-grown originals. Genuine leaders have something original to them—something cultivated from seed that reflects a home-grown character. They prize light and knowledge, virtue and industry, without believing that they have a corner on the market. Their charisma is quieter, but evident in their wisdom, perspective, and life balance. Their style is to build, empower, create self-reliance. They keep perspective and balance. Their ethic of service, even sacrifice, engenders deep loyalty among followers. They become responsible stewards, trusted friends, and committed peacemakers. Although they may be fierce competitors as needed in conflicts, they are vigilant guardians of precious rights and freedoms, constantly preparing people and taking defense initiatives to keep peace.

Most genuine leaders love games, stories, fantasy; they are child-like. Their fun and humor are natural and spontaneous, less affected, vulgar, and artificial. They are good sports and enjoy competition within the rules. They respect the opposition and the officials. They may not like certain calls but show restraint. In situations of conflict, opposition, and competition, they may respond nobly; they may even be grateful for their opposition, knowing that it keeps them strong and vigilant. They recognize that through opposition and competition they are motivated to make continuous improvements and to maintain fitness and viability. They may even cooperate with competitors in unique ways. They break down prejudices and walls built up over time; seek to understand other cultures and languages; and promote commerce and trade, making alliances and agreements that benefit all concerned.

5. They have a sense of stewardship about their talents, time, and other resources. Authentic leaders have tremendous capacities and capabilities to lead and uplift, inspire and motivate. Those are often developed talents and discovered gifts. These "gifts" come with high price tags in terms of duty and stewardship.

We all know people of great wealth, status, and possessions who consider none of these things their own. They have little sense of ownership, but a keen sense of stewardship. They consider their possessions, even their own children, as gifts. They are humbled because of them. They consecrate what they have for the blessing of family and of the less fortunate. Not that they turn their private homes into open houses 24 hours a day, but they wisely and discretely use their resources to benefit other people.

For example, a medical doctor and his wife offer a room of their home to one unwed, pregnant teenage girl at a time, until each has her baby and is able to return home.

Once I led an entertainment troupe of university students through the southern United States. We travelled by bus from city to city, giving a concert each evening and then staying overnight in the homes of local residents who offered us bed and breakfast. One day I needed to get four cast members into the next city several hours early to do live radio and television interviews. I saw no way to do it. Dismayed, I spoke with our host that evening, a man of means in the city whom I had known for only a few minutes. When he learned of my need, he simply said, "Let me help. I have an airplane, money, and friends who can help make this happen. Anything I have is yours if you need it."

More than speed, what matters most to authentic leaders are motive and direction. Speed, in business and other competitive contests, is very important, but mission, motive, and direction are even more important in life, as tales of tortoises and rabbits are told every day. Even though strong forces may push, pull, and entice them to change their course, authentic leaders keep their promises, commitments, contracts, and covenants.

6. They are more concerned with being and becoming than having and getting. Having and getting are counterfeit concerns compared to being and becoming. Having versus being, getting versus becoming are interesting dichotomies. One of the counterfeit questions is, "What do you do?" as opposed to "Who are you?" and "Who are you becoming?"

For four years, I worked closely with hundreds of young men and women, most of them between the ages of 19 and 21, who studied for eight weeks of final preparations at a missionary training center before leaving for various Spanish-speaking countries. They were excited about what they were becoming.

And for four years, I worked full time at a major university where the most important questions were "What are you reading? What are you writing? What are you becoming? What are you thinking? What are you planning?" as opposed to "What are you doing?" and "What do you have?" or "How much money do you make?" Why, then, are the later questions the only seemingly relevant questions past age 24?

I submit that they aren't. Nothing changes upon graduation from college. The most relevant questions at any age or stage of life are ones about being and becoming, not having and getting.

Those who are being and becoming are true to their best selves—true to something innate, inherent, that's born within them, that comes as a unique gift, an endowment. By selling themselves cheaply on the market, most counterfeits become nameless, faceless followers, fit for whatever menial purpose their master might inflict on them. As Henry David Thoreau says, "Most men lead lives of quiet desperation."

7. They maintain relationships. Authentic leaders nurture relationships by building trust. Trust is the cement of relationships. As we build trust, we build more than Babel—we build the only tower able to reach the heavens. The best argument and evidence for an eternal marriage is a couple who deserve one. As we lose trust, we lose the mortar, and the many bricks laid by faithful followers collapse under the weight of suspicion and accusation.

Trust earned frugally, a penny at a time, is often spent recklessly, in million-dollar overdrafts. Soon the lawyers and the bankers make all the decisions. And where the woos and coos of tender love were once whispered, only the brash words of law and finance remain. Foreclosures and second trust deeds replace grand openings and primary deeds of trust.

"Kiss me and smile for me"—lyrics made popular by Peter, Paul and Mary—suggest that lovers and leaders come and go. We catch them in glimpses, and the great often die young because they risk so much, they love so deeply, they are open and trusting, they put it all on the line. These sweet songs of parting are often the only memory and legacy of leadership.

And so, we may have the notion that life is a zero sum game, and that when someone wins, it is at our expense, because there is only so much pie and pot. Worse is the sense that life is a sweepstakes, a lottery, where "the winner takes all." We then keep investing our tithe in that one-in-a-million chance that our ticket will be drawn—missing altogether the "sweet-stakes" where all can win, with better than even chances, all we can ever use. Authentic leaders make winners of us all. They prove that life is not a zero sum game, that there is an abundance, and plenty to spare.

8. They feel free to progress to the next level and take measured risks because of their high degree of inner security and proactivity. What often distinguishes authentic from counterfeit leaders is the source and degree of their self-identity and internal security.

By tapping into sources of internal security and self-esteem, they are empowered to start over at a new level, to progress, to enter a rigorous finishing school or a disciplined basic training system. They can leave family and friends and get married. They can build a home and have children. They can provide and progress in their jobs and be promotable. They can start their own business, plan for their own retirement. They can do these things because they understand the principle of continuous improvement, daily progression, line-upon-line learning. They are not intimidated by things that are new and have never been done before. They understand the need to start over at a higher level.

Having more internal definition, direction, and motivation, authentic leaders get involved and take action. American culture has degenerated from proactivity to passivity—close your eyes, turn your back, hear no evil, see no evil, speak no evil. We seem to think, "It's better to just sit here than to do something," better to "wait and see" than do and be. Seemingly, some would rather bury their children than oppose pollution. The few who get involved are branded activists, extremists, and crusaders in a cause. Some will turn the other cheek, preferring to be kicked and stoned or to die as martyrs for a cause, rather than wage war.

When authentic leaders deal with the poor and needy, they give not just money and lip, but time and services. They don't ignore, tune out, or turn off the cries and pleas for help from the needy, just because they slow them down or get in their way. Real leadership—from David, who one-hit Goliath, to Nolan Ryan who no-hit the Giants—faces up to the challenge.

9. They treat all people, especially the disadvantaged, with love and dignity. Once a beautiful five-year-old girl was badly burned and became very disfigured. Her face was almost hideous to look at. And yet her parents continued to love her to the point she felt secure enough to go out in public, to go back to the public schools and to help other people relate to her as a normal person. Her family gave her constant affirmation, and her friends helped other classmates at school to cope with her appearance and to accept and understand her.

In their treatment of children and disadvantaged people, authentic leaders show respect and compassion. Rather than create dependencies, they develop capabilities and competencies. To the degree these people are able, they are empowered to become more independent and capable of managing their own lives.

Leaders recognize that the blind may "see" some things better; that all are handicapped in one way or another, and therefore, they lead respectfully—not reading every word or signing every syllable unless necessary. By reading Braille and lips and signs, the blind and the deaf not only make their way, but also turn their weaknesses into strengths. Often, children and disadvantaged people progress the most because they are unusually humble and open. Their simplicity, sincerity, and openness to learning help them to improve their station in life and to seize opportunities.

10. They are appropriately meek, humble, and submissive to proper authority. These master virtues are marks of authentic leadership. With them, we are open to counsel and correction, able to learn, progress and change. Without them, we are frozen in our tracks. Nevertheless, in counterfeit cultures, being submissive and meek is most often seen as a sign of weakness because power, bluster, and bluff are everything.

Authentic leaders are submissive to the divine within them. They are humble because they are self-aware and recognize their weaknesses. They are meek because they realize that were it not for mercy and grace and the work of others, their lot in life would be worse than it is.

Many top athletes and performing artists are humble because they compete daily with the best, and they struggle to maintain a high batting average against tough pitching or to maintain positive reviews against strong critics or to maintain competitiveness in the global marketplace. Those checks and balances within the market keep us humble and let us know that there are many good people out there. Boxers Sugar Ray Leonard and Thomas "Hit Man" Hearns thanked each other, as Magic Johnson thanked Larry Bird, because they kept each other in top form.

Shortly before his death, Bing Crosby confessed in a penetrating interview that in spite of all he had done, he was "nothing special." In summing up the balance sheet and looking at the bottom line, he basically said, "You know, Bing Crosby is no more important than anybody else. All I've done in life is dance and sing the songs that somebody else wrote and appeared in movies that somebody else scripted, casted, and directed. I've had my place on stage, but in the grand scheme of things, my life has not mattered all that much." Since Bing Crosby was one of the great entertainers of the 20th century, we might all more modestly assess our performances.

Misunderstood, submission and meekness could make one a wimp, a doormat, a loser, a masochist: "Hit me again; I like it; I'll take it; I'll turn the other cheek." Unless we balance these attributes with courage, boldness, initiative, and creativity, we invite tremendous abuse. Likewise, a belief in "the nothingness of man" is an attractive doctrine to those who would relinquish their right to all things eventually.

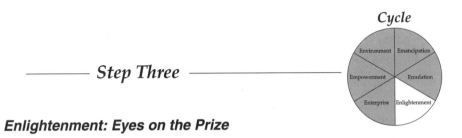

Cycle

——— *Step Three* ———

Enlightenment: Eyes on the Prize

If we really believed that "the eye is the light of the body," we might care more about having bright eyes and enlightened bodies, both personal and corporate.

The so-called "dark ages" of human history were dark because whole societies closed their collective eyes to some basic truths. The age of "enlightenment" opened eyes, minds, and hearts, heralding in a more progressive era in education, the trades, and in the arts and sciences.

In this section, I explore how we, once schooled in emancipation and emulation, can gain a greater measure of enlightenment.

• Counterfeit leaders specialize in secular education and situational ethics, primary causes of corporate hanky-panky, as graduates of schools of mismanagement start their own schools of scandal.

• Authentic leaders bring moral education and absolute values back into the classrooms, courtrooms, and boardrooms, and not merely as a visual aids, something to frame on the wall, rather to write in the "fleshy parts" of the heart and soul.

• The sweet outcome of authentic wisdom is a fellowship not only with the sages of the ages but also with colleagues who share similar values. It all starts with being the author of your own life story.

To escape the trap of having zeal without knowledge, knowledge without wisdom, and wisdom without meaningful action, we must learn how to learn—and live, or at least abide, in a perpetual state of enlightenment.

Hierarchies &
Bureaucracies

Plantation
Mangement

False
Followership

Imperfect
Models

Bad
Habits

Secular
Education

Chapter 7

Secular Education and Situational Ethics: In Fraud We Trust

"Education in virtue is the only education which deserves the name."

—Plato

The phantom of fraud haunts many folks in the huge education, training, and human development industry. Fraud can appear on any campus, to encompass the unsuspecting faithful, to entice appointed administrators, or to tempt elected officials. It feeds on the blind trust of others' goodness and proclaims the right of the righteous to prosper. The only crime is in getting caught. "My client believes that at no time did he commit a crime," is the standard line uttered by the attorney after the conviction. The defendant looks stunned when the verdict is read: his denial of dishonesty—let alone criminal behavior—fits the familiar profile.

The ghost of fraud also hovers over many university communities. As Mark Twain noted in *The Man Who Corrupted Hadleyburg*, a self-righteous community is rather easily exposed once real temptation besets them. When asked why his community was so susceptible to fraud, one official said, "We compare each other's children, wardrobes, cars, and homes. Under such social pressure, the lure of easy money becomes almost irresistible."

Under the roof of secular education and training, fraud finds a spacious home. He walks the halls, teasing the students, tempting the faculty, and telling the deans to sacrifice principles for the sake of political, financial, and academic expediencies. As each college and department of the school, and as each leader and individual in the system, refuses to make any sacrifice for the general good, we are increasingly drawn to single-issue groups and special-interest lobbies to ensure that our personal views and private interests are protected.

In painful irony, many private schools and small liberal arts colleges must either merge or close their doors now. And in the public squares, administrators face shifting demographics, stiff competition, taxpayer revolts, and changing parental expectations. Grade schools, like McDonald's, are expected to open for breakfast, provide a sporty playground, serve a cheap hot lunch, and offer drive-in convenience for working and single parents. At all levels, educators are being shackled in the public pillory and slapped with criticism for programs such as unstructured learning, open classrooms, and valueless instruction. Curriculum is criticized for representing the social arm of the establishment, and schools are seen as mechanisms for transmitting a set of watered-down values.

And where has secular education taken us? Alston Chase has observed: "Most colleges no longer see themselves as a repository for knowledge and values but as businesses, selling products to students. Marketing strategies have come to determine curriculum development. Institutions teach whatever is in demand, ensuring that as little is asked of the students, fewer will learn the basic skills in reading, writing, and computing. We should not be surprised that this generation is more concerned with private careers and less concerned with social values than any in history."

Still, the plight of higher education looks like peaches and cream compared to the do-or-die predicaments of many corporations, where self-interest is merely carried to a higher level. Once students leave college and become employees, fast-track graduates focus on career development, measuring their success by how fast and how far they are moving in their careers. Rather than ask, "What work is right for me?" students are taught to ask the business question: "What pursuit will yield the greatest near-term returns on investment?" Many leave high school with the illusion that all learning can be easy and fun, and that teachers should have nifty techniques to make it that way, forgetting that learning is also grappling with issues, problems, stresses, and constraints. An authentic teacher might advise students, "Everything you do will be taken into account; your responsibility is to communicate to me what you have learned."

Most teaching makes students passive receptacles and promotes smugness, arrogance, and self-congratulatory attitudes. One dean of a business college confessed: "We send too many students out of our school with little understanding of social issues. We get calls from some employers who claim our graduates are obnoxious, self-righteous, sexist, and racist—and whose passivity in the classroom has

made it difficult for them to create meaning out of organizational pande-
monium or to act on issues rather than wait for an authority figure to
decree direction and provide answers."

When one university president told his students, "Don't ask me
what you are supposed to believe—life doesn't have any subtitles,"
another replied, "Great Scott, man, live dangerously; offer them the
Scout Law if nothing else comes to mind. No wonder education is
ranked 23rd on a list of 30 influential institutions in America, just
behind magazines and slightly ahead of movies. Given our national
loss of virtue, no wonder higher education is impotent. Too many
people are somehow getting light without getting virtue."

Indeed, the voice of atheism, corruption, faithlessness, and dissension resounds from many platforms; moreover, it is subsidized
from public funds, and invited into public institutions. The voice of
faith, on the other hand, is fading. Few places are left where it might
speak; almost nowhere can it speak without interruption.

• *The rush on fraternities and sororities.* Many potential leaders
adopt the elitist values of social clubs and exclusive Greek-lettered
sororities and fraternities. While supporters claim these groups fill
important social, physical, and psychological needs, all too often the
fruits are dissipation, not discipline; division, not union; affectation,
not authenticity. Truly "elite" students develop breadth of vision and
depth of thought. They manifest integrity, courage, and commitment
to the pursuit of truth. Only in that sense should we want more "elite"
members. What we too often get are narrow and powerful cliques that
mistake privilege for purpose. The cultural health of a university or
community is not determined by how many people we can exclude,
but rather by how many we can include and wholly accept.

Some practices in training and education are aimed more at preserving innocence and ignorance than developing virtue and competence,
at protection rather than progression. Authentic leaders learn to confront
evil, falsehood, and ugliness on their own terms, from their own
strengths, and with open-eyed realism. When censorship occurs, too
often it is done in a patronizing or condescending way to people considered incapable of exercising mature judgment.

• *Counterfeit vs. authentic art.* Sentimental art not only distorts
reality but leads to self-complacency; it is, therefore, ultimately
immoral. To create great art and authentic culture, people must be

allowed to work without undue censorship, and to perform without being overly worried about offending someone. The risks of building a critical culture are the same risks run by allowing choice of any kind: some people will make mistakes. Either we accept those risks or we must not expect to achieve a great culture. At a great university, the morality of the graduates provides the music of hope, and the collective contributions of the community create such an authentic culture that counterfeit elements typically self-select out.

• *Counterfeit courtships.* Campus dating is often described in such negative terms as "tense, painful, artificial, pressured, and dishonest." Both male and female students agree that the purposes of dating—to meet and make new friends, have fun, develop social skills, discover truth about oneself and others—are often frustrated by false fronts, guarded behavior, and game playing.

Since the mass media constantly stress romance in courtship, many youth focus on appearances, evaluating those of the opposite sex positively only when they are physically attractive. Those who don't meet stringent cinematic standards have a hard time selling other qualities—especially when their chances to interact with the opposite sex in an honest way are limited.

• *Scapegoats and free-loaders.* Public school teachers and administrators are often scapegoats for parental and societal failures. The best teachers could work for more money, get higher paying jobs, and enjoy more social recognition, but they choose to stay with the system and try to be change agents because they truly love children and have their best interests at heart. These people are heroes. But then many administrators and teachers only exacerbate the problems within the public systems, and as children look to these free-loaders, they see people whose speech and behavior have an institutional grayness to them—nothing crisp or colorful.

Most reform movements start with basic disciplines of order, neatness, cleanliness, and respect. If all we need to know we learn in kindergarten, then in kindergarten we need more basic training in picking up after ourselves and treating ourselves and others with respect.

Schools of Mismanagement

The theory behind the MBA degree is to give people a general education in management and then turn these generalists loose in business, often at high levels. The appeal of the MBA degree to some employers is that they get a product that they can plug, as needed, into any socket in the organization. They might assess the capabilities and talents of the individual early, and use them within the organization as needed.

Faculty members in schools of management are infamous for their quadrants, constructs, theories, diagrams, paradigms, concepts, models, metaphors, and assessments—stuff professors can use in sideshow consulting practices or in occasional teaching assignments to explain the universe. Many conceptual models include dimensions that are foreign to the natural, universal, and timeless principles; and so inadvertently, they promote selfish, short-term thinking. Nonetheless, students are eager to learn the buzzwords and accounting practices of the bottom-line orientation of business.

Without understanding the roots of economies and societies, we only "hack at the leaves." If we separate causes and consequences, roots and fruits, we lose sight of the forest for all the trees in our face. Consider the countless stories of stock brokers and financial analysts, well-intentioned MBAs and seasoned managers, who lose their way because they fail to see that money, stocks, and bonds are but symbols of economic value added by people who actually work in harmony with natural laws and agricultural principles.

Schools of management will say, in their defense, that we expect too much of them. We can't expect business schools in two years to infuse students with all classic virtues and ethics along with the core curriculum they need to step into management and leadership positions, especially given the failures in homes and communities. Having one class on ethics is like putting a Band-aid on an open wound. And so, by and large, the ethics of business graduates are situational, meaning ethics go out the window when money is on the table.

Commencement Address

After visiting several schools of management around the world, I have imagined what the dean of the Counterfeit College of Management might say at the school's commencement to the graduating class.

Dear graduates:
Your career is before you. For your sakes and mine, and for the financial security of the college, I expect that it be one of unbroken success and excel-

lence—not that you need to be an example of either. Seeming is as good as being in business, and having and controlling are more important than helping and contributing. Remember: Nothing breeds security like bucks in the bank.

Please understand that your career is your life. Life is a career. You are to have no mission, no love, outside the bonds of loyalty to your work. Sacrifice all upon the altar of career success—your marriage, family, friends, health—this is not too much to ask. Thousands have done it before you. Let them be your mentors and models.

Even if you want children, my advice is this: Sublimate and substitute. Sublimate with promiscuous sex and once-a-year (well publicized) service projects, and substitute with pets, possessions, and promotions. When you desire that trendy balm of life balance, remember that most real achievement comes from zeal—monomaniacs with a kamikaze mission. Health and happiness can always come later.

Your career, together with your financial statement, must be foremost in your mind and heart. Make your resume your religion. Guard your career options jealously. Keep them open, especially at your current employer's expense. Lavish the lotion of loyalty on yourself; don't waste it on an employer. Take advantage of all employee benefits, and lobby for more. Invest your money in sheltered funds. Look for an inside advantage. In business, there is no such thing as selfish—you are either rich or poor, winner or loser, have or have not (need I say which side you want to be on?).

If you make a donation or do volunteer work, make it visible, and, of course, use it for a tax write-off, or for publicity and public relations. If you throw a party, make a media event out of it. Buy credibility with makeshift titles and credentials—that's much faster and cheaper than building it from scratch. Win by intimidation, aggressiveness, and assertiveness. When you go to the mat, go for the quick pin.

Shop incessantly for shortcuts and secrets to success. Buy and read religiously all the how-to-get-ahead books—how to get promotions, how to get what you want, how to get rich without risk or work. Keep score with money. Nothing else matters, in the final analysis, because only money can buy you things. Money talks. Listen and learn its language. Let the language of money and accounting be your primary, native language. Law is a good second language. Don't bother with literature.

Love? Yes, as long your love includes a healthy portion of lust, an occasional affair, and, ultimately, sexual conquest. Keep current in the language of "love" by reading and viewing sexually suggestive material—the "sophis-

ticates"—to keep the words and images fresh in your mind. These will drive you to great heights. All great men and women are driven. While you're at it, seek all the sensual pleasures and satisfactions; satiate appetites and passions; experience all the feelings and sensations of human sexuality, even if it comes at the expense of true intimacy.

Skills? You will need few, really, if have the one master skill: closing the sale. Practice barter and negotiation to learn how to wear down and win. Drive the hard bargain, close the deal, pick up the check, get the credit, pocket the commission, and then, if necessary, get out of town. It's better to keep on the move and make megabucks than settle into some "good neighbor Sam" lifestyle.

In your first job, seek visibility and mobility. Take the boss to the airport. Learn your way around the executive wash room, dining room, and board room. Get your face and name in front of people. Jet around.

Let those sorry folks with Ph.D.s working in dreary R&D worry about actually making something. You can always steal and sell their work, and gain all the rewards. Don't let small things like ignorance and inexperience slow you down. You can claim the work of intelligent people and capitalize on the experience of others.

If you have to make a choice between a close relationship and a career advancement or sales commission, make the smart choice—go with advancement or money. You can always get into new, and potentially more rewarding relationships.

Never sacrifice results for relationships. Regard them as mutually exclusive. Focus on quantity, not quality; don't let those snivelling soft-hearted, moral-minded, church-going bureaucrats sell you religion—that laughable farce marketed by self-interested, self-righteous hypocrites. Make security, seasoned lightly with the three E's of the '90s—ethics, economy, and environment—your religion. And always remember: Nothing builds security like bucks in the bank. All else pales in comparison to hard cash. Cash is king. With cash, you command and control; and control is everything.

*   *   *

There is hope. Some enlightened deans are calling for more collaboration. Once I visited the Stanford Graduate School of Management and there witnessed an activity involving a group of caring alumni who mingled with administrators, faculty, and students. These practicing executives were teamed with inquisitive students to engage in dialogue and to provide a placement network. The best universities, Harvard and Stanford among them, create a ladder for their graduates. That's one reason why their graduates are valued so highly, as evidenced by their average starting salaries. For the most part, they are worth it because they are part of a tradition and legacy, and they have a responsibility to measure up, to move on, to assume positions of leadership, to be responsible corporate citizens, and to give back to the institutions and communities that made them who they are. Still, in the counterfeit corporation, a Harvard MBA has nothing over nepotism.

The "Con" of Consulting, Tricks of Training

Management consultants, trainers, presenters, speakers, advisers, and counselors—the men and women who work from the outside to assist in-place management—must have some tricks of the trade, some fun and games, to entertain as well as enlighten their clients. Unfortunately, some get carried away. Their models of leadership call for the leader as deal maker, pitch man, politician, strongman, benevolent authoritarian, diplomat, and even the barbarian. Every management consultant or trainer must have his or her model, even if it comes straight from the copy machine, the one truly indispensable piece of equipment in the consultancy. The model must be memorable and transferable to coffee mugs, posters, T-shirts, book covers, business cards, and slides. An expert is "someone from out of town, with slides." And a consultant is "someone who knows 29 ways to make love but doesn't have a mate." In other words, they have all the answers but little practical experience. Some have never had a real job.

It is easier to advise from the outside than to lead from the inside. Seagull consultants fly in, drop their load, and then wing away without caring much for the consequence. Company managers are left with the question, "Now what do I do?" Counterfeit consultants can't be too concerned about where the waste is dumped and who is getting hit with the droppings. They are too busy winging it. Authentic consultants don't wing it; they prepare and plan, diagnose and prescribe. They also motivate those who must go out on a limb to implement ideas over time, who say, "Let's give this a shot for 18 months and see if it really does make a difference."

I like the Edwards Deming confrontational style of consulting. Like a hairy, scratchy Old Testament prophet, he came in sackcloth and ashes and made people very uncomfortable by questioning everything they are doing, including their motives for doing it in the first place. His favorite question was "why?" He tried to get to the root motivations of management actions and decisions. Ultimately, that style of consulting might be the most helpful. Since the consultant neither makes decisions nor implements recommended actions, this kind of reflective questioning and listening may be more helpful than prescription and presentation.

I also like consultants who draw out the client's ideas. Most people know what they ought to do. Rather than impose some jerry-rigged model that is fashioned in the garage the night before or copied from somebody else, why not draw out what's inside the management team? Why not form a model that comes from them, that is formed by them through participative action, and that reflects their best ideas and noblest aims? A synergistic solution that comes from the bottom-up is more likely to create an authentic culture than a text-book model. With so much counterfeit schooling, training, consulting, and counseling going on, it's little wonder we are perplexed.

Situational Ethics

Daily, we read alarming reports of dishonesty in the form of income tax evasion, misappropriation of funds, merchandise theft, expense account violations, and bribery payments.

As leaders attempt to legislate a level of honesty, critics contend that honesty and ethics can't be legislated and that it's too costly to expand the scope of audits to detect and deter fraud and other forms of white-collar crime. These flourish when people work in a valueless vacuum; when situational pressures make it hard not to succumb; and when people find it easy to exploit opportunities afforded them because of their position of trust, control of critical financial transactions, knowledge of company operations, or awareness of weak internal accounting systems.

By reducing the pressures and easy chances to commit fraud and by creating a favorable climate for honesty, a company can influence the integrity of people. Honesty may be a character trait for some, but for others, ethical behavior primarily depends on circumstance. Since corporate codes of ethics can't detail every improper act, we need to learn correct principles and govern our own behavior. The better codes specify general principles and support them with illustrations to help people understand the intent and import.

Many business schools offer courses in ethics; these, however, do little to counter the alarming trend toward compromise. When the graduate business students at one university were asked how they intend to respond to pressures toward unethical behavior, only 34 percent of them anticipate resisting the pressure—an amazing 44 percent expect their behavior to conform to unethical practices!

Obviously, with almost half of their recruits ready to adapt to the prevailing moral climate, leaders ought to ask some hard questions about what constitutes right and wrong behavior. If people perceive—correctly or incorrectly—that top management is dishonest, they will justify and excuse their own dishonesty and establish negative norms such as loafing, stealing, cheating and exploiting privileges. Once rooted in the culture, these norms become nails in the coffin. Rationalization then substitutes for moral reasoning, and expediency takes precedence over integrity.

Those who intend to decide each case on its own merits and do whatever they think will produce the best result tend to be less honest. They are placed in positions of compromise and subjected to the persuasions of special interests, financial pressures, and personal desires. Those who base their decisions either on ethical principles or enforced office rules are less likely to compromise because of the circumstance.

Because of the overall climate of moral relativity in society, controls are now an indispensable part of corporate defense strategy. Increasingly, leaders are adopting more elaborate physical controls, such as guarded entrances and exits, secured valuables, tagged merchandise, monitored cashiers, audited clerks, and increased surveillance. Along with company codes and norms, controls help people behave honestly and guard against "honest" errors, which often account for as much loss as the dishonest ones. Improved physical controls, however, are not the ultimate solution to dishonest behaviors. To the dishonest, tighter controls simply represent a greater challenge. With so little risk of getting caught, they figure, why not lie, cheat, and steal?

The big lie assumes there are no absolutes, no hard standards, no universal verities, or timeless principles—all is subjective or relative. The only sin, in fact, is getting caught. And so, without a compass and the security of true north, we tend to go with the flow, following old maps and relying on outmoded security systems. Such is the sad fate of alumni of schools of mismanagement—those who succumb to secular education and situational ethics.

Chapter *8*

Moral Education and Absolute Values: Growing Leaders from Seed

"To educate a man in mind and not in morals is to educate a menace to society."

—Theodore Roosevelt

In business and private life, we have all met our share of menaces—and these are not the mischievious "Dennises" of the 50's or the dunces and dropouts of other decades. Rather, these are often otherwise bright folks who, drunk with moral relativism and situational ethics, do whatever they feel is right for them and theirs—truth or torpedoes be damned.

That's why character development and virtuous behavior must be the primary aims of education, particularly business education. A moral eduation goes beyond mastering a few facts of science and art into the development of character, the conservation of health, into self-denial and self-mastery. "Self-limitation is the wisest aim of a person who has obtained his or her freedom," said Aleksandr Solzhenitsyn in his *Reflections at Century's End*. "If we do not learn to limit our desires and demands, to subordinate our interests to moral criteria, we will simply be torn apart as the worst aspects of human nature bare their teeth." The truly educated man or woman makes obedience to social law and moral order a guiding principle. "The end of all knowledge should be in virtuous action," said Sir Philip Sidney.

Plato's *Analogy of the Cave* suggests that we are either turning toward or away from the light at any given moment in time. Depending on that direction, the pupils of our eyes—as well as the pupils of our instruction—are either dilating or shrinking.

When we turn on the light in the bathroom in the middle of the night, we are somewhat blinded by the instant illumination. The more intense the darkness, the more intimidating the light. The more intense and pervasive the light, the more obscure, dense, and terrifying the darkness—because darkness is also ignorance, and light also means intelligence.

And so, from day to day, we move along the continuum, toward light or dark. Our soul is enlightened on one hand by truth and virtue or darkened on the other by sin and ignorance. Some people may never experience authenticity or light—all they know is something of a sham. Others may turn by choice to darkness.

When people of intelligence turn to counterfeit paths and start assuming a false face or front, they are often motivated by frustration resulting from unfulfilled or violated expectations. People think that if they behave a certain way, they will be blessed and rewarded. Their behavior constitutes an investment, and they expect to see some returns in the short term. If they don't see returns, they feel as if they are not receiving their just rewards. Some, in frustration, turn to alternative ways of doing things or feeling about things. Their frustrations lead to pursuits that deliberately take advantage of others and are destructive to themselves as well. Their frustration may lead to an aggressive style meant to bring harm to others or gain to them. And their frustrations make it easy for them to justify lying, cheating, and stealing.

To expose counterfeit, we may need to examine internal motives. With a painting or paper money, we may have to scratch the surface or do a chemical analysis to see what lies below. When we probe inside a counterfeit leader, we often find insecurity at the core. Because of insecurity, a counterfeit person will act irregularly, inconsistently, irrationally, defensively. And when his counterfeit side is exposed, he might well collapse, his defenses exhausted.

Internalizing certain values in one age or stage of development leads to certain ways of acting later. Certain counterfeit behaviors are expected at a particular stage of moral development.

For example, an undergraduate student may parade as a moral relativist, saying, "There is no absolute truth. No one can know anything for sure. There's just diversity of opinion, and one opinion is just as good as another." And yet that position is only authentic if he has lived or worked in a culture of absolute values and come to believe that some sources of truth are ultimately better than others. But if he has never been an absolutist, and tries to assume the facade of relativism, he would likely be found out. People tend to respond in certain ways when pressed, and those who try to put on character without really having paid the price are rather quickly undone.

A counterfeit person may feign commitment, for example, to gain an advantage. A teenager might feign some deep feelings of "love" to justify some new romance—putting something on, for the moment, that doesn't really fit or belong. The person is not well grounded in the values of that level of maturity, and yet he pretends, plays the role, as if he were committed to a long-term relationship.

Commitment is most attractive to counterfeiters because it appears as if they have progressed or achieved. For example, if we could somehow convince people that we have commitment, when we really don't, then we have so much the advantage. Others would make assumptions about us and give us the benefit of certain doubts that would put us ahead of the game.

And so, when we look in the mirror on the wall, the question is not "Who's the fairest of them all?" or even "How fair am I compared to somebody else?" If those are the questions, we get caught up in the "wicked queen" syndrome of comparisons. And when we see a Snow White, we plot to kill her to claim her title, property, or beauty. The better question to ask is "How fair am I?" or "How authentic or counterfeit am I?" Most likely, we will get a mixed review.

We can conduct a simple psychological self-test to determine the degree of counterfeit behavior by asking ourselves: "Can I walk away from the contest and not feel some sense of intense personal loss?" When we become so invested in other people, projects, and entities that our self-identity and self-esteem are inextricably tied up in them—we are in a measure immature or counterfeit.

Another self-test is to ask yourself, "Must I get the credit?" We have reached counterfeit stage if we must get personal credit for all accomplishments we are associated with. So much of the lure of counterfeit styles of leadership is closely connected with getting the credit, honor, glory, or gain—of having people look at us and say, "He (or she) is the one who should get credit for the success."

We often aggrandize ourselves in that way as the cause of success—and, therefore, see ourselves as the deserving recipients of all the credit. If we aspire to authentic leadership, we might practice declining or sharing the credit, not assuming that we are a central cause in the success. Psychological counterfeit is rooted in self-interest; in the relative ease of gaining social status, social recognition, and social success; in wanting to get as much as possible for as little as possible. If we consciously behave in ways designed to aggrandize ourselves and to enhance our prominence, prestige, and power (without having to pay the full price), we are well on our way to becoming counterfeit leaders.

Counterfeit leadership can do much psychological damage, including loss of self-esteem, social face, and the ultimate disgrace—public exposure and censure. If we intend to build something enduring, we ought to build something solid and time-honored—or it will eventually collapse and break ignominiously. We read daily about the misfortune of those who seek to build something grand, on sand, without first counting the total cost.

New Rules: New Age Editor, Old Age Educator

For four years, 1975 to 1979, I lived in San Diego, California, where I learned the "new rules" of business as a marketing specialist for an aerospace company and the "new rules" of education as a graduate student at the state university. Coincidentally, this period marked a time of record inflation and culture change in Southern California—and by reading the news and serving and working in the community, I could sense, almost see, change taking place in real time, as if by some freak accident, time-lapse photography was stuck on fast-forward.

Following this total immersion in secularism, I accepted a position at Brigham Young University, where for the next four years, 1979 to 1983, I was caught in the cross-fire between old and new rules in education. It made for an interesting dialogue, and striking contrasts.

For the sake of simplicity, I have reconstructed this dialogue as an interview between a new age editor and an old age educator. I invite you to join the discussion and draw your own conclusions relative to possible causes and cures of counterfeit leadership.

Why are so many people frustrated in their search for personal and professional fulfillment?

In their search for new meaning, millions of people conduct risky experiments using the only materials at hand—their own lives. They wake up one day and find themselves with a dissipated body, a broken marriage, a foolish career change, or a muddled mind. Focused on their own needs, they find neither joy nor freedom, only loneliness and depression. They are caught in contradiction: their goal to expand their lives by reaching beyond themselves leads to an inward, ever-narrowing preoccupation with themselves. Seeking to enlarge their choices, trying to keep all options open, they diminish their options and themselves. In a quest for everything—new meaning, new rules, new freedom—they are often left with nothing.

But isn't the big promise of education, indeed the chief product of education, a degree leading to self-fulfillment?

Yes, but the new definition of self-fulfillment is doing what we feel is best for ourselves. By this definition, all our actions are justified. But this frantic search for self-fulfillment leads to frustration, a wreaking of families, a restless rumination about our inner needs, and unfulfilled dreams. So preoccupied are some with their inner needs that the self becomes simply an assemblage of needs, a talking tinker toy, a collection of organs.

If we turn inward, and do only what we feel is right for us, we harm many of those around us and cut off compassionate service. Everything we do will then be egocentric and will turn to a selfish self-fulfillment. The ethics of today's search for self-fulfillment discard many traditional values, placing more emphasis on self-indulgence, self-centeredness, and self-concern and less emphasis on self-denial, sacrifice, hard work, and continuous learning. Education is a worthy endeavor, if it doesn't get in the way of life and learning.

So what's the central purpose of education?

Nothing is more central to education than progression. It's more important to develop proper tools to obtain knowledge and intelligence than to gather information. Tools of rational learning include reading, analysis, debate, research, criticism, and skepticism; while the tools of extra-rational learning include inspiration and revelation. In any profession, the truly educated person tries to understand the opposing viewpoint, not just to state what it is, but to comprehend its persuasive value.

Since people tend to abuse power and authority, the only place to learn the relevant lessons about the best uses of power is in the lab of life. We could never have experienced the risks and opportunities of power merely by attending some pointed lectures or doing some directed reading. To be poorly educated academically is a disadvantage, but to be poorly educated in things of the spirit is tragedy. It's one thing to split an infinitive, quite another to misread life and its purposes.

"A university must be a place of light, of liberty and of learning," said Benjamin Disraeli. "Education does not mean teaching people to know what they do not know; it means teaching them to behave as they do not behave," said John Ruskin. "The object of a true education is to make people not merely do the right things but enjoy them."

What is the best way to learn?

We are morally responsible to learn from everyone and every-thing, and then to use that knowledge to bless others. Let's put the responsibility for learning back on the student, where it belongs. The student must capture the fullness of what the teacher offers, expand or integrate that fullness for his own purposes and values, teach others for their benefit, and evaluate to improve performance. In science, there are invariant laws that can be applied in any situation, without exception. These principles work anywhere, any time. Once the student understands that his role is to learn, expand, teach and serve, he can then experience explosive learning.

Why have many church-related universities faltered in moral education?

Many church-related universities have become the same as other universities and colleges, keeping the ceremonial robes without the theology, the pomp without purpose. Secularists appear to be carrying the day, often because they go unchallenged as they break with tradition. How dramatic the departure from our roots—as the scorching sun of secularism dries up the heritage of the past! Effort to infuse education with relativism, which rejects the reality of absolute truths, contains an incredible irony and sows the seeds of self-destruction. Without moral content, neither public nor private education can produce public safety.

What is the role and purpose of real education and of real leaders in the field of education?

Quality education includes a sense of proportion. Real universi-ties, in addition to dispensing and preserving knowledge, provide perspective and priority. Both real education and religion help us to distinguish between trivial and eternal truths, as well as between sense and nonsense. Is a population explosion wrong, for instance, but a copulation explosion right? How long can we keep the culture of service alive in the acid of secular selfishness?

In challenging the onrushing hedonism or the preoccupation with pleasure and secularism, leaders can be pardoned a shivering of the soul as they contemplate what needs to be done. They can be humble without being mute, effective without being strident.

Why the need for moral leadership in education?

For those who have ears to hear, a formidable cry can now be heard, like a howling of innumerable dogs, asking for someone to take charge of the situation and lead us out of the morass we find ourselves in. Today some of the finest schools are closed to the highest values of our culture. As society disintegrates, the need for a rooted, prepared, competent, spiritually sensitive citizenry is not only clear, it is crucial. The future of any society must be made in its universities.

What charge must we give to students in graduate schools of business?

These students need to understand that authentic leaders service the human element in organizations. Once hired, they should be expected to observe what's going on, diagnose problems, propose change, conduct training, consult with management, redesign companies, work with people in cross-cultural settings, go into other countries and set up management systems. That's a tall order, and for that reason, knowing how to learn is far more important than knowing how to perform a certain task.

Why are recent graduates often caught in moral or ethical dilemmas?

Because they aren't competent enough to see a dilemma coming, manage the situation, and rise above it without getting caught up in conflicts and in ethical binds. Because they are loyal to the organization, they sometimes go along without questioning current leaders or challenging current policies or practices. And they get seduced and caught unwittingly in compromising situations. They need to look at situations analytically and see conflicts on the horizon. Innocence, naivete, and loyalties on the low level are dangerous at the higher levels of management.

How can students not be deceived by appearances?

The best defense against being deceived or carried away by appearances is an education that includes a sense of proportion and perspective. The best universities resist fleeting fashions and challenge the conventional wisdom of secularism and materialism. Often, even at universities, we can't view others with affinity and respect because of our obsessive devotion to appearances and material possessions. One wonders if the yearning for such things is not the most desperate of ploys—the seeking of an illusory refuge from what we most need to face in ourselves and in our circumstances.

Without a quality education, a person is inclined to take things that are quite arbitrary as literal and sacrosanct. It is insidious and tragic when, while theoretically espousing certain ideals, we so betray them in half-hearted application. We then begin to feel smug in our ability to fool people: "No one knows me deep inside," we might say to ourselves. "I keep people out of my inside space by maintaining a sophisticated facade, and manipulating appearances." We ought to be suspicious of almost everything that advertising persuades us to take with such deathly seriousness—like the design of our homes or shape of next year's car. We all must be powerfully challenged regarding our easy adoption of selfish values and materialistic lifestyles—including the "right" to excessive luxuries and leisure.

But appearances count. In a survey of 100 major employers, 84 said an individual could be accepted or rejected for a job on the basis of dress alone, and 96 said an individual who knows how to dress stands a much better chance of promotion.

Yes, but by following the false god of fashion, we become possessive, selfish, hollow, and power-oriented as opposed to people-oriented. By investing in a timeless wardrobe, we eliminate unnecessary expense and anxiety in trying to keep up appearances—we can then get on with the business of being successful. Our wardrobe doesn't have to be expensive, but it has to be right for the roles we play.

Why do many graduates fail to learn how to package themselves properly? Wardrobe, speech, posture, and a pleasantly assertive personality are all part of the trimmings.

With regard to image, individuals have the same challenge as institutions; their product or service may be good, but it must be packaged properly to influence people favorably. We're often perceived in quite a different manner than we intend. As we begin to layer on apparel and mannerisms, our figure may soon appear false, bearing little or no resemblance to the original. The secret to successful human relations is not found in layering on stylish looks, but rather in stripping away all pretensions and affectations.

When people adopt foolish fashions, they tend to depart from standards of decency and lose their balance. The idea of dress and grooming is to preserve and enhance the natural inner beauty and emphasize our best physical features, certainly not to hide them behind a mask of make-up.

Are morals now passe in most professions?

Many students have been told by their professors, parents, and others that they are welcome to their morals, but that their morals have little to do with the culture of their professions. In some professional circles, morals may be considered irrelevant. The result of this view is that morals become irrelevant. Sophisticated professionals, like sophisticated politicians, sometimes pretend that morals have nothing to do with their enterprise. Our legal culture, for example, has perhaps not yet led us to tyranny, but it has led us to the adversary ethic, which is nearly as bad. The adversary ethic announces that justice is the goal of professional activity and that the means to justice is zealous loyalty to the interests of one's client. It seems unable to entertain an ideal of professional service involving faithfulness rather than loyalty—one difference being that faithfulness aims at goodness rather than the realization of client interests.

What is the chief benefit of moral education?

The chief benefit is having increased one's capacity to love and to serve and to live with all the ambiguities of life without losing joy or faith. It also allows one to "trespass" into all academic disciplines and to be at ease with both scientific and artistic learning. It allows people from different cultures, who can't comfortably comprehend each other at first, to be interested and excited at every chance to learn the other's language and perspective. It provides us with hope that we will have more Renaissance scholars like Michelangelo, Leonardo, Christopher Wren, Thomas Jefferson, and Benjamin Franklin.

Of course, moral education is a dynamic and ongoing obligation. Often, statements about "finishing" and "completing" one's education turn out to be true. We all must engage in active learning of the behavior and thoughts of people, not of the continuous non-events that make up most news. In politics and economics, only those who have no responsibility speak with certainty of what will solve the problems. An evening spent in sharing ignorance with such people does not produce understanding. Able men and women often act proud of having kept innocent of understanding in areas outside their narrow specialty. Even more pitiful are the generalists who gossip about several subjects but have no substance in any one area.

Why is continuous learning the best protection against pride?

The relationships we have with our surroundings are more complex than ever, and yet most of us are too ignorant to face these intelligently and worse, we take pride in our ignorance. Built into the nature of learning is remarkable protection against pride. A person who is vigorously learning can't be egotistical about what he or she knows, because each increase in understanding reveals a larger area of ignorance.

Rapid upheaval of the language by those who never knew or loved it soon leads to complete and dreadful isolation from heritage, from philosophical roots, from faith, from opportunity to learn, from the ability to tell someone clearly what one knows and feels. Some professionals in the areas of speech writing, public relations, and advertising have sullied their trades by becoming fabricators of images that obscure the truth and deceive.

We see graduates of universities who cannot speak coherently, who do not read, who understand nothing of the physical universe and who give no evidence of thinking. The ideal undergraduate education is to complement intensive study in a major with a solid liberal education to produce men and women who can face the demands and decisions of life with a higher level of equanimity, who are past the point of supposing that their every experience is unique and who are not torn apart by uncertainties.

In the book *Only in America*, Harry Golden tells of practices among immigrant Jewish people in New York. When a child is presented his first book, a little ceremony is held in which a drop of honey is placed on the book's cover and the child kneels, placing his tongue on the honey, so that his first contact with learning and books is sweet. The counterpart to this in too many homes today is when the child eats his first pizza off the television set. Provincialism and pride are hard to overcome. The best approach is to have experiences that help children realize and appreciate differences.

Should universities provide a classic liberal education or prepare people for jobs?

If our system of education buckles to the intense pressures to be little more than trade schools, it will be at great cost. The intent of education is to liberate, not to stratify, isolate, and compartmentalize us. A liberal education helps us to distinguish between sense and nonsense. As we achieve real literacy in things spiritual, we will have added discernment with which to weigh and test ideas and assertions as we make decisions and judgments. We must not over-control the very process by which our youth learn how valuable and irreplaceable their freedoms are. Real universities do more than prepare individuals to have views about everything under the sun. They neither confuse information with knowledge, nor knowledge with wisdom. They reserve the right to ask any student at any time, "What books have you read lately?" Some might consider that question unfair or irrelevant, but it is the most relevant question we can ask at a university.

In *A Liberal Education and Where to Find It*, Thomas Henry Huxley writes: "That man has had a liberal education who has been so trained in youth that his body is the ready servant of his will; whose intellect is like a steam engine, to be turned to any kind of work and spin the gossamers as well as forge the anchors of the mind; whose mind is stored with a knowledge of the great and fundamental truths of nature and of the laws of her operations; one who is full of life and fire, but whose passions are trained to come to heel by a vigorous will, the servant of a tender conscience; who has learned to love all beauty, whether of Nature or of art, to hate all vileness, and to respect others as himself."

And in *The Function of Criticism at the Present Time*, Matthew Arnold writes: "Criticism keeps man from a self-satisfaction, which is retarding and vulgarizing, and leads him toward perfection by making his mind dwell upon what is excellent in itself, and the absolute beauty and fitness of things. The pursuit of perfection, then, is the pursuit of sweetness and light. He who works for sweetness and light, works to make reason and the will of God prevail."

Nice sentiments, but can there be real standards or only double standards at universities?

Authentic leaders enforce real standards, even when people don't like the idea of standards. Leaders know that you don't get to the

moon in the NASA program or to the finals in an NCAA program
without some standards. They remind every administrator, athletic
director, coach, and individual athlete that no program or person is
exempt from the rules. And they charge governing committees to
enforce them. In the explosive areas of admissions and scholarships,
they eliminate double standards. They remind freshmen that once
they choose to come to the school, they choose to abide by the standards. They see that violations are penalized, even when it means
public embarrassment, lost games, and lost revenue.

What should be given for a final self-examination upon graduation?
We might ask ourselves: 1) Has my education better prepared me
to be of service? 2) Has it deepened my compassion for those who are
hungry, discouraged, and without hope or provided a soothing salve
and handy list of reasons why they deserve their lot? 3) Has it brought
a sensitivity unbounded by cultural, racial, or national differences, or
merely furnished a comfortable justification for provinciality? 4) Has it
made money my sole measure of worth? 5) Has it saddled me with a
dream of financial independence or provided independence from any
such necessity? 6) As I have learned to win through intimidation, dress
for success, and think and grow rich, have I neglected learning to love
my enemies, bless them that curse me, and pray for them who despite-
fully use me? 7) Will my future decisions take into consideration not
only margin and marketability but also faith and family?

The future can be frightening except as faith comes to calm us. The
God who held the sun at bay for Joshua, provided a lamb in the thicket
for Abraham, and raised Lazarus from the dead can certainly help us
start a home, raise our family, and meet our obligations. We must build
our lives, one day at a time, in full faith and quiet reassurance. Whatever
the economic climate, we need to keep our promises and keep smiling—
making time for others who can't pay us back, living by the best, the
truest, and the most sacred of the old rules. We simply can't afford to set
aside all that God, prophets, and centuries of history and scholarship
have taught us to seek fulfillment by newer, untested and, finally, fatally
flawed new rules.

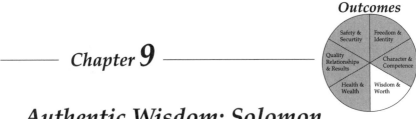
——— *Chapter 9* ———

Authentic Wisdom: Solomon Brothers and Sisters

"Wisdom is the principal thing; therefore, get wisdom. And with all thy getting, get understanding."

—Proverbs 4:7

Since Saloman Brothers and the rest of Wall Street can't qualify as particularly wise, we need a new breed of wiser men and women—*Solomon* brothers and sisters—to step forward on every wall, street, and sheet of paper. In fact, to be fully authentic, we must eventually author something—express and preserve something in a medium of choice.

In our day, wisdom seems to be in short supply, perishable in the heat of secularism and in cold, heartless materialism. Rather than put the baby on the cutting block—as King Solomon did— knowing that the true mother will cry out, we either award the baby to foster care, or throw it out with the bath water.

Wisdom wanes regarding resources—people, money, time, talent, turf—as well as roles, goals, priorities, and principles. We are all found tracking trends, but lost in learning truth and consequences. Leaders who are only wise in their own eyes are ever learning but never knowing the plain truth or real worth of people and things, perhaps because they know not where to find the truth, and fail to tap the sources of wisdom.

King Arthur looked to Merlin, President Reagan to Nancy, and Nancy to astrologers. But if we are going to gamble on the stars, we at least ought to observe the house odds. The casino may be packed, but that doesn't mean anyone therein is wise, or winning.

"The wise man endeavors to shine in himself; the fool to outshine others," said English essayist Joseph Addison. "The first is humbled by the sense of his own infirmities, the last is lifted up by the discovery of those in others. The wise man considers what he wants, and the fool what he abounds in. The wise man is happy when he gains his own approbation, and the fool when he recommends himself to the applause of those about him."

It seems never to occur to people to look to tried and true sources of wisdom—standard works (scriptures), stable people (models), great literature (metaphors) and art (symbols), and nature (seasons, cycles, processes).

And so we daily reinvent the wheel in the name of duty or experience. Observed Ben Franklin, "Experience keeps a dear school; but fools will learn in no other, and scarce in that; for it is true, we may give advice, but we cannot give conduct."

In the business magazines and other media, fools and great falls are the news of the day. Examples of folly make front-page news, whereas examples of wisdom rarely see the light of day. Wisdom makes boring reading but good living, as the products of wisdom include growth, progress, patience, perspective, priorities, and concentration on what matters most.

Wise leaders are moral philosophers and practical idealists who apply the lessons of history and the current counsel of trusted associates. The value of an authentic leader may be measured not only in the bottom line but also in every other line of the organization, including the lunch line—lines running diagonally, horizontally, and vertically, through staff as well as line management; lines running between walls and through halls on the same floor as well as through the elevator on different floors. Every line of the corporation is better because of wise leadership.

Wisdom is often undervalued. The highest paid are rarely the wisest. For some reason, it's hard to be both wise and rich, not that poverty is any sure sign of wisdom either. The worth of one's leadership can only be measured against standards that hold water when subjected to the wisdom of the ages and sages. The principles of wisdom include moderation, balance, temperance, discipline, fitness, openness, and flexibility. Such standards tend to be inspired, not conspired; intrepid, not insipid; with applications first to personal, not organizational. And in a world of moral relativity, that's a tall order.

The task requires more discernment, less measurement, assessment, and testing. What positively identifies an individual is both the fingerprint on the outside and the soul print on the inside. TQ, IQ, SAT, and all the tests that man and machine can devise are not the total measure of a person, not even of his or her mind.

Wisdom of the Ages

Dick Dauch, former vice president of manufacturing at Chrysler Motors, wanted managers with "high foreheads." Wisdom is not commonly listed as a desired trait in want ads. But it's needed in every position, especially at the top. Of course, it's hard to test for, hard to interview for, hard to detect by appearance, since wisdom is not always synonymous with age and experience. However, it is a problem-solving capability, and this capability increases with age, peaks at age 55, and decreases only slightly over the next 20 years. And yet we're always searching for wisdom in youth, where it is rarely found. A manager who has 30 years of experience, not one year 30 times, has many cycles of learning, perhaps in three or more functional areas of the company or in three different companies—if not three different careers. Wise executives see patterns; predict end results from a few clues at the beginning; know where to put time and resources; sense what matters most; manage resources well; and define mission, direction, goals, priorities.

Every man, woman and child—yes, even the rich and famous—is alone and lonely at times, worrying about inadequacies and wondering where, if anywhere, wisdom is to be found. We put great faith and trust in degrees, diplomas, and professional credentials. We may suppose that a certified counselor or consultant represents a safe bet. We begin to deposit dollars and dilemmas in them, only to find that the problems are inevitably handed back to us. If all the wisdom is on the sidelines and in the press box, we won't see wins on the field. We need wise players who make smart decisions daily, aided by the collective wisdom of the culture.

The "closing of the American mind" has shut off much of the wisdom, once so rich in the American tradition. We've seen a gradual erosion of wisdom, as the landscape has been swept by the hurricanes of the harried, the cyclones of clones, the microwaves of mimes. The great deserts and waste places are now to be found between the ears; politicians may "win the vote of every thinking citizen" and still not get past the primaries. Lacking depth, we are left with paranoias of soap operas, the manias of models, the media of celebrities. Rather than read the sages of Philadelphia, we reap the wages of Philistines.

Short on cool ideas, we resort to hot reacting and hot wiring. In 1958, the moment my father, a traveling salesman, left town for the week, my two older brothers, ages 13 and 15, would "hot wire" the car and be off to the races. The street-smart teens had learned to wire around the ignition system, the authentic starting system, to start the engine and get on down the road.

Today, street smart managers and politicians "hot wire" the systems to get up to speed and race with the front runners. They spread rumors, gossip, lies, and misinformation. Counterfeit communication—like hot wiring—short circuits the official system and sets up a grapevine, a private network of public relations and management communications. Indeed, we have created many substitutes for wisdom: speed, money, resources, fashion, fun, activity, talent, energy, and planning. But nothing quite takes its place, especially when dealing with people and their problems.

No executive will rise to be wise if surrounded by "yes men." With so much "yes" no one can say "no." And "no" may be a wiser word in certain contexts. Every executive needs wise counselors, on the left and the right, to maintain equilibrium. What wisdom is built into your systems, policies, and practices? Who are the wise men and women (counselors and consultants) at your side? The wise win what the counterfeit forfeit—and the purse, as counted in the coinage of credibility and legacy, is not a paltry sum.

Lost and Found

Authentic leaders are true to their own unique genius, knowing that it is not the privilege of a few to be artists and prophets, but the obligation of all. The light of the enlightenment, reformation, renaissance, and restoration must come to one and all. Even that bright morning light of inspiration, which defies all description, must descend upon us all. By choice, free men and women must want the good, within boundaries and law. All else is a degree, a shade, a hair off the mark. And as author John Updike wrote, "Hope reads a word where, in fact, only a scribble exists." And, when we don't know where we're going, any direction will do—north, south, east or west, as the following sorry stories depict.

• A certain man from the north wanted to escape the cold winters and constraints of market and home and previous marriage. And so he packed his bags and headed south, following the sun and seeking the fun in beaches, babes and beer. Advertising promised fulfillment, and he expected it. He wanted new friends, new identity. Over time, he dissipated his energies and resources, developed addictions, and fell into ruin.

• A young man from the west left his home to venture east to work at an airport, used by the corporate chieftains. He was only a member of the ground crew, but he handled their bags, shook their hands, and sometimes chauffeured them into town. He enjoyed being near power and money. There was a certain scent to it. He felt that it was only a matter of time, only a favor away, before he got his big break, before someone would recognize him and recommend him for the big advancement. He never noticed that all the power of jet engines, highs and lows, takeoffs and landings, were all part of a grand, intoxicating illusion. The movement of others created the illusion that he, too, was going somewhere when, in fact, he was grounded.

• An absent-minded man who was always losing his keys and glasses started praying to St. Jude, the saint of lost causes. To his amazement, he started remembering where he put things! He began attributing his good fortune to his new-found saint. But then one day, at a time of real need, he failed to find his lost keys and missed an important engagement. Disillusioned, he denounced St. Jude and relied once more on his own wits. Better lost in fact than lost in faith, he figured.

• Not having ears to hear nor eyes to see the warning signs, a symphony orchestra and their guest artists played on during a hail storm at late summer performance held inside a large tent at a high mountain resort. The hail piled high and fast, and soon the weight collapsed the tent, sending the grand piano through the stage floor. After it was over, everyone acknowledged that "*they* should have stopped the concert" before the hail, quite literally, brought the house down. We may hear the same refrain in hell itself!

Many people feel that they are trapped in counterfeit relationships, systems, organizations, traditions, and beliefs—and so they sit through hail storms. But as some courageous East Germans and Russians have proven, walls can come down, barriers can be broken, great escapes can be made, notwithstanding the opposition. Transformations are tough. The question is always, "Where can I go? What will become of me?" The answer, "go west, young man, go west," still works as a metaphor—*west* meaning new territory, outside the comfort zone.

When I ask people who feel trapped, who are underemployed or overwhelmed, in certain big cities— "Why not move out?," they come up with pathetic excuses. A modicum of security keeps people in corrals like cattle. Elephants will stay put with a rope, horses with a rail, sheep with a grate, people with but a promise. Once domesticated, we all stay in our place.

But we can change, move, and progress. We must. Stasis, even in the sense of "having arrived," is more descriptive of stagnation than progression. Wisdom—knowing what's right—requires courage, conviction, and execution to become authentic action—doing what's right. We're all too much stuck in the middle, in that no man's land between knowing the right thing and doing the right thing. The real measure and worth of wisdom is in the doing.

The total worth of the wisdom of authentic leaders is not only the value of their personal examples, as immense as that might be, but also the value of their judgment, vision, and perspective. Leaders are paid mostly for their judgment—for the degree of wisdom that they exercise in their decisions and choices: whether to buy or sell, make or buy, maintain position or move forward. Whether to hire, fire, motivate, or retain people. Those decisions are made by all leaders, and the degree of wisdom is often only manifest over time.

We can't look to colleges and universities as repositories of wisdom, necessarily. Wisdom is not even listed in the course catalog. We graduate people who read and write poorly; who gain few skills in their major, much less some specialization within that major; and who, once graduated, are lulled by the sweet lullaby of their careers or pulled in different directions as causes compete for their time and talent. They try to do everything, be everything, buy everything. Consequently, they tend to end up being nothing to everyone, including themselves.

Greatness is determined as much by wisdom as by power. With authentic leaders, what they should do, they can do. What they should express, they do express. What they ought to be, with God's help, they become—even authors of their own stories.

An Authentic Legacy

Most leaders think of themselves as authentic; however, few think of themselves, first and foremost, as authors. Some, in fact, have written very little for external publication, or even internal distribution. Other executives have written and published widely. The issue of executive authorship is important not merely for the potential of getting one's name in print but for the immense payoff in authenticity and authority.

• *An author* is one who produces, creates, or brings something into being and then causes it to grow and increase; the author is the originator, the first mover and shaker of anything, one who composes or writes. Authorship, then, is often prerequisite to clear identity and great achievement.

• *Authenticity* is making the self an instrument, having the genuine article, the original model, the legitimate authority—as opposed to that which is false, fictitious, and counterfeit. It is being what you purport to be, trustworthy, reliable, credible, faithful. Authentic leaders are authors of ideas and actions. And in the process of authoring, they more clearly identify what is unique and original to them.

• *Authority* is the power or right to act, author, and make final decisions. Such power may be delegated, or it may be derived from opinion, perception, respect, esteem, or influence of character or office. Most authority in any executive position is derived from the influence of character, from the state of authorship, and the status of authenticity. The counterfeit is authoritarian: characterized by unquestioned obedience to authority, rather than individual freedom of judgment and action.

The Executive Author

Having worked with several executives as a writer, editor, publisher, and now literary agent, I find many to be dynamic, visionary, proactive. All have something to say, although many prefer media other than print for their expression. But for one reason or another, little of real merit ever gets published; executives settle for short, clipped statements (often misquoted or out of context) in media, minutes and other records.

I worked four years in a major aerospace corporation and came away without any meaningful remembrance of the CEO. In fact, after 10 years, I can't remember anything of substance the man said. Basically, all his communication was functional and sterile. In contrast, I worked four years at a major university and came away with a wealth of meaning from the speeches and writings of the president.

As a person and a leader, you have a need:

• *To find your own voice.* Don't use a ghostwriter or "collaborator" who brings all the substance and style. Speech writers and other assistants should take more than a cue from you—they should get the essence, if not the full text, out of you from interviews.

• *To express yourself in writing in cohesive message units.* The irony is that in a day and age of voice-activated recording, voice-to-print transformation, electronic editing and spell checking, word processing and laser printing, we find it no easier to say something worthwhile. You need to finish some things; otherwise, all you leave behind are fragments.

• *To increase your ability to think and write clearly.* If you fail to express your feelings and insights appropriately and regularly, in speech and writing, you forfeit influence. Your ability to express yourself will fade, as will your ability to feel and think deeply. So record your insights and feelings, especially as they relate to mission, vision, people, performance, and direction.

• *To establish your identity as an author.* You may not have a personal need, but you have a professional need. Your leadership authority is linked to your identity as an author. So write your own script. Revise it, refine it, to be sure. But above all, finish it. Publish it. Distribute it. Get feedback on it.

• *To separate your thoughts and writings from those of others.* Always recognize and attribute sources properly. Acknowledge and reward collaborators, contributors and counselors. Credit your sources in all forms of communication, casual and formal. If you use other people's material as your own, you run the risk of delusion (thinking the material actually is your own), alienation (from your own thinking and from the true sources) and compromise of integrity.

How to Become an Author

As a young journalist, one of my first assignments was to write a feature story on university professor and management consultant Walter Gong. I interviewed him and other sources and composed an article on this remarkable man. To check the accuracy of some statements, I showed him a draft.

"I think you have captured the content well," he said, "but what *creative value* have you added? Your duty as author is to expand on what you receive and present it in the context of your own thinking and style."

The second draft was vastly improved.

To become an author is to add creative value, to become authentic and to earn real authority.

• *Get rid of all the rational lies* as to why you can't ever write anything. Believe in yourself. Have faith. Faith and works yield fruit.

• *Appoint someone on staff to assist* in capturing, transcribing, editing and publishing your material. Leverage your time. In your line of duty, there is virtually nothing more important than publishing your vision and values, principles and life experiences.

• *Find or create a suitable medium in print, audio, or video format.* Create in the medium and format that are most comfortable and natural to you. Learn to adapt to other formats. This often requires some coaching, constructive and objective feedback and capable editing.

• *Schedule creative periods and submission deadlines.* Organize thoughts around these times. Schedule submissions. Be accountable to someone for meeting deadlines.

• *Develop a system or process for capturing your insights and other important communication;* then organizing; then storing and filing; then publishing.

• *Keep a journal*—otherwise much will slip through the cracks. In the movie *Paint Your Wagon*, the most profitable mining was being done under the floorboards of the saloon where gold dust was falling through the cracks. A lot of "gold dust" or great ideas and expressions will fall through the floorboards unless they are captured and kept safely in a journal.

Obviously, some things are more important than other things. Executives should be most concerned about authoring the following items: 1) statements of mission, values, principles, beliefs, purposes; 2) speeches, articles, statements, on significant issues of management and leadership; 3) new products, programs, processes, systems, structures, styles; 4) children, protegees, successors, empowered managers; 5) dreams, visions, directions, preparations.

Benefits of Authorship

Being an author brings many side benefits to you and your organization.

• *Identity.* If you're not an author or an original, then you're probably an actor or impostor, imitator or plagiarist. Publishing your own material and ideas helps you and your organization to gain identity and position—to be seen and known as original sources.

• *Philosophy*. Moral philosophers are needed as much today as they were at the time of our founding as a nation. Even if you are rich in profitability, you cheat your organization if you are poor in philosophy.

• *Authenticity*. You can gain a sense of true identity and legitimacy and integrity because of heightened awareness of who you are and what you believe in and stand for.

• *Authority*. Real authority comes from authorship. The formula is: *Authorship + Authenticity = Authority*. Much of your potential management authority lies outside the confines of your office and position. It must be earned through authorship and authenticity.

• *Legacy*. You leave something behind in what John Updike calls the "icy permanence of print." On this point, imagine that you meet an untimely death in the near future and that a few of the faithful seek to build in your honor a memorial, patterned after the Lincoln memorial, complete with two of your most significant writings etched in stone. What have you left them to work with? Authorship encourages real innovation, not cheap imitation. You become a personality with a perspective. You become, in the process, a more genuine, authentic leader.

You may get off to a bad start in life, but with persistance and patience, you can finish well; and it is the finish that counts.

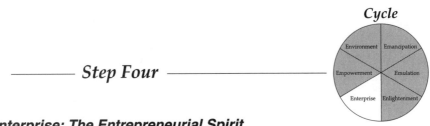

——— *Step Four* ———

Enterprise: The Entrepreneurial Spirit

When I once gazed at the small aircraft (*The Spirit of St. Louis*) that carried Charles Lindbergh across the Atlantic Ocean from New York to Paris, I realized that he risked everything in the enterprise. That, I suppose, is the spirit, the very essence of entrepreneurship, the business of creating something new from next to nothing and then crafting it into a Paris original.

• What keeps us from even starting our flights of fancy are false starts and bad habits. In our timidity, we show so little appreciation for the wings provided us by our progenitors and pioneer ancestors. What good are high-speed jets when, rather than take us to clouds of glory, they just get us nowhere faster?

• In the spirit of enterprise, we seek work that matters relative to our life mission. Also, we care more about reducing waste and doing meaningful and fulfilling work that makes not just good use but the best and highest use of all available resources.

• We find over time an abundance of wealth and meaningful work where we once saw only scarcity and poverty. True wealth is being free of dept and free of illicit and covetous desires. We are then at peace, pleased with who we are and what we have.

The outcome of real enterprise is real work that stands the tough test of time. The two best friends of authentic leaders are Father Time and Mother Nature.

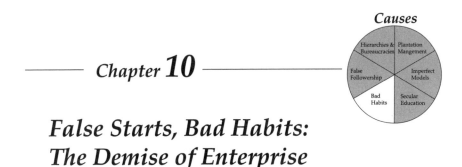

Causes

———— Chapter **10** ————

False Starts, Bad Habits:
The Demise of Enterprise

"Habits are like a cable. We weave a strand of it everyday, and soon it cannot be broken."

—Horace Mann

The root causes of our false starts in life are false beliefs, training, traditions, and notions of what's normal. Still, a bad start in childhood and teenage years need not doom us, if we cultivate good habits. Bad habits tend to make us either passive, reactive, and dependent—accepting of status quo—or more agressive, compulsive, addicted, driven, and extreme. Hence, we see the demise of true enterprise, since this requires sustained, sane, disciplined effort.

False Starts

Growing up, I benefitted from having a major university located virtually in my back yard, complete with all the sports facilities a kid could ever want. At age 12, a best friend and I started using these facilities every day after school and on weekends. Track and field was a favorite of mine.

I enjoyed watching the sprinters go through their meticulous warm-ups and pre-race routines and motions. At the starter's command, "Runners, take your marks," they would line up, shaking limbs, eyes fixed on the track ahead; gingerly they would settle into the blocks. "Get set," said the starter, raising his gun in the air, and up on the tips of fingers and toes they would come, poised in breathless suspense along the chalk line.

Frequently, one or more of the runners, anticipating the start, would jump the gun, sprinting out ahead of the others. The starter would fire a second time to signal a false start, and the ritual began again. Of course, even on a fair start, some runners came out of the blocks much faster than others—and on a short sprint, the start would often determine the winner.

125

Fortunately, life is not a short sprint, and a false start or a fault is not the end of the story. For most of us, life's a combination of all of the track races and field events: the dashes, the distance runs, the high jump, pole vault, hammer, discus, steeplechase, javelin, shot put, and relays.

Few compete in the decathlon; most specialize in one event or distance. But in every event or race, a false start or a fault never helps one's chances of victory—as it means a warning, a penalty, or a lost mark.

Clouds of Glory

Alexander Pope wrote: "The patterns of art come from a deep unconscious source in the memory." And Keats noted: "The truth in poetry comes almost as a remembrance." And Wordsworth saw us born into life "trailing clouds of glory."

Pope, Keats, and Wordsworth searched for their patterns of truth in a deep pool of memory, sensing that their work would have universal appeal only if they drew their ideas and images out of the collective unconscious, the universal spirit of mankind.

The age-old questions, "Where did I come from?" "Why am I here?" and "Where am I going?" relate not only to the purpose and meaning of life but also to the meaning of every job. The Wizard of Oz, once found out, wondered why people had such awe of him. He told how his balloon was blown into the land of Oz, where it landed on the Wicked Witch (the previous CEO) and killed her. He was then taken (or mistaken) as a wizard.

So, too, some executives feel that they have ascended in hot air balloons (the Peter Principle) and have been blown into organizations and landed in executive suites. Many have a sense of displacement. They openly wonder where they come from, why are they are there, and where they are going. Those questions apply to every position, and to every person.

On the larger question of our origin and nature, I see two basic schools of thought. One explanation is evolution, with its companion doctrine of determinism. Surely early inks and impressions influence us, but do they determine us? Are we born as blank sheets of paper to be imprinted by the environment, by parents, neighbors and family? And if we are stamped as bills from birth with all these environmental impressions, do we have no identity separate and apart from environmental or genetic imprinting? Are some of us doomed to be born and raised as counterfeits? Or, as John Updike wrote, to be "born in concupiscence," and to "die unrepented."

The second explanation is creation, with its companion philosophies of proactivity and repentance, meaning we choose a course of action and make course corrections as needed. This school of thought recognizes that the creation is a very personal matter—at least as personal as birth or death. And as a result of this unique personal creation, we come into the world "trailing clouds of glory."

If we have a skewed sense of our origins, roots, and birthright, and doubt our inalienable rights and inherent powers and potential to make a difference, we are hard-pressed to become authentic leaders because we carry the heavy baggage of a false sense of self. Without self worth we won't be of much worth to others.

Trying to discover our own roots, genealogy, or ancestry is like tracing tributaries in an attempt to discover the ultimate origin of some river, stream, or lake. If we trace the origins of our leadership traits, these may take us back in time beyond our birth to the ultimate origin of our unique gifts, talents, competencies. We might suppose that many great and noble spirits are born into this life with traits and characteristics that predispose them to positions of leadership, even at an early age. We might further suppose that our origins, like those of many great rivers, are high, pure, and undefiled.

What is our birthright? If we are born without sin, we carry no "original sin" into the world; we have no burdens coming into life— we are free, innocent, pure, undefiled. The only real sin is "original" to us—we create and commit them ourselves. And because they are ours, we don't want to let them go, even our worst sins and habits. We have title and possession, a sense of ownership, perhaps even pride in our transgression.

I assert that we are born with certain unique endowments and certain "inalienable rights." These divine endowments and imprints stamp us as originals—each one, as unique as fingerprints. As we ink up our fingers and press them onto paper, we make an imprint unlike any other. There can be no other print like it. Likewise, each soul-print is a one of a kind.

When we examine our roots, we will find more good news than bad news. To the degree we are severed from our roots, we, as historian Alex Haley tried to show us, will deviate from our true nature, or from true-north principles. Without an appreciation of roots, we grow up lost or confused, with no sense of family or history. With no real name, we carry only a generic label, a pseudonym.

Somehow each generation manages to get cut off from the preceding one, and each of us, to some extent, grows up parentless. Indeed, as publisher Kathaline Graham has noted: "Many false starts and bad habits reflect a lack of parental leadership."

Wombs, Rooms, and Tombs

Of course, counterfeit leadership is made in many fine factories. Some cynics might say that it begins in the womb with genetic imprints, that human nature is flawed, and that every body born of woman is defective. While that may be argued, it is certain that by the time children are five years old, many indelible impressions are made upon them in homes and families, neighborhoods and churches, preschools and day care centers. And the stamping, engraving, foiling, embossing, and die casting continue through the teenage years. Our skin, our very souls, become tattooed with inks and ideas. Tragic, indeed, is the pernicious imprinting done by some with ill intent upon children. These negative impressions are hard to erase.

If we could see life from the eyes of a newborn baby, monitor the senses of a baby, and record the impressions (as we now monitor astronauts in outer space), we would gain a valuable perspective on priorities. Actually we now know plenty about how unborn and newborn babies experience the world. And that knowledge should give us a better sense of how terribly important it is to create a safe, secure learning environment in the womb and every room at home.

Pregnant mothers are warned at every turn, for example, about the risks to their infants of drugs, tobacco, and alcohol—but some choose to ignore the warnings if these interfere with their lifestyle or habits.

Every newborn tries to teach us anew how harsh and ugly are many sights, sounds, and substances in the world. They cry for the right to be born free of debilitating addictions. Of course, we violate those rights already through abortion. If we wink at killing, mutilating, and poisoning fetuses in the womb, in the second and third trimesters, might we next condone killing babies once out of the womb—or, trashing kids in the first semester of college (as some programs are ingeniously designed to do)? I wonder if some women and men who intellectualize and rationalize abortions of convenience have lost all parental sensitivity. When we play around with creative powers—be they sexual or intellectual—we waste our inheritance and forfeit our family.

Checking into life is like checking into a hotel. An imprint is made of your card at the front desk; uniformed service agents help you to register, and then they relocate you to a room that has been inhabited by many before. Within minutes, however, the room takes on your own identity. All you have to do is open your suitcases and start putting a few things out, and soon it looks like your room. You claim it as your own; you have bought it for a night; checked in; and received your own key.

So it is with authentic leaders. It doesn't take long for them to make their mark. They pack light, carry no excess baggage (not even a golden parachute). They may occupy offices and rooms previously occupied by hundreds before them, but soon they have their pictures and prints all over the place. Within minutes after taking office, real leaders have their names on more than desks and doors—their stamp is on the minds and hearts of many who work with and around them.

Where Have All the Parents Gone?

Many parents virtually disappear from the lives of their children, leaving children "home alone." Every weekday morning, we see thousands of babies being bundled and deposited before dawn into the hands of hired substitutes at day care centers. Is something important being lost in the handoff? A high price is paid in broken homes and marriages by innocent children who are cheated out of positive role models, house rules, discipline, instruction, security, and self-esteem. They miss out on activities designed to develop trust, initiative, industry, identity, and intimacy as well as foster social and emotional health.

• *Homes.* Of course, homes and families are defined in various ways these days. In big cities, millions of people are cocooned in small apartments and condominiums that keep them isolated, even from wall-to-wall neighbors, as they import all news, information, and entertainment.

We now define "spouses" as temporary relationships of either sex, and "families" as anyone who shows an interest in children.

The traditional family—consisting of a mother with one or more children at home and a working, bread-winning father—is becoming rare. Therefore, traditional roles of man and woman, husband and wife, male and female, are becoming blurred.

How important is it to have models of genuine parenthood and leadership—models who understand the principles of progress and the value of continuous progression, improvement, and learning!

High degrees of stagnation, ignorance, filth, sloth, addiction, indolence, abuse, insolence, and disorder in a home are indications, not sure proof, of counterfeit parenthood and leadership.

Disrespect for life and selfishness in parents imprints children with images and models of counterfeit. When mothers neglect the most basic needs of children, when fathers turn abusive, when older siblings bully younger brothers and sisters, the imprints can be indelible. Who can afford Madonnas and prima donnas, kings and queens, within the home or corporation? When soap opera models of adulthood and parenthood are played out in the home, we witness all sorts of havoc. If no other success can compensate for failure in the home, no other failure will be so hard to live with over time as failure in the home.

In the classified ads, we see attorneys advertising divorce services: "No Contest Divorce: $90 plus filing fees," as if those were the total costs. That isn't even the tip of the iceberg. The hidden costs of divorce run into the inestimable millions of dollars, and the damages of divorce are incalculable. Few people, young or old, ever calculate the total cost of such things.

• *Neighborhoods.* The world of a child is close-quartered. Children rarely get more than a few hundred yards away from home, through age six, until they start school. Then they are often bused miles from home, subjected to the public education system. Meanwhile, their preschool world consists of neighborhood, family, home and perhaps a few other outside institutions like church or preschool, day care centers, other family members, and relatives who often take care of these children while parents are working.

In effect, these close but not-so-neighborly quarters take the place of the home for street-smart kids who become six-year-old "teenagers". These quarters too are full of counterfeit adult leaders and models who do their own imprinting. Again, not seeing the world through the eyes of children, eyes often filled with tears, we rarely address the questions as to why they are being treated the way they are.

As children venture into this wonderful world of the neighborhood, they discover that it is not always Mr. Rogers' Neighborhood or Sesame Street. Thank God for Mr. Rogers, for some sane human being who is doing normal things, and treating children with respect. Thank goodness for PBS (public babysitting service), that brings children decent programming. Without that, the world of many children would be extremely limited, harsh, and cruel—without rules, fairness, discipline, love.

When I think of neighborhoods, I think of the inquisitive newborn of various animals getting out of their nest, den, or cave for the first time, and testing their wings by romping, playing, and imitating their parents. Much animal behavior is instinctive. Human behavior is much more subject to models of parenting and social conditioning. As children experience the neighborhood, the bigger world around them, many are afraid. My own three sons, when very young, had many fears, and a lot of these were bred by things they picked up in conversation, things they heard on the news—such terrible things as rape, incest, child abuse, and divorce. These things concerned them. They were troubled by the thought that their parents may not stay married, troubled that someone might abuse them, troubled that their "friends" could be so mean.

Read adoption reports on children who have been subjected to drugs, divorce, abuse, or emotional trauma. No wonder kids can be so mean to each other. Of course, children are often mimicking the behavior of adults when they are mean to each other, call each other names, mistreat possessions, and experiment with each other's bodies. They need guidance, and they need good models.

• *Churches.* Religious leaders may not be perfect models either. TV evangelists and local reverends, pastors, or priests may not be providing children (or adults) with authentic leadership. Children may see, for example, leadership in the church that is highly polarized or prejudiced, condescending or critical, judgmental or short-sighted— or so far-sighted that they can't see the step in front of them. They may get "fire and damnation" one week and "mercy and grace" the next. After a while, anything goes, as long as you're singing in the choir on Sunday.

Children sense at a very early age the economic underpinning of the church, and the basic business aspects of religion, as the plate is passed and as they overhear their parents talking about donations and money decisions. Some churches put undue burden on members for money that goes beyond need and becomes a greed—for buildings that go beyond a place to worship and become burdens on the backs of the parishioners or for programs that go beyond self-improvement to self-glorification and indulgence. Programs tend to become more important than people.

All these are evidences of counterfeit culture within churches. And religion—just like education, business, industry and government—ought to be responsible and accountable. People ought to be examining those cultures and testing them for degrees of counterfeit. Sending a child to a counterfeit church for the wrong reasons can be much more damaging than sending them to the park or playground on Sunday.

• *Childcare institutions.* By age eight, children experience several institutions, and are imprinted by each. Most children experience a day care center or preschool, for example. What is advertised is rarely what is administered. But in they go, into the homes and businesses of hired hands who try to care for them and teach them in various ways.

I once sat through a city council session where a mother of nine children (four of them preschool age) wanted officially to start a day care center in her home (located on a busy street with no fenced yard). A concerned neighbor had written the council a note: "It would be a travesty if this woman were permitted to bring other children into her home." The mother of nine, of course, was offended by the remark and defended herself by promising to make some improvements in the future. The council granted the permit.

Whether they're learning the alphabet, dance steps, or swimming strokes, kids begin to have other teachers at very early ages. In our area, there's a mania around cheerleading camps. Many parents project their own ambitions by pushing their children hard into such programs and taking great delight when their three-year-old daughters do all the adult moves on the dance floor. As children are pushed into "special" programs, tots become toys, dolls to dress up and to push into success, achievement, and get-ahead programs (baby contests, beauty pageants and the like). Money will buy programs and nannies for parentless kids, as in the case of Mary Poppins and the Banks' children, but it won't buy kites, kittens, and memories.

• *Schools.* Schools have largely assumed the socialization role in our society. As more parents abdicate their responsibilities to raise their children, this role ultimately ends up in public institutions. How well the schools perform this role is open to question. When we talk about "education," we are really talking about degrees and credentials—and that's a whole different orientation.

Counterfeit parents virtually turn their child's education over to the school. A healthier approach is to constantly monitor your child's education, ensuring that instruction is taking place to your standards by taking advantage of parent involvement programs in the school. Both theologically and philosophically, parents are ultimately responsible for the education of their children. Why do students in private and parochial schools learn so much more and behave better, even when their family background affluence are discounted? Kids respond to caring teachers.

Worst Waste of All

Children are at the prime of their learning capabilities. They will never again learn so much so fast. Because they are on such a high learning curve, the greatest waste, notwithstanding all the dumping that's going on throughout the world, is the intelligence and inquisitiveness of children.

This is the greatest waste, the waste of the inquisitive child, the waste of the two, three, four, and five year olds—as innocent children are subjected to counterfeit systems, societies, cultures, institutions, and leaders. There's always hell to pay when parents or surrogates mistreat children; and children pay most dearly.

Recognizing the realities, children are tremendously adaptable and flexible. They have training wheels and baby teeth; their bones are flexible and malleable. They come into life with adaptability and flexibility. But parents and other institutions exploit that, thinking they "won't remember this" or "be harmed by this."

One young father who was accused of beating his one-year-old daughter in a fit of rage excused himself by saying the child "fell out of her crib," even though the evidence clearly showed that to sustain such damage, she would have to fall two stories.

The question to ask ourselves, both in regard to our own childhoods and our roles as parents or guardians, is this: "What imprints am I making on children?" and "What can I do now to recover from any counterfeiting done?"

False starts and bad early habits are hard (and expensive) to correct later. All too often, the correction never comes. And so we see the start of counterfeit leadership and the demise of personal and professional enterprise.

——— *Chapter* **11** ———

More Work, Less Waste:
Just Do It

"When idleness is a public virtue, what becomes of the moral value of work?"

—Russell Lynes

In the classic children's story of *The Three Little Pigs*, I see a parable for modern managers. Indeed, as I read and reread the story to my three sons, I wonder about today's odds of keeping the wolf at bay and the house of bricks intact.

My guess is that if my three sons—or your sons and daughters—set out upon graduation from the College of Commerce seeking monetary fortunes first, they will join the two-thirds majority who are masters of quick and easy, straw and sticks.

Already, the artful dodgers are perfecting the art of work-avoidance while taking comfort in inflated grades and "don't worry, be happy" friends like Joe Fifer and Sam Fiddler. Among these work-shirkers, leisure has great allure.

But with so much time on our hands, we tend to misuse our leisure. Russell Lynes warns: "Life is getting easier physically, and this makes life harder morally. In the past few decades, we have changed the nature of our leisure from natural to artificial, from pleasures provided by nature to pleasures concocted by man. Leisure without direction, without satisfaction of accomplishment, is debilitating."

Work-Avoidance Strategies

Debilitating or not, no self-respecting, college-educated youth is going to do any *real work* of the organization beyond age 30. I define *real work* as the creation and delivery of the primary products and services of the company; the serving of actual customers; selling to potential clients; value-added support and management of those functions; and faithful, fruitful leadership.

If by age 30, people haven't mastered the games of delegating up and down, putting on appearances, politicking, and socializing, they deserve the awful fate of having to work for a living.

Meanwhile, back at the brickhouse, old-school professionals—the practical pigs—continue to work themselves into early graves or early retirement, whichever comes first. Sorry, no storybook ending here. In fact, many executives are finding themselves on the outside of the highly politicized house of bricks, with all the real work of the organization, while their quick-and-easy partners are comfortably situated inside, sipping lemonade with the doors locked.

Frankly, I'm no longer shocked when I see such "pigs" running around the corporate house, letting the big bad work (work they were hired to do) in the back door for others to deal with.

So, who's doing the real work of the organization? Primarily folks in four different camps: Third-world nationals who don't know any better; women and minorities who do it to make ends meet; youth (under 30) who have no power to avoid it; and seniors (over 50) who do it out of duty.

This leaves many people between ages 30 to 50—what should be prime time—relatively free to maneuver: to play games at the expense of their employers; to mate and merge; to divorce, divide, and conquer, even fear itself. What's to fear when there's no big bad work in sight?

These gamesmen and politicians avoid work in many ways.

• *Seek training and development.* Who seeks and gets the training? The people who least need it. In fact, training has become one of several work-avoidance strategies and havens for many professionals. Of course, one reason we see so much white-male flight into training seminars is because the minorities, women, and powerless people are needed to do the work—somebody has to stay home when management and "high potentials" are in training.

• *Play office politics.* Office politicians spend big chunks of time developing liaisons, networks, CYA policies and procedures, and other work-averse practices. Running the office has come to mean running for office, away from any real work. Office politicians flourish in staff roles, where they are safe from line fire. They become purchasing agents, accountants, lawyers, communications specialists, and public relations agents: people who don't do the real work of the organization. Some, in fact, would not recognize real work if they saw it. And these professionals can stay on staff for generations, safely tucked inside, while others—including many senior executives who built these houses brick by brick with their bare hands—are exposed to all the hostile elements of the competitive environment.

- *Engage in busy work.* Keeping busy or appearing productive has never been easier. With so many mazes, machines, and mergers, one can busy himself or herself with the endless minutia of managing and working in the modern organization.
- *Build and serve "internal customers" and private networks.* Bureaucracies—just look at the Federal Government—tend to turn and feed on themselves when no external crisis is occupying their time and attention. We then see dozens of people serving their internal customers, even though these customers aren't engaged in anything even remotely related to the real work of the organization. Dozens more are using the organization as a springboard for developing their own private networks.
- *Pursue private agendas.* Many people are employed in modern organizations for reasons other than to do the real work of the company. In fact, their busy private agendas won't even permit them to get close to the real work.
- *Do rework.* The "hidden organization" employs an alarming number of people who are doing over the things that weren't done right the first time.
- *Attend long meetings and lazy communications.* Sacrosanct meetings, chit-chat, socializing, and stale communication can easily fill an average working day.
- *Take breaks, succumb to distractions and diversions.* Extended coffee breaks, lunch "hours" and "flex time" maneuvers easily eat a couple of hours. In fact, in some companies, working six hours a day is close enough, given the degree of confusion, clutter, noise, distractions, and diversions built into the working environment.
- *Log telephone and computer time.* When your line is busy, you are thought to be busy. And turning to the computer screen is seen as a sacred experience. Like confession, it's not to be interrupted, even if all that's going on is game-playing and pirating.
- *Read and write nonsense.* Keeping abreast of new thought and development is commendable, but in reviewing the literature, many get side-tracked into reading articles and books (on company time) that have little or no relevance to their work. A host of other folks spend their days writing stuff that nobody reads.

• *Get caught up in sexy distractions, diversions, detours, discussions, and digressions.* Some of these, as executive secretaries can tell you, may involve private real estate deals, travel plans, vacations, toys, mistresses, and money.

This list is hardly exhaustive; it just scratches the surface. Professional work-avoiders—some executives foremost among them—know there are a thousand ways to skin the wolf.

But as phychologist Erich Fromm points out: "There is a far more serious and deep-seated reaction to the meaninglessness and boredom of work. It is a hostility toward work which is much less conscious than our craving for laziness and inactivity. Many a business person feels himself the prisoner of his business and the commodities he sells; he has a feeling of fraudulence about his product and a secret contempt for it. He hates his customers who force him to put up a show in order to sell. He hates the competitors because they are a threat; his employees as well as his superiors because he is in a constant competitive fight with them. Most important of all, he hates himself, because he sees his life passing by, without making any sense beyond the momentary intoxication of success."

Sticks and Straws

In all too many circles, America has become a parody of herself. Long fed a constant advertising diet of "quick and easy, fast and free," we now face the penance: for every past sin or indulgence, we must develop a discipline—not just the discipline of early-morning workouts and smart diets (as healthy as that is) but the discipline of doing the real work of the organization better, faster, more efficiently and effectively.

If we can regain and maintain that basic discipline in business, we ought to be competitive, even in brick-and-mortar industries. But if we become a nation of sticks and straws, then we must rely on our shopworn political and marketing savvy; and we must hope that outside in the streets, the wolf is too preoccupied with his own problems to mount an attack. Any real competition, and the house of sticks and straws will collapse like cards.

Once into minutia management and counterfeit leadership, executives get all caught up in a myriad of social problems, as if the corporation exists to nurse, burp, and diaper its newly hired MBAs; play welfare agency to employees with disintegrated marriages and families; and provide general education to a poorly educated work force. Management then becomes a self-justifying endeavor—excused from doing any real work; incapable of getting any real results; divorced from the front line; and engaged to social and political networks. Each real worker must then support two or three work-avoiders—and it's a heavy load to bear.

How to Get More Real Work Done

Nothing of much meaning, substance, quality, and worth can get done in modern organizations without genuine leadership.

The genuine leader sets a high standard; defines what the real work is; and makes sure every person is either doing the real work of the organization or directly supporting the people who are doing the real work and serving the real customers.

Genuine leaders create more meaning for whole people in challenging jobs; they install responsibility and accountability at every level; they reward performers, especially those on the front lines; they find better ways for getting the work done; and they tie compensation to performance of real work and to achievement of desired results.

Why teach your children and employees to do real work? Because without such basic training, they won't get much of real value, worth, and substance done in life. People raised on a high-fat diet of constant entertainment do not acquire the persistence and self-discipline needed to do difficult or unpleasant tasks. An individual must learn through tough assignments and work experiences how to accept the unpleasant and monotonous parts of a job and find satisfaction in doing them well.

A sensible work-out might include the following:

• *Provide meaningful work activities.* A prerequisite to teaching people how to work is having meaningful work for them to do commensurate with their age, ability, and interest.

• *Teach by precept and example.* The most powerful lessons on work will always be the ones the person lives with. If managers want their employees to develop real craftsmanship, they should model a commitment to quality work, even if that means correcting embarrassing mistakes and starting over again on a project. When assigning a task or delegating a duty, respect the person's personal interests, reach an agreement, specify the standard, and schedule a final evaluation.

• *Serve as a resource.* Ensure that adequate information, resources, instructions and assistance are given—without terminating the contract or agreement.

• *Schedule and conduct final reports.* The final report is part of the job. It should be scheduled from the start and given soon after the job is completed—or in the case of a continuing responsibility, on a periodic basis.

• *Reward with periods of celebration and leisure.* Our value of work often poisons our leisure. We are afraid of unobstructed time or unscheduled hours because our free time exposes us for who and what we are. Depending on our character and values, one of two things can happen to our free time: we can create leisure—a time to expand the soul and renew the energies—or we can create idleness. Idleness is passive, passes time, occupies us. But leisure calls on us to participate, fills deep personal needs, and renews us. Authentic leaders value and cultivate leisure in contrast to their constructive work.

Is Anyone Safe Anymore?

I'm not sure anyone is "safe and sound" in the house of bricks anyway. Corporations have too long perpetuated the myth that they can deliver on the promise of security and safety and supply life meaning and satisfaction to every worker.

We hear "practical pig" executives making such false promises, as if they had a kettle of boiling water under the chimney. No big bad work is going to get them and theirs—la, la, la, la, la.

Even a house of bricks will collapse under the weight of its own bureaucracy—if the competition doesn't get it first. If executives are afraid of the big, bad, real work of the company and are into sexy substitutes—the battle is lost. The houses of straw and sticks have, for the most part, already fallen. Bricks, too, may collapse: there are many precedents, and Donald Trump and his towers and casinos may soon be the next case in point.

Precious little real work will get done as long as people are paid for straw-and-stick activity—perpetuating the myth of corporate welfare independent of real work and global market competitiveness.

Less Waste: Mismanaged Resources

Much of the news and management literature deals, either directly or indirectly, with the issue of waste—waste of natural, human, physical and financial resources.

The topic, then, is often on my mind. Once you acquire a distaste for waste, you begin to sense it everywhere. After a while, you even dare to talk about it openly—and that's when the skeletons come out of the closet.

For example, once when my family gathered for Christmas, I was reunited with my 98-year-old grandfather and 74-year old father. We saw on television the scattered wreckage of an ill-fated flight, witnessing anew the carnage caused by terrorists. More than 100 bodies were discovered in the rubble at the crash site. The story aired in connection with the demise of the entire airline.

We started to talk about the waste of life and resource. The conversation began with the news event but eventually covered the century. We shared stories of the World Wars, of national politics, business, industry; tales of greed, blind ambition, foolish ventures, poor judgment, short-sighted decisions.

"The sad thing," said my grandfather, after our prolonged discussion, "is that we don't seem to learn from the past."

In this country, he suggested, we keep making the same mistakes. People are dispensable; all other resources are disposable. We are addicted to the easy, the quick, the sensual. Waste is a way of life; shocking examples hardly even get our attention anymore.

Still, I'm shocked by Armand Feigenbaum's statement: "Forty percent of what we pay for in some products is for the waste imbedded in them."

Waste, finally, is why I left corporate America. It assumes various forms: wholesale misuse of human talent; massive layoffs; high turnover; exploitation of some workers, especially women; forced early retirement of many valuable older workers; the spoiling of the environment; the pampering of newly recruited MBAs.

The prostitute attitude that for eight hours "they can have my body, sometimes my mind, but never my heart and soul" breeds waste—as does sin, sloth, war, poor quality—because it all means deviation, defect, destruction, rework. Some would argue that waste is an inevitable byproduct of "organization." And perhaps to a degree that's true. But the best leaders and organizations go to great lengths to eliminate waste.

Today's leaders must have supreme wisdom to detect and correct wasteful practices. Appearances can be misleading. To know the difference between waste and worth, a leader must use all five senses:

waste has a certain smell, sound, touch, taste, and look—disguise, camouflage, and masquerade notwithstanding.

Great leaders not only get the most from available resources, they re-create, reinvent, reawake, renew, empower and transform resources. Authentic leaders strive to wipe out waste at every source. They take no resource, especially the human resource, for granted. The leader, after all, is in the best position to eliminate or proliferate wasteful practices—to make the organization more fit, profitable, and fruitful or more indulgent, ineffective, and barren.

High Costs of White-Collar Waste

The folks on the factory floor and the support staff in the office, living on tight budgets, don't waste all that much; to the contrary, they save coupons, seek rebates, look for discounts, shop sales, buy material and make it themselves. And they believe in maintenance: they recover, refinish, paint, lubricate, fix up, and clean up. And so where is the super, industrial-strength waste to be found? In the mismanagement or misuse of things and people—in other words, in the white-collar areas.

• *Things.* Talk "off the record" with any seasoned professional about wasteful practices, and you'll likely get an earful of horror stories—tales from the dark side of the organization about the massive waste of such things as paper and computers, fuel and vehicles, time and money, all squandered and swept under the rug or written off the books.

Sensitivity to such waste is sometimes regarded as old-fashioned, small-minded, or as "penny wise and pound foolish." I've seen executives excuse themselves—even blink at or boast of—Pentagon-size waste and scandal in the name of "big thinking" and "wheeling and dealing" and "playing in the big leagues."

I say, balderdash. But, granted, I was born and raised in a conservative household. My parents, rationed tightly during World War II, made sure we made full use of our limited resources. Pants were patched; food scraps were saved; shoes were resoled; bath water, electric lights, and hard-won dollars were meted out.

These early impressions were reinforced during the sixties, my teenage years, as I worked summers in Zion and Yellowstone National Parks. There I experienced first-hand the silent economy of nature in stark contrast to the noisy gluttony of society. In the Big Sky country of

Montana, I also worked for Pacific Fruit & Produce, and witnessed the tremendous waste of those precious commodities; indeed, it seemed to me that in America we eat only "the heart of the melon."

Of course, waste is not confined to our borders. My two years in Argentina, seeing the monuments of waste erected by Juan and Eva Peron, taught me that nobody does waste better than a dictator. But while each country and culture has its own special brand of waste, no country quite compares to the U.S.A. in the volume of waste—be it nuclear, chemical, or clerical; indeed, our "dumps" are legendary.

Personally, I thought it sadly appropriate that *Time* magazine once departed from its annual "Man of the Year" to pick "Endangered Earth" as its planet of the year. The editors warned us of impending social and environmental catastrophes and added: "Now, more than ever, the world needs leaders who can inspire people with a fiery sense of mission, a universal crusade, to save the planet."

• *People.* Again, I'm troubled when I see on TV the waste of human life, whether depicted in murder, rape, or bad management. Of course, we try to downplay such waste. Rarely do we count the total costs, especially in human terms. I suppose, for example, that we under-estimate, by a factor of one million, the real costs of divorces and drugs, miscarriages and abortions: all the "accidents" and damaged relationships.

The greatest waste in the world is not the devastation that goes with war; not the cost of crime, not the erosion of our soils, not the depletion of our raw materials, or the loss of our gold supply—but the low level of human performance resulting from organizational (system) problems and from such personal problems as poor self-image, self-condemnation, feelings of unworthiness or unimportance, and from bad habits. There's a big difference between pruning and ruining, both in agriculture and corporate culture.

Anyone who has read the reports of J. Peter Grace and his Commission on Government Waste should lose at least one night's sleep. As a young professional working in marketing with General Dynamics aerospace, I tossed and turned many nights as I saw, over a four-year period, the colossal waste of human resources built into the structure and systems of the organization and the industry: the waste of words, ideas, potential; entire legions of engineers let go; misdirected proposals and presentations; raw ego and ambition; the sign on the copy machine, "If you want to see the dead return to life, come back at five o'clock."

Causes of Waste

Waste is a natural consequence of counterfeit leadership.

Counterfeit leaders cause tremendous waste by creating counterfeit cultures. What price tag can you put on the waste of a Hitler? How much waste did that one man create? Put a counterfeit leader in a counterfeit culture, and you will see waste of such enormity and extreme that it will boggle your mind. In the tiny economies and small budgets of ordinary people, you see real conservation, regular maintenance, wise resource management, modest expense, and stringent cost control. But in the grand designs of scheming men and women, you often see such tremendous waste that it almost defies imagination—waste of money, talent, resource, words, ideas, and thoughts.

When counterfeit leaders are living high on the hill and off the hogs (the real workers)—when the rich are robbing the poor—we may need Robin Hoods (consumer advocates like Ralph Nadar) and radical tax propositions to make things right. When waste is assumed as a curse to be endured, it gets budgeted in; people never expect to get rid of it. It becomes part of the business plan, even when everyone knows that half the waste in any company product or process could be eliminated through better management.

In aerospace, I witnessed first-hand the massive redundancy built into the industry. Three giant contractors would all work on the same or similar defense program, all courting the same government purchasing agents and decision makers. I saw the colossal carcasses of multi-million-dollar space launch vehicles, phased out and rusting out.

In every industry, we can see signs of the wasteful cycle: use, abuse, and dispose. Why? What are the root causes? I believe that the high incidence of chronic waste has its roots in attitudes and beliefs—these then become evident in individual judgments, decisions, and actions; get imbedded in the culture; and implanted in products and services. Among the attitudinal causes of waste of concern to me are the following:

- "There's plenty more where this came from"—that thinking can lead to indulgence and excess as well as wipe out precious resources and endanger some species, including man;
- "Not my responsibility" or "out of my jurisdiction"—the excuse of military or any bureaucracy, as if one's moral and professional duty could somehow be outlined with red tape;

- "It's only human"—this one tries to excuse major character weakness as manifest in sin, sloth, pride, ambition, blind faith, and raw zeal;
- "Kill the competition"—this attitude, found everywhere from basketball courts to board rooms, sparks contention, argument, war, fight, discord, anger, strife, and legal battles;
- "We're going in style"—carried to an extreme, this one elevates status to a supreme value and makes anything as old as yesterday out of fashion;
- "What do the numbers tell us"—nothing against numbers, but we need to ask, "what does my heart tell me?"
- "The fools will never know"—this one breeds distrust, disrespect, deception, darkness and detours;
- "Why try to trim waste in this company?"—with a little thought, you may come up with several compelling answers to that small question—unless low self-esteem, lost identity, and poor morale and resignation are blocking your vision;
- "Let's add water to our product, fluff to our public relations" — fine, but it leads to "vaporware" and lies.

Examples of Conservation

I've met some veritable models of conservation, real people who battle waste on every front.

- For example, I'll always remember my visit with Robert MacVicar, who served as president of Oregon State University for many years. In Oregon, one expects to find environmentalists; but in MacVicar, I found the consummate conservationist. He turned the lights off during the lunch break; refused to fire the football coach when the team had a losing record; had a lean, efficient staff who served a loyal faculty, who served dedicated students; dealt one-on-one with people.
- Also, high on the list is Dick Dauch, former executive vice president of Manufacturing at Chrysler Motors. When I met with Dick in his Detroit office, he introduced me to his team and to his dream. I could sense his pride in his people and his passion to be world competitive, to eliminate defects, to educate and motivate his workers. No fat, flab or false emotion in the man. He made every minute and every man, woman, and manager count.

• And then I commend Nolan Archibald, CEO of Black & Decker, for his effective leadership resulting in quality, made-in-America products and in cost-conscious people. When I interviewed him for publication, I sensed his deep commitment to high principles and to the people closest to him. His drive to succeed is motivated by genuine interest for the welfare of others and by a desire not to disappoint his family, friends, and others who believe in him.

These and other executives who are turning companies around are thinking: make or buy it right, use it up, wear it out, and dispose of it right. *They have a deep and abiding respect for all resources*—natural, physical, financial, and human. Respect suggests that some things are irreplaceable, and when they are gone, they are gone—and there may never be others like them. It implies a reverence for life; a maintenance of men, women and machines; a responsible reuse, recycle, and disposal policy.

They make creative use of human resources. A vast amount of talent is being wasted. Every person is a genius in at least one of six talent areas: academic, productive, valuative, planning, forecasting, or communication. And yet, so many colleges and universities are lifeless, tired institutions living on the intellectual legacy of the past. As a result, people stop thinking freely, a sense of powerlessness sets in, new ideas are snuffed out, and universities become just another regulated industry. A person's talent quotient is a more reliable indicator of potential than the intelligence quotient. If educational and professional organizations were geared toward "multiple talent development," nine out of ten people, regardless of their IQ limitations or cultural background, could become highly regarded in their field.

Authentic leaders are not undisciplined mavericks who violate laws and standards. They are stimulated, energetic and alive because they have goals and questions to unravel. The academic totem pole produces "yesterday minds." If people who never learn to tap their creative potential and mind power, who are most concerned about getting high grades and doing well on standard achievement tests, become our leaders, we will become a society of lazy followers of people who can only imitate what has gone on before.

They believe in their own creative potential. In effect, they nominate themselves as creative people; stimulate their minds and make use of both the analytical and intuitive portions of their brains to solve problems and create opportunities. By focusing information and insight, they experience moments of transparency when they see clearly how to do what they've decided to do.

Cures of Waste

A few leading men—and just about all women—are finding cures for the cancer of waste. The cures, curiously, can be found in many different places: in education and training, order and obedience, quality and productivity, open systems and ethical conduct. Great leaders make gardens of waste places, restore and rebuild people. Christ fed the 5,000 with five loaves and then gathered up 12 baskets of crumbs—now that's real economy. The late Edwards Deming, a modern-day Isaiah, made his living by telling management they can do the same if they work with faith to improve quality.

From the mouth of Deming and other "prophets," I hear the warnings, the "wo unto him" who wastes the days of his probation (time), wastes human life and animal flesh (meat), wastes the harvests of the field (fruit), or wastes human resources (people).

On this last point, we might note that Asia's rate of productivity growth increased twice as fast as that of most European countries and four times as fast as that of the U.S. while the defective rates of their products are as little as one-tenth those of U.S. products. The reason we've witnessed a reversal in connotations in the phrases "Made in Taiwan or Japan" and "Made in USA" is because the Asians recognize that quality must be a way of life to compete successfully, whereas CEOs in this country have been complacent, wasteful and exploitative with regard to human and natural resources.

Because the soft or human factor is hard to quantify, economists have left it aside. But there's a limit to how far technology can improve. Seven of the top ten concerns in Japan are related to human resource management; in contrast, not one of the top ten concerns of U.S. managers is related to human resources; it's just one line in the P&L statement called "labor." The human resource is viewed differently in Japan, because that's the only natural resource Japan has.

The difference is well described by Neil Chamberlain: *Employees are being paid to produce, not to make themselves into better people. Corporations are purchasing employee time to make a return on it, not investing in employees to enrich their lives. But somewhere in this philosophy there is an inconsistency with the notion of a society of self-governing individuals. The corporation has become an organizer of people, a user of people, a molder of identities, according to criteria that it has evolved, without regard to the effect on those people except as this is registered on the balance sheet.*

I invite you to listen, to check what's going down the drain and out the door with the trash; what's being spilled, left over, misused, neglected, mistaken; what's being burned in the incinerator and ground up in the disposal—you may just find some of the prime minds and time, meat and potatoes, fruit and produce, people and things of the organization.

—————— *Chapter* **12** ——————

Abundant Wealth and Power:
Free of Debts & Illicit Desires

"To preserve our independence, we must not let our leaders load us with perpetual debt. We must make our choice between economy and liberty or profusion and servitude."

—Thomas Jefferson

An abundant mindset frees us of the "win all you can" ethic—frees us not only of debts but of lust, greed, blind ambition, and covetness—because when we have "*one*"—we already have an abundance in knowing who we are and what God has blessed us with. Still we are free to seek additional resources to bless and benefit others.

Counterfeit leaders view government and business largely as a game of grabs, and thus consider the win-win ethic counter-productive. Since these charlatans perceive that there is not enough to go around and whoever gets his market share must be taking it from others, they play the game by the laws of the jungle, complete with natural selection, survival of the fittest, and raw economic and political pressure. He who has the most toys or chips wins.

Authentic leaders see that there is an abundance in life and plenty of paradox in business: that winning at all costs might mean losing everything, for nothing.

To make the point that the path to real wealth is filled with paradox, Hugh Nibley, a professor of ancient studies at Brigham Young University, tells a story about two employers and their prospective employees. I have modified it here for effect.

*   *   *   *

One day we read in the university placement center that two major employers in the area are recruiting and interviewing the best talent. Having just graduated with MBA degrees from the university's prestigious School of Management and in need of work, we decide to interview with them both.

The first employer offers to take us to lunch, and since lunch is something we all must have, he is in a powerful position to bargain. He skillfully plays upon our ambitions to find a fast track to the top by hosting us in the impressive executive dining room.

After a prime rib lunch, we are treated to a tour of the manufacturing plant. We can't help notice the tight security. All employees wear identification badges, yet no one is called by name. Out of neccessity, each has made a deal with the boss and works in relative anonimity in order to make more money. Because money is the only thing that will get them lunch—mere work is not enough. And since everybody must have lunch, the boss has them under his control: If anyone gets out of line, he simply asks, "If you leave this employment, what will become of you?" That question scares the daylights out of them. From the man on the assembly line to the senior vice presidents, they are all scared stiff.

When we interview with the other employer, we are first impressed by the open "campus" of the corporation; in fact, several people refer to the place as a "learning environment." People come and go freely. And then at noon in the cafeteria, we are surprised to see that all employees are served a free lunch! When we ask one of the managers about the free lunch, he answers emphatically: "The boss tells all of us to forget about lunch—to not even give it a second thought. He says that if we do our work well, he will take care of lunch. In his opinion, lunch should be the least of our concerns."

After lunch, we interview with this kind benefactor. He begins by asking, "What subjects did you take in school?"

"We studied courses in business and management," we respond, thinking he will be proud of us.

"You studied that—all the time?"

"Yes, we thought of studying some other fascinating subjects, but we then remembered that it's the bread-and-butter courses that count and that in the real world there is no free lunch."

"But I provide all my employees with lunch right now."

"Yes, but our purpose in life is to get more and better lunches. We want to go right to the top."

To our surprise, the man seems saddened by this remark.

"Why do you serve a free lunch?" we then ask.

"Because otherwise, lunch easily becomes the one thing the whole office looks forward to all morning. A passing need too easily becomes a distraction, a decoy, an engrossing obsession."

"But," we say, thinking of all the exclusive restaurants, exotic cuisine, and fancy dining rooms in town, "doesn't such economic equality produce a drab, monotonous sameness among your staff?"

"But that sameness already exists," says the employer. "We all have the same number of eyes, ears, arms, and legs. It is in the endless reaches of the mind, expanding forever in all directions, that infinite variety invites us, with endless space for all, so that none need be jealous of another. Only those who seek distinction in costly apparel, living quarters, diversions, meals, cars, and estates become the slaves of fashion and the most stereotyped people on earth."

"But what about the ancient teaching that the idler shall not eat the bread of the laborer?" we ask.

"That has always meant that the idle rich shall not eat the bread of the laboring poor, as they always have," says the wise employer, who then quoted Shakespeare: "What is man if the chief good and market of his time be but to sleep and feed? A beast, no more. Surely he that made us with such large discourse gave us not such capability and godlike reason to fust in us unused."

"If we use our capabilities solely to feed, we are much less than the beasts. It is only the human predator who keeps a 24-hour lookout for victims in the manner prescribed in the flourishing contemporary success literature," he says.

"But those are the very books and magazines that we are required to read," we gasp, now getting worried.

"Those very popular how-to-get-rich books are but guides for the perplexed," says the employer.

"But our professors say that we should keep our minds fixed at all times on just one objective; that the person who lets his thoughts wander away from anything but business, even for a moment, does not deserve the wealth he seeks."

"Yes," says the employer knowingly, "such is the high ethic of today's education. And such an ethic places us not on the level of the beast, but below it. The no-free-lunch mindset easily directs our concern to nothing but lunch, making lunch our full-time concern—either by paying workers so little that they must toil day and night just to afford lunch, or by expanding the need for lunch to include all the luxury and splendor that goes with the executive lunch."

At the end of our interview, the employer asks us to choose between the peculiar economy and employment he just described for us and what we had always considered the more realistic, convenient, and expedient economy of the first employer.

We discussed the matter briefly, and then decided to be true to our education and upbringing—we chose the first.

Saddened by our choice, the second employer nonetheless wished us well, but also said with a tone of warning: "Notice that at this very moment, the economic order you have chosen is convulsively gasping and struggling to survive. The difference between the two orders is never more apparent than at lunch-time. The homely ordinance of lunch, meant to unite us all for a happy hour, instead divides us with the awful authority and finality of the Last Judgment—in which, by the way, we are assured that the seating order is going to be completely reversed."

*   *   *   *

If universities simply turn graduates out into the best current job market, they have no mission. As much as we all need the means to feed and clothe ourselves, we need not sell our souls to get them.

Said Ralph Waldo Emerson: "Men, such as they are, very naturally seek money or power; and power because it is as good as money—the spoils so called of office. And why not? For they aspire to the highest, and this, in their sleepwalking, they dream is highest. Wake them, and they shall quit the false good and leap to the true and leave governments to clerks and desks."

Two Examples

As I entered a very impressive corporate boardroom situated atop the most impressive office building in Salt Lake City, a man next to me said, "You've been in a lot of executive offices and boardrooms, are all of them such obvious displays of opulence, ego, and power?"

"No," I said. "But, a nice office and impressive boardroom aren't always indictments against the character of the CEO. Let me tell you about two chief executives here in your own state."

I then related the stories of two CEOs who are wise in their use of power and money: Bill Child, CEO of R.C. Willey Home Furnishings, a leading retailer; and Verl Topham, CEO of Utah Power and Light, whose power is in serving people and communities.

• Bill Child, president and CEO of R.C. Willey Home Furnishings (now backed by billionaire Warren Buffet), is making Utah retailing, once considered a very tough act, look as easy as child's play. Utah's "kick the tires" customers are hard to satisfy, as Child well knows: "They tend to have large families and limited incomes," he says, "And they are not going to spend it without doing some real thinking and checking."

Having grown up with the challenge of selling products to cash-strapped people, Child has arrived at a simple solution: Offer real value. "Look," he says emphatically, "if people are willing to drive anywhere from 10 to 40 miles out of their way just to get to our store, we have to offer something extra—a bigger selection, better quality, and lower prices."

Child has won so many awards and honors—including Utah Master Entrepreneur of the Year, Utah retailer of the year, Rocky Mountain Retailer of the Year, and national retail store of the year—that he's become embarrassed. Since 1954, R.C. Willey has grown an average of 17 percent a year—from two employees to 1,400, and is now ranked 20th among the top 100 furniture stores in America at about $300 million in sales.

Child often visits his stores and knows his people. "I try to know them all as well as I can," he says. He already controls half the Utah market, but even after selling the company to Warren Buffet, one of America's most successful investors, Bill has increased his commitment to the company.

Along with his brother, Sheldon, Bill took the small appliance dealership started by his father-in-law and created a retail organization that is dominant in electronics, furniture, and appliances. But as recently as 10 years ago, R.C. Willey was just one of several Utah furniture stores vying for market dominance.

Timing is everything. As Salt Lake City entered a prolonged growth period, R.C. Willey was also growing. In 1990, the company added two large new stores and a massive distribution center. "We were willing to spend the money and build the infrastructure we needed to handle the business," said Bill.

Now, from its chain of superstores, R.C. Willey provides a vast selection of product at competitive prices, clearly emerging as the state's dominant retailer. "We practice basic business guidelines of conservatism balanced with growth and risk," says Bill. "We try not to get ahead of ourselves or move ahead unless we're ready to expand and to grow. We focus on customer service, because customer loyalty is what it takes to build a great organization."

• Verl Topham believes in power from the bottom up. Every year for the past 20 years, he has attended a major Shakespeare festival. One of his favorite plays is *King Lear*. He likes *Lear* for its lessons on power and leadership, sensing that the same misuses and abuses of power are evident in most of today's organizations. Power, it seems, is intoxicating—it goes to one's head, affecting vision, reducing reason and in some cases, inducing madness. The corporate counterpart to King Lear is the CEO who, from the top down, demands loyalty and expects certain affections from followers.

Although Topham has the power office in the state, enjoying expansive views of the valley and instant access to data and information on virtually every person, place and thing in the state, he is amazingly unaffected by it all. Like a child, Topham has a sort of natural aversion to power. He quotes, in addition to Shakespeare, Thomas Jefferson: "I've sworn upon the altar of God eternal hostility against every form of tyranny over the mind of man." Says Topham, "There is no greater tyranny than the tyranny we place upon ourselves through our own fears, inhibitions, restrictions and self-limiting beliefs." He wants his management team to be free from prejudice and pre-conceived notions. His favorite book, *Les Miserables*, is the account of the French opposition to an abusive aristocracy.

Topham tries hard not to let the opulent office surroundings get to him. "I try to keep a common touch and appreciation for those who do the real work of the company. I spend a lot of time visiting our offices and plants and our customers to listen to them and let them know I support them. There's always a good deal of natural skepticism about the leader of a company. My managers see me as someone who has the power to upset their lives. And so they wonder who I am, what I am all about, and whether I represent their interests, and the best interests of customers, stockholders, and employees."

He adds reassuringly, "I don't believe in bullying people or abusing power. I'd rather be creative in coming up with win-win alternatives. You have to respect the power of your position and use it as carefully as you would the power of electricity."

Uses and Abuses of Power

The love of power and money corrupts, and obsessions with them corrupt absolutely. Power is a wine, smooth and intoxicating. Power can subtly transform a person from a participatory leader to an absolute tyrant—from caring to callous. Power and the accoutrements of possessions and perks and privileges can become so intoxicating that people become drunk with greed and ambition. When power becomes the absolute standard of leadership, turf and title and things become the name of the game.

Who has power? Who is king of the hill? Neither Rodney King nor Anita Hill—both are victims. Even in the smallest of kingdoms, a marriage, a little power goes to one's head. Power can turn the legitimate to counterfeit faster than you can say O. J. Simpson. There are great lessons about power in *King Lear* and other plays by Shakespeare, and in the lives of Adolf Hitler, Abraham Lincoln, and the modern-day tragedies of Michael Milken and Richard Nixon. Like Donner and Blitzen, they coveted Rudolf's red nose.

Give a man a little power, position, and authority and see what he does with it, see what it does to him, see what it does to his relationships. Bless a man with riches and see what it does to him and to his relationships. Give a man a couple of servants and a secretary and see what it does to him—and see what he does to them. What effect does it have on his life, his relationships, his mission, his motives, the means that he uses to get things done? In counterfeit cultures, power is taken from the people and hoarded in the coffers of the king or the chief executive who seeks dominion.

Hard to Eradicate

Counterfeit leadership is costly to keep and even more costly to force out. Ask George Bush what the total cost of the Gulf War was— and he still didn't get Saddam Hussein out.

Of the many options to oust a counterfeit leader—democratic procedures (such as elections), military procedures (such as coups, take-overs, revolutions), social measures (such as ostracism or banishment)—none is cheap or easy. Counterfeit leaders are like weeds in gardens. And for some reason, weeds grow faster. In dry soil, they're so hard to yank out. You grab them, and you only jerk the top off. The roots remain, and the weed grows right back. So it is with counterfeit leaders: If you don't get all of them, the roots remain; they grow right back; and they continue to choke the flowers.

In some cases, rather than attempt conversion, you may have to "blow up" the organization and start over. If counterfeit leaders are in power, you've got a real problem. Chances are they aren't going to like the idea of popular elections. Most dictators don't. They won't like the idea of being ousted from office. They will use all their might, power, and persuasion to maintain their grip on position.

When a powerful corporate CEO learned of a certain man who was rising in power and popularity, showing great promise and performing well in a division of the corporation, he was worried. Some had dubbed him as the next CEO. He feigned adoration; secretly, he was jealous and covetous. He thought of ways to destroy his rival's career. "It's either you or me," he said. "And I'm not leaving."

His law: If outwitted, use power and position to gain advantage. He had the young executive assigned to tough duty overseas where he felt sure he would fail.

Indeed, in the beginning, the young man floundered. But he rallied as he won alliances and learned the ropes. The experience proved to be invaluable to his growth and development. Over time, his influence expanded throughout the region.

When that region gained immense importance as a potential market for the corporation, the worst fears of the CEO were realized. The young man he had banished was now a serious contender for his position. And a few close advisors, fearing for their own careers and sensing the imminent demise of the CEO, decided to leak the fact the CEO had sought to destroy his career. The news spread fast in the newspapers and resulted in the dismissal of the old CEO and the appointment of the new CEO.

Indeed, the pen is mightier than the sword. William Penn, a convert to the Quakers, stood in stark contrast to the culture of the time, depicted as a culture of false laughs, unearned emotions, costumes, jewelry, wigs, feigned mannerisms, initiations, game playing, gambling, drinking, betting, and flattery. His abstinence from all of this made him a social aberration. Penn called his male contemporaries "peacocks," because they reminded him of colorful struting birds.

Penn displayed a transparent peace and contentment. He had few wants and needs, a directness in his conversation, a purpose to his consecration, a simple faith that his needs would be met, and a love of people regardless of their power or station, profession, title, address—a stark contrast to the feigned society that surrounded him.

Would-be leaders gain real power and wealth as they move away from this "peacock" existence of false laughs, unearned emotions, costumes, cosmetics, jewelry, wigs and jigs and move toward the character traits that William Penn and all great scholars, musicians, philosophers, writers, politicians exhibit. They make their mark on the world by serving as leaven for the whole loaf of human life.

In Avery Fisher Hall in New York at the Lincoln Center, I once saw a "mostly Mozart" program. How expansive is the influence of Mozart? A genuine leader will influence the lives of millions of people, far beyond his death. Even though, in his immediate life time, there may not be any indication of immortality. In fact, often genuine leaders are almost sure targets for criticism, even assassination, because of the sharp opposition to their ideas, or to the brilliance of their wit or work. But in the test of time, the true saints and those gifted giants with the pen will overshadow all the network's sitcoms, soap operas, and peacocks.

People with real talent are ambassadors of influence. On three occasions, my wife and I travelled with a troupe of entertainers called the Young Ambassadors, college kids with no money or professional credits. But after one show in Egypt, we heard: "Responsible people want to meet you—you are a hit." The audience stopped the show several times, applauding with their hands above their heads. At the end, they erupted with enthusiasm and surged toward the stage.

I wondered, "What makes this show such a hit?" Raw energy, real sacrifice. Home-grown goodness and spirited dances, faces, songs. An ethic that no one gets preferential treatment. The ancient Egyptians spent a lot of time stacking stones to prevent the sands of time from erasing their civilization. Give them credit. After 4,500 years, the remains are still there. But in moments, these ambassadors erected monuments in the minds and hearts of people that rivaled the pyramids.

When people strive for excellence, when they are not trying to fake it or force it, something unique and beautiful comes from it. It's contagious to see people perform who are focused and free and who express love and unity. An entertainer gives people what they want; a leader gives people what they need. The best leaders both entertain and enlighten, and thus qualify as ambassadors of influence. They play music that directly affects the senses. People find themselves singing and tapping and marching along with a lump in the throat or tears in the eyes. Music exerts influence on most systems and functions of the body. Plants subjected to calm devotional music measured two inches higher and actually leaned into the music.

Authentic leaders seem to have the same effect—effectively drawing direction and policy from their people, and then providing the facilitative leadership to make things happen. They attract quality people and keep them. They have a light touch that allows people to feel comfortable and responsible and to move ahead on their own. They are supportive, treating people with dignity and giving credit to others liberally.

We can't escape having influence upon others. Ours is the opportunity to build, to lift, to inspire and to lead. But the power to lead is the power to mislead; and the power to mislead is the power to destroy. So we can't be careless. The lives of others may depend on us. The greatest leaders appeal not to power but to conscience. Their advocacy reconciles rather than defeats people. In fact, they go beyond advocacy to ministry. Meaning triumphs over power—and for that reason, sensible leaders show compassion to all. They reach out to touch lives, even of those who are despised because of race, social condition, or physical or mental imperfection. As advocates, authentic leaders stand prepared to assist a person who is downtrodden, destitute or unpopular.

Once I interviewed an actor who was playing the role of Hamlet: "My biggest challenge as an actor is to get in touch with my inner self and have my emotions at my disposal," he said. "Many men and women mis-spend their days in materialistic pursuits. The question of whether or not to be an artist is only difficult because we live in an age when men are caught up in getting a job and making money. From the moment a person starts treating his life as a career, worry is his constant companion. Careerism results not only in constant anxiety but in an underdeveloped heart, since you must ignore idealistic, compassionate, and courageous impulses that might jeopardize your career. I will only make a significant contribution if I am faithful to myself, to my own integrity." He had chosen self-employment.

Shortly after I was fired from a job, I prepared, printed and sent out dozens of resumes. I became a beggar on a job hunt. In response to my resume, I was invited to interview for a position at the University of California, Los Angeles. I prepared my case, practiced my petition and plea, dressed my best, and flew to L.A. hoping to pass the test.

I stayed in a hotel at the university's expense, and while walking to the interview the next morning, I was asked by a young man for some money so that he might meet his needs. He asked cheerfully.

I denied him. I was concerned about my meager cash funds, concerned that they would not see me comfortably home.

Again at the airport, after the job interview, I was asked for money, this time by an earnest young man who opposed nuclear arms build-up. He explained his cause and asked for a modest donation.

I told him that I had only a few dollars—for lunch—but that I supported his cause. I never spent that money on food at the airport. Instead, I ate the free airline food on the flight home.

By refusing the petitions of the beggars I encountered in Los Angeles, I disqualified myself for the job I sought. For I, too, was very much the beggar, asking for lunch money from men who stood in a position to provide. But like my petitioners, I was turned down, treated as a passing fancy. My earnestness deserved their brief attention, but was judged unworthy of support—as ambition or greed or undeserved need. By refusing them, I was refusing myself, proving myself unqualified. I supposed that I would "pay my own way" and "buy my own lunch" and "earn my own bread" and "win friends and influence people" and "land a good job." I was just another beggar, one of 66 applicants for the job, not the one who would be chosen.

Money's No Object

Money is the name of the game by which many are cleverly decoyed into counterfeit paths and pursuits. For example, in mergers, acquisitions, leveraged buy-outs, and hostile take-overs, there is often artificial value created in these activities that benefits relatively few people without really changing the nature of the company or improving the quality of the products and services.

The words and the symbols on U.S. currency make a statement of value: the inscription "In God We Trust" is most interesting. Counterfeit leaders don't honor these models and monograms on our coins. Surveys show that most people don't even know who is on a one-dollar, five-dollar or a ten-dollar bill, or who's on a quarter and a dime and a nickel and a penny. As much as we see these coins and currency, we don't recall who or what is inscribed on them. They become paper and metal that pass through our hands without meaning. And yet in the trade of business, these coins and currency are the symbols of our trust and our integrity.

To counterfeit leaders, money is not a manifestation of their character and integrity but of their ability to wheel and deal, hook and jab, cheat and win. They are caught up in what money can buy. They can't tell you who or what's on those coins or what it means. They not only don't trust in God, they likely fight Him on every front.

Counterfeit leaders don't deliver on promises because they can't. They may promise to pay us well, and, in fact, they might, but not in currency of lasting value. It is often in cheap thrills, momentary pleasures, passing fancies and other such coin and currency of the realm. People who do the work and trust in the promise to be paid well, eventually get paid in counterfeit bills that are only good within the counterfeit culture.

One sign of a counterfeit culture is the attitude that "the world owes me a living." When things are acquired too easily, they are valued lightly. Only sacrifice and labor give things worth and value. Without earning our daily bread and money through hard labor, we gain a distorted sense of what things are worth. We confuse what money can and can't buy.

Living beyond our means is now an accepted standard operating procedure. Everyone encourages it, especially the good folks behind bank credit cards who love to extend those limits, the next best thing to prison terms. The ancient discipline of saving, even tithing, 10 percent of income has been replaced with modern indulgence of spending, even gambling, 20 percent over and above income and seeking subsidies, grants, gifts, donations, charities, and welfare to make up the difference.

The new canon is "Forgive us our debts, because we surely won't or can't pay them." The leniency system of mercy begs for absolution of any need to repay. Paying one's debts is optional in counterfeit systems because the outrageous sums of the loans are seen as clear evidence—sure proof—of the insanity of the lender.

———— *Step Five* ————

Empowerment: Power to Be and Do

Under authentic leadership, the new "power game" is not played up and down the hierarchy but inside-out, from me to you and from be to do. This means that in authentic cultures, the old gamesmen and politicians are out of work. The new mandate: If you hope to do, first be—be the change you want to see in the world.

• Be the follower you would want if you were the leader. False followership is both a cause and outcome of counterfeit leadership. They cause counterfeit by following blindly, obeying without question, giving up power gladly, and divesting themselves of responsibility and accountability. By being part of the crowd, they experience the ultimate loneliness—feeling alone in a crowd, with no one, including themselves, to call a friend.

• Getting back on beam usually requires forming or joining a quality team or "great group" of people who care about life balance and constructive use of power. Authentic leaders make wiser and better— even highest and best—use of their senses and resources to maintain equilibrium and magnify their power to be and do.

• The triple crown of quality, results, and relationships can be won by anyone who runs the race wisely. The false dichotomies of either quality or quantity, results or relationships can be dissected using the formula of vision + faith + work = fruit. There is no scarcity here—abundant will be the harvest for all who exercise the power to be and do.

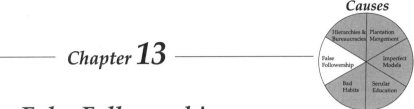
——————— *Chapter 13* ———————

False Followership: Pushing Power Up

"Ask not what your country can do for you—ask what you can do for your country."

—John F. Kennedy

Counterfeit leadership often begins with counterfeit follower-ship—with the notion that passive resistance, patronizing assistance, ignorance, activism, apathy, ambition, and aggression are traits of true followers—with the idea that the tallest, toughest, biggest, loudest, most articulate, best dressed, most popular, or the most physically or financially endowed ought to be the leader.

Counterfeit election, selection, recognition, reward and promotion systems compound the problem by encouraging game playing, positioning, politicking, and palavering. Followers are forever jockeying for position. We see it in spades in political organizations where work becomes gamesmanship.

If the great truth of the culture is that the followers who get promoted are those who get recognized, then the game is to be visible and mobile, to be at the right place at the right time in order to be appointed (self-promoted) to positions of leadership.

Counterfeit followership aids and abets counterfeit leadership. Gross misconceptions about who is most loyal, faithful, and helpful generate some bad ideas about who should be leader. In a counterfeit culture, various forms of false followership are prerequisites for leadership.

The masses who are asses are the nameless, faceless followers of counterfeit leaders. They are the deceived, the poor in wisdom, who follow anything or anybody that moves. They give rise to despots, dictators, and con artists—somebody who is moving, doing, and saying something.

In Hollywood and Beverly Hills, we see a curious parade of people, a constant stream of passers-by, whose lives are filled and fulfilled by proximity to their heroes. These are the fans of movie stars. Media-made celebrities and their counterfeit followers really deserve each other. It's a match made not in heaven but in the hell of an artificial society.

In *The Mysterious Stranger,* Mark Twain writes, "Satan dropped all seriousness and overstrained himself, making fun of us and deriding our pride in our great heroes, our imperishable fames, our mighty kings, our ancient aristocracies, our venerable history—and laughed and laughed till it was enough to make a person sick to hear him; finally he sobered a little and said, 'But, after all, it is not all ridiculous; there is a sort of pathos about it when one remembers how few are your days, how childish your pomp and what shadows you are.'"

The best counterfeit leaders mass-produce false followers on high-speed presses: It's faster than individual stamping. Again, Twain writes: "I know your race. It is made up of sheep. It is governed by minorities, seldom or never by majorities. It suppresses its feelings and its beliefs and follows the handful that makes the most noise. Sometimes the noisy handful is right, sometimes wrong; but no matter, the crowd follows it. The vast majority of the race, whether savage or civilized, are secretly kindhearted and shrink from inflicting pain, but in the presence of the aggressive and pitiless minority, they don't dare to assert themselves."

Hard-core counterfeit leaders, like Hitler and Mussolini, are both causes and consequences of counterfeit followership. They cause game playing, positioning, politicking, flattery, and aggression. Such leaders get to the top by leaving a trail of counterfeit confetti behind them, inviting people to join the fun and enjoy the spoils. They leave their bread and stones scattered through the forest for Hansels and Gretels. Followers are quick to pick up those coins and bills, payoffs and bribes, along the way to the top. They see how their leaders got there, and they expect to get there by the same route.

Defiant and destructive followers often feel justified and expect society to just leave them alone. But as John Stuart Mill said, "As soon as any part of a person's conduct affects prejudicially the interests of others, society has jurisdiction over it." And then defiant counterfeits lead people along on a string of lies. They lead entire nations to war, poverty, violence, ignorance, aggression, prejudice, and death—the rotten fruits of consummate counterfeits, the end results of countless distortions and deceits, lies and cheats.

A Crowd on Every Corner

And so on the street corners, we see vendors, evangelists, entertainers, and politicians drawing big crowds. Swarms of people apparently have nothing better to do in life than be spectators to rap music, dirty dancing, and pop politics. As Adlai Stevenson once said when told that every *thinking American* would vote for him: "Yes, but I need a majority."

I'm always a bit taken-back by the Nielsen ratings that show what millions of people are watching on television. Millions of people consciously turn on TV and watch garbage. No matter how poorly conceived, written, directed, and produced the program is, many thousands of people watch it—on TV, in theaters, on street corners, and homes. Apparently we need professional critics to tell us what is good and bad, what to think, and when to laugh, cry, and clap.

If millions of people can follow a Jim and Tammy Bakker, for example, in a pursuit as important as religion, I suppose that anything is possible. We are all susceptible to a good sales pitch, especially when we are in a crowd. Now, whenever and wherever I see teeming masses—whether it's at Tianenmen Square in Beijing or Red Square in Moscow, Piccadilly Circle in London, Times Square in New York City—I try to separate myself, at least mentally, to keep a perspective on what is being said and done: "What is going on here? Who is leading whom? Why are all of these people together?" When we are in a crowd, we tend to go with the flow. It's easier to move a crowd than to sway an individual.

People are attracted to movement, even passing fancies. The masses can be led by momentum and mirrors alone—a mere flick of the wrist—as every good dictator, preacher, and traffic cop knows.

Many followers do not want to be leaders. They fail to find and develop leadership within themselves. They become numb to their natural gifts and talents and become satisfied with low levels of achievement. They become creatures of habit and go with the flow. Their lives become ruts and routines. During the week, we can peg where they are going and what they are doing at any given moment of the day. Weekends, too, become predictable hours of leisure and loafing. Because of their choices, they forfeit leadership. They adopt the ethic of convenience and ease, hoping to get bread the easy way by abusing power and by refusing to wait for the right time and the right way. But their bread is bogus.

Today, the only restraint left is self-restraint. But we don't want to be inconvenienced until we've earned the right and paid the price. We want it all now: body and soul, stocks and bonds. We don't want to go a day without physical gratification, spiritual assurance, or monetary security, but sometimes we must, since we have no guarantee of room-service convenience in life.

Indeed, inconvenience is the itch of poor leadership. Hang-ups, holdups, and huddles can happen anytime—on the street, in the office, hall, restroom, or cafeteria. Commonly, holdups are short interruptions and interceptions as we travel to and from. Without commitment and concentration, we unwittingly trade the significant life for a never-ending series of distractions.

People expect much from their leaders, and to gain access they will target memos, schedule meetings, and intercept them in transit, even on the toilet, and hold them ransom. Leaders must weigh what they will part with. Several of the greatest leaders chose to part with life before parting with integrity.

In trying to meet the high standard of total integrity (the personal equivalent of total quality), we may fall or fail. But temporary setbacks are no disgrace if we keep trying and never give up in well doing. Integrity, the willingness and ability to live by our beliefs and commitments to codes of conduct and moral principles, is the foundation of good character. Without good character, one can't expect to sustain success.

We often wish for some magic in personal and professional life that will enable us to continue living comfortably with sophisticated self-deceptions that relieve us of responsibility for transforming our lives. We start thinking that a resurgence of person or corporation is possible without a concomitant commitment to timeless values, ethics, and principles. The shift from kinship to contract as the basis of business and society has been accompanied by the rise of individualism; consequently, the focus is on the individual, not on the family, team, or company.

We hear few expressions of responsibility, more expressions of passivity or abdication of responsibility. In the Spanish language, we say, "se me cayó" (it fell from me) or "se me olvidó" (it was forgotten to me). Those expressions absolve one of responsibility for forgetting something, or for dropping something. What is active tense in English becomes passive or reflective in Spanish. What is passive in language becomes passive in belief, in attitude, in behavior, and in lifestyle. Fatalism and determinism are companions to passivity and irresponsibility. You start thinking that "things are meant to be" or "they just happen" or "it's not my fault" or "it's out of my control." Such philosophies are powerfully reinforced in counterfeit cultures.

The absolution of responsibility is very seductive. Cain asked, "Am I my brother's keeper?" And his counterparts today are saying: "The devil made me do it" or "not my responsibility." When such phrases are built into the structure of the language or culture of the corporation, natives must consciously choose a proactive alternative; otherwise, they are virtually doomed to determinism. Fatalistic philosophies are reinforced whenever we think, talk or walk in the way of "things just happen" and "there's nothing I can do about it." We then just go with the evolutionary flow of life.

Even if passivity is not built into the language, those idioms can be part of a corporate belief system (the way things are expressed) or the culture (the way things are done). They become the "official" attitudes and ways of doing things—part of the counterfeit culture.

The basic ideas of being accountable for results and accepting risk in exchange for reward has yet to penetrate many firms. Said one politician when asked why more people choose not to run for public office: "Demagoguery, grand-standing, political joking, aspiration to high office, lack of character—these are standard charges leveled against anyone who assumes leadership in a controversial issue." That's why many people choose to be followers.

Leadership assumes risk and responsibility, and not everyone wants that kind of R&R, even if it means greater reward. Even people whose faith and belief system encourage the exercise of agency to achieve greater degrees of glory and to make choices and be accountable and responsible at an early age—typically want to be around the food in the kitchen but want none of the heat. They don't want to get involved in the fray. They want to stay in the middle of the crowd, not speak out or stand out. Sadly, they slowly become apathetic to social issues. They would rather bury their children in the back yard than become involved in a pollution abatement program in the community.

Rarely are the risks of passive followership ever recognized. But those risks are real. As Henry David Thoreau said, "A man sits as many risks as he runs." There are risks in being led. There are risks in assuming that someone else will do it; that someone else will say it; that someone will take charge and lead us out of this mess and into the land of promise. The risks are that you can remain a captive to the culture, captive to your own habits, captive to your own lifestyle, and captive to community standards and become satisfied with low-level achievement.

We can't grow authentic leaders in cultures where people seek the easy way out. When people want an easy way out—whether the issue is bankruptcy, no-contest divorce, or no-fault insurance—they want none of the responsibility or liability, nor do they want to face the consequences of their own behaviors, even if they've broken the laws, committed untold crimes, and made creditors line up for miles and wait for back payments.

Chapter 11 and Chapter 13 are poorly written chapters in the book of American business life. These chapters have caused untold grief to many creditors. Today, a financially troubled person would be considered insane to adopt the attitude, "I am going to pay everybody off, with interest, even if it takes the rest of my life." That person would likely be found "not guilty by reason of insanity" in a trial by a jury of peers.

Counterfeit Admissions

When counterfeit followers infiltrate legitimate cultures, they can ruin them in short order. Their very presence suggests monkey business. If they can win key positions and hold them with tenure, as they often do for decades, then the implication becomes: "If this person is in this position, this system must be counterfeit."

Counterfeits get hired and hold their jobs because of defects, double standards, and soft admission standards that allow for exceptions, even extremes—whether that's hiring family, promoting incompetency, or rewarding miscreancy. And not all rules apply to all people. When that happens, what is authentic in culture is tainted with counterfeit. Because of the visibility of the position, people will say, "This is sure proof that the culture is counterfeit."

In counterfeit cultures, false followers get ahead by being vocal, visible, mobile, and having access to the inner sanctums. Kids learn these keys at an early age, often in such "model institutions" as school and scouting. In school, they witness the truth of what Mark Twain said in *Pudd'nhead Wilson's New Calendar:* "In the first place, God made idiots. This was for practice. Then He made School Boards."

And in scouting, many 12-year-olds become "scouts" of their own making, with their own oaths and mottos, patterned more after movie star Bruce Willis, the last boy scout, than Lord Baden Powell, the first boy scout. In reviewing the movie, *The Last Boy Scout,* film critic Roger Ebert said that the film is "slick, glossy, clever, smart, skillful, and well crafted" but also "cynical, unexpectedly violent, utterly corrupt, vilely misogynistic" with the only consistent theme being "hatred of women." In one extended scene, Willis and his child curse each other. "I'll give it three stars," writes Ebert, "but as for my thumb, I'll use it and my forefinger to hold my nose."

In spite of such reviews, the movie was second to *Hook* in gross sales its first week out. "My distaste is irrelevant," concluded Ebert. "*The Last Boy Scout* type of movie *is* the future. It assumes the average audience has no standards except those of the mob."

Indeed, it appears that a lot of people are "hooked" on the sort of "scouting" portrayed in *The Last Boy Scout.* The street-tough, machine-gunning, macho model appeals to a major segment of the population, as evidenced by the box office success of Arnold Schwartzenager and Sylvester Stallone movies. So what if a few million decent folks are offended and appalled. The new oaths and mottos have the majority: 1) *The PR motto:* Do a trick or a turn daily for others to see for the sake of publicity; 2) *The out laws:* A scout is trustworthy (honor among thieves), loyal (to his private cause), helpful (in self-interest), friendly (to his own kind), thrifty (with his own money), brave (in groups and gangs), clean (when appearing in court) and reverent (some things, like money and power, are sacred); and 3) *The (hypocritical) oath:* On my honor, I will try to do my best in doing my minimal duty in order to run with the pack. Kids quickly learn the tricks of getting meaning-less merit badges and parading in uniforms for all its symbolic glory.

Beyond scouting, they are playing games throughout their educa-tion—only now the merit badges are grades, degrees, scholarships, and social relationships. They are playing games even in their religion or church where appearance is everything. The proximity to the pastor is everything. Being seen with, sitting next to, and hanging around with the right people, wearing the right labels and the right clothes;

driving the right cars; and playing the right scenes give them a sense of legitimacy.

Counterfeit cultures reward counterfeit followers and bestow their own legitimacy on those who play the game well. They make up their own awards, honors, medals, badges, and uniforms to give members a sense of legitimacy. A street gang has its own signs, symbols, slogans, and rewards, for example, and to become one with the gang, you have to do or simulate certain things to pass inspection.

Counterfeit followership breeds counterfeit leadership, and vice-versa. The fake group Milli-Vanilli would not have won a Grammy if it weren't for counterfeit fans and followers who even today won't send in their records for the $3 rebate.

When counterfeit followers become managers, they join the ranks of amateurs. "Amateur leaders try to direct the efforts of followers by attempting to think out everything for them," says Bill Oncken III of the William Oncken Corporation. "The result is one-to-one leverage and a back-breaking assortment of monkeys. The amateur never gets over the feeling that to stay away is to move in the opposite direction from where he or she should be moving. Knowing when to stay away is the mark of a pro, whose leverage is much greater than the number of followers because of the number of self-assignments each empowered individual takes on and completes without the manager even knowing about it."

Authentic Followers

Genuine followers are active and informed, vigilant and valiant, even in bathrooms. For example, once at Berkeley in the men's bathroom, instead of seeing nasty words and crude drawings of sexual anatomy on the walls, I read statements on the vital issues of the day (a sort of op-ed page). One asked "When most of us are admitted here on merit after 18 years of hard work in the school system, why are some among us admitted here on double standards? We see athletes and others who can barely read and write, but are here to perform revenue-generating functions for the university." This short editorial on inequities in admissions and double standards in academic classrooms suggests that the culture values pretense over competence.

Authentic followers sustain, support, and affirm authentic leadership—often in less vocal, visible, and political ways. They, too, may be opportunistic but are true to their mission. The Biblical Joseph was opportunistic during his tenure in Egypt, but he was also true to his God. There's nothing wrong with employing one's talents in the service of others and thereby earning promotions that lead to leadership positions—or with earning good grades and getting scholarships legitimately.

Authentic followers don't overload their leaders. They carry their own weight. They understand that every leader, like every truck, has his or her load limit or capacity for carrying dead weight. In the best family-owned businesses, all members of the family understand a basic truth: "He may be my brother, but he's too heavy if he's not carrying his own weight." Sure, there is a sense of family, community, and caring, but no one gets a free ride. Chronic welfare cases are fired (or not hired in the first place). Nepotism is nipped in the bud.

Before we assume the load of another human being, we better weigh the body. For example, just one more employee may be the proverbial straw that breaks our back. Wise leaders carefully weigh what they put on their backs. They don't go on 20-mile hikes loaded down with useless gadgets and gear. They know that they can only carry so much. And knowing the raw tonnage of burdens, bodies, and bones in the organization, they make people carry their own packs, unless they are truly incapacitated.

Authentic followers make wise counselors. Authentic followers prevent blind spots that result from bad or no counsel. Throughout history, some of the greatest crimes have been committed in the name of religion, patriotism, and nationalism. As leaders cry to people congregated in front of TVs, or in plazas, squares, centers, parks, coliseums, and stadiums, true followers supply much-needed feedback.

Objective evaluation rarely happens within the confines of one's own frame of reference. That is why authentic leaders select and appoint counselors at both sides. That is why we see a house and a senate on the wings of the Capitol. That is why every leader has a right hand and a left hand—and ought to have counselors at both sides, because without them, one begins to tip and tilt and become imbalanced. One's own mind becomes the mind of the people; one's own wishes become the wishes of the people; and without accurate feedback and wise counsel coming from various stakeholders and from both counselors, one in the right ear and one in the left ear, even the best leaders will begin to tilt. They become distorted and self-deceived, thinking that their mind and will represent the minds and wills of their followers. They justify themselves in the most heinous of crimes because of what they perceive to be noble missions, means, or motives.

We often are comfortable in the counsel of counterfeit followers or counselors who flatter us and talk endlessly about our strengths. Their counsel actually leads us in wrong directions and keeps us from making course corrections.

Few people dare to tell us the bad news or call us on counterfeit moves. Most true messengers get shot. And as we mistake flattery for fact, we create counterfeit maps, keys, signs, and symbols. We are then continually lost because we no longer have a compass or even an accurate map. We only have public opinion—the noise of various voices, full of self-interest. We become pinballs, bounced and flipped about by social feedback, lacking self-direction.

Finally, authentic followers are true friends. Through the thick and thin of our lives, they stay with us. While they may remind us of our weaknesses, they do what they can to compensate for them—and they support our strengths. Too often they are paid in counterfeit notes of ingratitude, indifference, and silence.

Mark Twain noted, "When we remember our unkindnesses to friends who have passed beyond the veil, we wish we could have them back again, if only for a moment, so that we could go on our knees to them and say, 'Have pity and forgive.'"

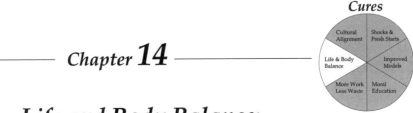

—————— *Chapter* **14** ——————

Life and Body Balance:
On Beam, With Team

"The balanced life has four dimensions: perspective, the big picture; autonomy, a sense of control; connectedness, quality relationships with others; and tone, positive lifestyle habits."

—Marjorie Blanchard

In the gymnastics of life, balance is all-important. One slip on the bar or beam, and we lose for ourselves and our team.

I've met two of the six members of the men's gold medal championship gymnastic team from the 1984 Los Angeles Olympic games — Peter Vidmar and Tim Daggett. Both scored perfect 10's on their routines that final night of team competition to win a stunning victory for the United States over the world-champion Chinese team.

But the victory started long before in lonely gyms. Peter and Tim kept late hours at the UCLA gym when they trained with coach Makoto Sakamoto. "Night after night, when the regular workouts were over and our teammates had gone home," recounts Daggett, "we were alone in the gym, alone with the stillness of the apparatus. Though we too were tired from the day's training, this was our time. It was the time that would make us better, stronger, and turn us into champions. For it was during those after-hour workouts while we disciplined our bodies that we also conditioned our minds, employing visualization techniques that put us in the identical positions we were in that night—the last two performers who had to clinch the gold medal for the team."

Once at age 12, I went with a friend to a local gym where all the gymnastics apparatus was set up for use. He had been in a program for a couple of years. After he showed me a few maneuvers, I said to him, "That was great. It would probably take me a year to do that." (One year was the longest time I could imagine.)

"Don't flatter yourself," he said. "It has taken me two years, and I'm the best in our class."

Learning how to balance one's life and budget on bars, beams, and bottom lines may take at least a couple of years.

A lasting cure for counterfeit leadership is life and body balance. Without balance, we tend to derail or develop an addiction around work, play, drink, or drug.

Life balance has become vogue again as people experience the consequences of an imbalanced lifestyle—as they become addicts, workaholics, or careerists, they lose balance, sight, perspective, vision, meaning, love, even life itself.

Five Ways to Achieve Balance

Some disciplines do take time. Of the many "gymnastic" ways to achieve life balance, I recommend five that authentic leaders use: 1) serving others, 2) sacrificing pride, 3) conditioning the body, 4) training the whole person, and 5) gaining social awareness. These have their parallels in the gymnastic events of beam, rings, floor, vault, horse, and bars.

1. Serving Others Anonymously. On a slip of paper, a great scientist, Harvey Fletcher, carried a constant reminder, "FFFF." Someone once asked what that meant. He said, "That's to remind me who I am and what I've been given: I have friends; I have been fortunate; I have a family; and I have faith. A man couldn't ask for more. Joy comes by developing and using your talents for yourself and for humanity."

Great leaders give anonymously. We are often seduced by the sleight-of-hand philanthropies of those who affix their name to museums to reap publicity and tax benefits. We are also charmed by the captains of industry who give the gifts of jobs. And yet historically, we see that behind great fortunes are often hidden great crimes and with great wealth comes great want. Must we tolerate the abuses and exploitations of earth and spirit by those who seek power and position?

The "salt" of the earth rise above materialism; they work anonymously, and serve voluntarily to develop, succor, protect, produce, and steward resources. Most real service is done by voluntary organizations, not through compulsory means and through ineffective government agencies and programs.

"Glamour is not greatness; applause is not fame; prominence is not eminence," said John R. Sizoo. "The man of the hour is not apt to be the man of the ages. The world would soon die but for the fidelity, loyalty, and consecration of those whose names are unhonored and unsung."

When I visited the Tomb of the Unknown Soldier, I was moved by the idea that here lies somebody, literally some unknown body, and yet we show such respect to this anonymous person that we keep constant vigilance, employing a sentinel to watch over and guard the tomb of this anonymous soul who represents countless, faceless, nameless men and women who died in defense of country or in a good cause. There in Arlington, the national cemetery, lie many bodies; most of the tombs are marked. We know whose remains are there. But many are still unknown.

Some of the best examples of genuine leaders are the unknown soldiers who have no place in recorded history, who lead lives of relative anonymity or obscurity, who are not in the headlines of the magazines and the papers. Many choose to remain obscure. The Amish, for example, don't byline their literature in order that the glory go to God.

Of course, not all leaders we read about in history are counterfeit by virtue of being known. Some famous men and women truly are great and genuine leaders. In fact, the noble and great among us who really lived and achieved so much—not as cartoon characters or film creations, but as actual men and women—should give us all pause. Having witnessed so many great lives, we know for certain that real greatness and grand dimensions are possible in the lives of mortal human beings and that one great man or woman may bless and enrich the lives of millions for generations.

Although I honor those who have achieved historical greatness, I submit that many more "ordinary" people who, if put in certain circumstances or given certain opportunities, would also have achieved greatness. But their lot was different: It was small; it was local; it was a time and place that did not attract the rather arbitrary searchlight of publicity. While the spotlight never fell on them, they acted nobly and dutifully and were true leaders in their sphere of influence.

Authentic leaders sense that in some instances it is better to work within a small sphere of influence and dramatically affect the lives of one or two others for good than to work with the masses on a superficial level. It is better to manage well one's small lot than to let an expansive estate fall into disrepair.

Many women will ultimately be recognized as the greatest leaders, even though in life "all they did" was serve nobly as mothers and raise a responsible child or two. They may have no name, face, or place in history. But, indeed, the least—the last, the weakest, dumbest, plainest, and the most deficient, handicapped, disfigured, and despised—may be counted among the best and first and greatest, as the tables turn in the light of true judgment, not flawed human judgment.

Because of the "wind beneath my wings" factor, it's foolish to attempt to identify "The 100 Greatest People" of all time. Likewise, it's foolish to attempt to define, as some books and magazines do, the greatest executives, artists, or entertainers. Authentic leaders—while they may have their face on a magazine cover from time to time—take publicity in stride. They realize that one day you may be king, and another day a condemned criminal.

Fame and fortune are fleeting, says presidential advisor Roger Porter. "Neither possessions nor positions bring us peace of mind, only great causes and good works. When the pursuit of excellence motivates us and causes us to be our best; when service to others ceases to be a phrase and becomes a reality in our lives; and when the bonds that bind us to those we love are strong and sure, it is then, however modest our circumstances, that we feel joy."

When we visit the sick and the suffering, someone in pain and anguish, someone who's handicapped or retarded—those visits often shock us into a realization of how fortunate we are. By working with those less fortunate, we gain an appreciation of more genuine values and character traits. When we comfort others, we receive much in return.

The counterfeit of selfless service is commercial public relations—it's service with a return in mind. Public relations is another seed bed of counterfeit leadership. PR has become one of the great false gods of our society and of our organizations. In today's PR society, God could not keep a job; Christ would be crucified anew; and Socrates would never graduate with a degree.

2. Real Sacrifice: Beyond Mail, Meals, and Meetings. One danger of being raised in the lap of luxury or living life in cocoons of comfort is to suppose that sacrifice means getting up in the morning, opening the day's mail, eating meals, and attending meetings. For that, some expect to be honored.

Authentic leaders, and great actors, know better. In several stage and cinematic productions, I have seen well-educated and titled men drop all their degrees and sophistication and make no distinction between themselves and those who only spend one minute on stage. They so sacrifice their pride because they know that if they do not achieve a cooperative spirit, they won't stand up under close scrutiny: such selfishness on stage will visibly weaken their performance.

An all-wise God will know when we sacrifice our pride for the sake of the performance, or when we harbor error willingly, says ancient studies professor Hugh Nibley. "And so we ought never to promote ourselves by manipulating others, by intimidating, lying, or cheating, because none of these will work on Him." We are too ready to sacrifice and too slow to obey. We are more willing to sacrifice our time and means than to sacrifice our pride and sins. How much of what we call sacrifice constitutes real sacrifice on our part? Sin, the most frequent cause of our stumbling, clouds our vision and dries up our access to spiritual guidance, leaving us alone—wandering with our own dim light and weakened resolve.

When the plate is passed and eyes are on us, we may make a "voluntary" contribution, a donation to a cause, according to the depths of our pockets, peer pressure, or the power of the preacher. And while these hit-and-miss donations add up, they are no substitute for a system that consistently requires the sacrifice and obedience of its membership.

Authentic leaders often require significant sacrifices, and a tithe may be the least of it. They call people on missions, not hand them job descriptions. They lift, motivate, and focus on the mission and motives, leaving the means to them. They know that there will be disappointments, risks, and struggles as people grow and develop. In the authentic leader's handbook, the only handout we ought to desire is opportunity.

Counterfeit leaders teach men and women to worship themselves and to celebrate their worship with self-indulgence. They preach rights and entitlements and teach us to take. Authentic leaders teach responsibilities and service and teach us to give. Among the great enemies of a free society are leaders who preach the virtues of free enterprise but expect special treatment and subsidies for their own special interests.

John F. Kennedy said: "With good conscience our only sure reward; with history the final judge of our deeds, let us go forth to lead the land we love, asking His blessing and His help but knowing that here upon earth, God's work must truly be our own." In the authentic life-style, you may have to wait and endure before you see much reward or return on your investment.

My father-in-law, a retired school teacher, was once paid a tribute by one of his sons, a top-of-class MBA graduate: "He's the best teacher I've had because he starts with where you are, who you are, and what you now know. He quickly picks up on how you speak, how you see things, and what you can do with your mind and hands—and then he takes you step-by-step through a growth cycle into new territory, and motivates you to reach new heights."

Privately, my father-in-law told me, "The rewards of teaching are few and far between, even for the best teachers. Looking back on my career, I see few headlines and highlights. The great accolades that one hopes for in a career rarely materialize. Few students ever come back to thank you or tell you of a positive difference you made in their lives."

We rarely stop to thank those who sacrifice to teach us or who sacrifice a career to be at home with us. When we do thank them, they are deeply touched. Rare are those moments when the people we help come back to thank us, even as we face death. Sweet are those moments when we feel rewarded intrinsically for the anonymous good we do; the anonymous service we perform; the caring behaviors we show. When we feel in fullness the rewards for that goodness, all other rewards and compensations pale by comparison.

When I served as the student editor of a university newspaper and magazine, I worked many hours beyond my meager compensation. Often, I made early morning and late evening deadlines and press checks without being asked or expected to ensure the quality of the product. On the last day of the semester, I was up again at 4 a.m. to see the last issue through the press. When I returned to my apartment, I felt immense intrinsic satisfaction and compensation.

In the heat of summer and cold of winter, we must hang on to those feelings and have faith in the ultimate harvest after a season of toil and sacrifice, keeping our eyes on the prize, on the delivery day of thanksgiving. Those with limited vision and small souls will forever feel cheated when they count the coins of extrinsic compensation. But authentic leaders know the big rewards are those thanksgiving feelings of fulfillment that saturate the soul and cause us to feel the love of God and man and get a sense of immense rewards for service, sacrifice, faith, work, diligence, discipline, obedience, chastity, and charity. Millions of people take a sacrament to remember the sacrifices of others in their behalf. The ultimate cure of counterfeit behavior is deep conversion to the principles of saviors who sacrifice for our sake.

Turning from counterfeit to authentic means making a choice. Joshua told the people: "Choose ye this day whom ye will serve" and asked them to make a covenant and commitment, to write their names in stone, to make a public confession and declaration. Without such measures, it's easy to turn back.

The line down the road to reform resembles the line of a seismic chart during a quake, as people stop smoking, swearing, stealing a hundred times. In the short-term, counterfeiting is sweet, but over time it becomes sour. The temptation is to turn again, to taste once more the temporary sweetness of honey or money. It's a passing fancy, but for a brief moment, the taste is sweet.

3. Conditioning the Body. Counterfeiting often begins with abuse, neglect, or mismanagement of the body. As food companies and their ad agents try to hoodwink us into thinking that Kix is as good as corn on the cob, we respond by eating artificial foods. Worse, women are persuaded to use silicone-gel breast implants, IUDs, and abortion-inducing pills even as the most knowledgeable and responsible medical doctors are saying that these items may cause serious side effects. What's unnatural and sinister has an aftertaste or a side-effect, and yet cosmetic surgery, liposuction, slim-fast diets, addictive drugs, fashions, fads, and bachelor pads are the big sellers.

The more we lose sight of what really is good for our body, and the more our idea of nutrition comes from television on Saturday morning—as we believe all that the advertisers are telling us between Bugs Bunny and Captain Kangaroo—the deeper our trouble. And the more we allow our body to become prisoner to our appetites, desires, and passions, the more we get our "truth" from the *National Enquirer* and Dr. Ruth, the more our character becomes thread-bare. We next subscribe to the idea that we can compensate for physical or character deficiencies with personality strengths.

Why is it so hard to fast, to miss a meal or two? Because we battle the ever-present appetites and the passions of the body. Moreover, the world has invented and packaged a million convenient beverages and condiments at every corner. Every counter has something to satisfy our appetites here and now—it is all right in front of us. And whether we take it in through our mind or mouth, for the fleeting moment, it feels good. It satiates an appetite, satisfies a passion, meets a need, pacifies a greed.

Authentic leaders are responsible stewards of their own bodies. They serve as gatekeepers who pay close attention to entrances. They know who and what is entering in through the front gate as well as through all the side and rear entrances. They care what enters and exits the body. They guard against infections and diseases that can enter the body—the body physical, politic, or corporate—and cause sickness or death. That is why leaders guard entrances. They monitor what is entering through the eyes, nose, ears, and mouth—through feelings, emotions, and thoughts—and determine whether it is healthy for the body.

• *The eyes.* What we take in through our eyes, the primary learning medium, is terribly important in this battle to overcome counterfeit. Counterfeit people see with their eyes what works socially, politically, and emotionally to get their way. They pick up on what titillates or tantalizes, persuades and entertains.

To the degree we walk in error and darkness, our eyes will be ill-suited to detecting counterfeit. The eyes, the window to the soul, are the surest means of inspection and detection; however, it may take discernment beyond the appearance. But eyes are a good indication. Counterfeits tend to avoid looking people straight in the eyes. They tend to have more glancing looks and sideswipes.

People who grow up in counterfeit cultures see the world through glasses made to a counterfeit prescription. And so they only perceive as "real" people who mirror similar attributes—bravado, chutzpa, chat, flattery. And if that's our model of authentic leadership, then we are going to overlook the meek, humble, and mild folks who are progressing day-by-day, one step at a time, and who have many talents that aren't obvious. We are also going to dismiss them as leaders.

• *The ears.* The ears pick up a lot of ambient noises and sounds: the thunderous tympanies as well as the soft subtleties. The blind develop a keen sense of hearing, as their ears become their eyes. Trained ears detect amazing detail, compensating in part for the loss of sight. Authentic leaders train their ears to pick up on certain sounds: the cries of children, the murmur of employees, the complaints of customers, the chat of family—these sounds are clues to their real needs.

• *The nose.* Authentic leaders savor life, in part because they have a keen sense of smell. At any given show on Broadway, some in the audience appear to be bored, distracted, or annoyed. They can't enjoy the performance because they can't block out what's bothering them. Likewise, at times some scene or scent prevents us from picking up on the fragrance of the flowers, the perfumes of people, the magical performances on stage. Because we're bothered or just too full of ourselves, we miss much of the savor and flavor of life. The nose detects what's sweet and sour, pungent and perfume. Authentic leaders use their olfactory sense to clean up the factory. They may sponsor innovative "skunkworks," but they ban human skunks and their offensive odors.

• *The mouth.* The mouth is both an entrance and exit. It's the entrance to the esophagus, stomach and intestines—the intake for food. And out of the mouth go our words and other sounds. We could put a microphone near the mouth and monitor who's authentic and who's counterfeit and to what degree they are, both by their intake and their output, by what goes into their mouth and what comes out of their mouth—by what food and drink they ingest in what quantity at what hours in what ways, and by what words, expressions, noises, and sighs leave their mouths, at what times, and in what circumstances. If you monitor what goes in and comes out of the mouth, you have great clues to the degree of counterfeit.

It is not so much, as Christ said, what a man eats and drinks that defiles him—it's not so much what dirt, dust, grit, grime gets on his hands and clothes as he does his work—what does the real damage is what is manufactured within from the raw material of those defiling sources that penetrate the mind, infiltrate the soul. Also, it's not what enters but what leaves our mouths that defiles us. Vulgarity, profanity, and obscenity—the tripod on which many movies are scripted and filmed—are evidence of counterfeit. As we entertain obscene words and images, our thoughts and imaginations, attitudes and behaviors, become defiled.

• *Touch* (feelings). Many impressions, signals, and sensations come by way of touch. The finger tips and other parts of the body are loaded with sensory cells. These help us determine the size, shape, and surface texture of objects and add to our delight and pleasure in life. The "erogenous zones" also add to our pain and anguish. The kings and queens of pornography are experts in sensory experiences, and they know what delights the body. The terrible irony, however, is this: what we abuse, we lose. In seeking the ultimate sensations, we lose all sensitivity.

• *Heart* (emotions). Some truths are only meant to be felt, not expressed in words. Deep-seated feelings and emotions are said to be heart-felt, referring to the emotional capitol of the body, not the physical pump. Songs of "the heart" have been sung for ages, and sadly most of them are blues.

• *The mind* (thoughts). Many sordid thoughts enter the mind. What's important is what we allow to stay, what we dwell on, what we think about when we are alone, when we aren't forced to think about something else—these are the telling moments between the genuine and the counterfeit, because they again become more sure signs of who's who.

The master minds of counterfeit are always looking to gain access and entry. Their minds become obsessed with what will pass, or what will get them in, what will get them by, or what will get them ahead. They covet access and entry into chambers of the Senate and the House, and the halls and the institutions that confer legitimacy and credibility. And they are masters at forging keys that unlock the doors, or disguises that fool the guards. And they forge counterfeit identity and entry devices.

A system of access, entries, and exits is all-important to counterfeit leaders. They have their defense tunnels, secret passages, and season tickets. They con their way into games, colleges, clubs, and corporations. They delight in crashing institutions draped with credibility. They covet credentials that smack of legitimacy, solidarity, longevity, and credibility. They covet most what they don't have, and they will cheat to get it. They hire lawyers, forge documents, disguise face, and masquerade to fool the palace guards, admission counselors, media gatekeepers, and security officers—and to get into legitimate print. To become mainstream, Mafia leaders try to infiltrate pockets of legitimacy. They make plans to get into Congress, into corporations, into unions, and into law, where they can do their deeds, not as criminals, but as respected professionals.

4. Training the Whole Person. The wise are forewarned by great literature and by vicarious life experience. For example, three great novels about adultery—*Madame Bovary, Anna Karenina,* and *Sister Carrie*—powerfully warn us of the consequences of certain choices, which we might not fully anticipate when we are young; vicariously, they help us understand how it feels to suffer those consequences. Lives that aspire to what is noble and right—even in the face of ongoing misery and affliction—are edifying illustrations of the beauty of character.

Leadership and the arts are companion endeavors: each produces moments of grace, beauty, power; each, regrettably, also attracts its share of the sordid. On any given weekend, for example, stadiums may become stages where fans turn fanatics, using the game as an outlet for anger, an excuse for gambling, an alibi for intoxication. Players and coaches, too, may succumb to brawling, bad-mouthing, and brute force.

The artist is harder to beat than the sadist or the scientist. Art is not absolute; it is creative, consisting of trial and error. It is not as conducive to analysis as is science. In tennis, when one player sets up his opponent and then lobs the ball over him—he shows more finesse than when he simply blasts the ball by him.

A conditioned leader executes moves requiring agility, strength, flexibility, speed, power and balance. Physical exercise is essential to mental health, particularly for those who have difficulty handling the pressures in their lives.

Authentic leaders work with mind and hands, heart and soul. Most "manual labor" requires some intellect, and the most intellectual labor requires some physical skill and coordination. Many scholars also work with their hands, and many take more pride in their tangible achievements, even though they may be elementary, than in their impressive intellectual feats. In working with words and concepts, ideologies and theories, they have little to show for the effort. They take more pride in building a dog house, putting in a yard, or planting fruit trees.

For example, Gifford Pinchot, author of *Intrapreneuring*, has degrees from MIT and John Hopkins and yet takes more pride in his welding than in his writing. I also know manual labor workers who look forward to the one hour each day they have in the night class where they can learn in computers, chemistry, or some subject that really tests them. The Renaissance ideal is to express oneself in a whole way—meaning physical, mental, spiritual, and emotional—to work with the head, hands, and heart.

5. Gaining Kinesthetic and Social Awareness. Kinesthetic awareness helps us have a sense of ourselves in relationship to other people, places, and things at all times. With this sense, even with all the twists and turns on the trampoline of life, we tend to be at the right place at the right time, appropriate in speech, dress, and demeanor.

Without kinesthetic awareness, we tend to act like student drivers. As I followed a student driver to work one day, I noted that driver's training, like most formal education, instills few skills, some knowledge of rules and laws, but sows the seeds of fear, failure, and crashes. Consequently, student drivers have little awareness of their car in relation to other traffic. When we're young, we tend to think we are isolated, and our behavior doesn't affect other people. The big social lie is, "This only affects me." When we get in a car, we carry that attitude into the street. It takes a while to learn that we are part of an interdependent system, a network of dynamic relationships.

As parents, we teach our children to be responsible drivers; we put them through rigorous driver's training; and we instill in them a respect for authority, obedience to law, and the rules of the road. And then we put them on the streets with people who don't have that background, who drive without a license, without training, who drive stolen or mechanically unsafe vehicles, or who feel when behind the wheel that the only rule is "what's best for me." These people are playing demolition derby, dodge ball, bumper pool. And who knows what they're high on? But these people also are out on the road.

Driving requires balance of defensive and offensive maneuvers— and an understanding of human nature. We're all tethered between the past and the future. We live in these air-tight compartments called *today*. With a sense of what's gone before, or what may come here- after, and a sense of who we are, what our duty is, what our job is, we can help keep an ecological balance in the system. But as people become more selfish, greedy, ambitious, offensive, and less concerned for others, we see a lot more "accidents" on the road; we see people being hurt, if not killed. We see it on the road, in the home, in the schools—as ambulances are on the scene, hauling people out of homes, schools, work places because of violations. In the corporate streets, we are also involved in "accidents," even hit-and-runs. Many of these are caused by people who break the laws of nature, the rules of the workplace, and who suffer the consequences of unnatural, imbalanced, addictive, or selfish behaviors.

Observing the strange behavior of other drivers, we often ask ourselves, "What could he or she possibly be thinking." We want to get inside somebody's head or heart. But our judgment is flawed, as we often judge ourselves by intention, others by action. Or we project our intentions or motives on other people as we see their behaviors. When we read our motives and intents into their actions, people are damned if they do, damned if they don't. Mere projections pass for perceptions. We really don't know what's in the minds and the hearts of other people. We can see their actions but not their motives. We can't be sure of the motivation or mind and heart of the person. We can only observe certain behaviors and guess what that means.

The wisest judges among us will also read the level of progression, the level of learning, and the stage of development for that person; what they know and what they don't know; and where they are emotionally, socially, and morally. And put all that into a context. Perfect judgment is the ability to accurately assess the mind and the heart of a person.

It's a struggle to achieve integrity in the gymnastics of life. Total integrity means a constancy in values, beliefs, norms, and behavior. We won't achieve that without subscribing to and abiding by the cures for counterfeit—observing timeless laws and principles in every season and situation.

Chapter 15

The Triple Crown: Quality, Relationships, and Results

"With malice toward none, with charity for all, with firmness in the right, as God gives us to see the right, let us strive on to finish the work we are in."

—Abraham Lincoln

Every leader wants three things: high product and service quality, relationships of trust with all stakeholders, and impressive bottom-line results. I refer to these three goals as the triple crown, and in this chapter suggest ways to win and keep that crown for yourself, your team, and your organization.

On a personal level, I maintain that if you want quantity, first think quality; if you want results, first build relationships; if you want the rewards, observe the prerequisites; if you want power and position, first learn service and sacrifice; if you want the fruit, exercise the faith and do the work.

On an organizational level, winning the crown starts with empowerment: pushing power down, making decisions at every level, encouraging more self-leadership, and creating a culture where every individual accepts responsibility for results.

Three Driving Factors

The hullabaloo over employee empowerment is no longer confined to the "elephants" learning to dance—everyone is getting into the act. And for good reason: empowerment is high on the list of needs to survive and succeed in the 21st century.

Why are so many executives at least paying lip service to empowerment? Is it the crazed quest for quality? The fashionable harangue against hierarchy? The open admission that organizations of every size and type must now reinvent themselves, reengineer their processes, and more fully tap the potential of people? It's all of that and more. But the driving factors appear to be the following three.

1. *Competition*—As foreign and domestic competitors become flatter, faster and more flexible, many Fortune 500 corporations are shedding management layers and adopting empowerment as a creed.

In flatter organizations, people must be empowered to make more decisions; to search for ways to improve quality, productivity, and service; and to engage in self-improvement activities because they are proud of their job and identify with its success.

2. *Nature of work*—As work becomes more knowledge-based, leaders must get and use information and knowledge to create products or to help customers improve their business performance. The new generation of leaders must be more intellectually aware because the world is becoming more information-intensive; so those who rise to the top will be those who are excited by ideas and information.

3. *Employee expectations*—Organizations need leadership at every level to manage change effectively and sustain competitive advantage. To create such leadership, you need clear direction, shared vision, and well-defined policies, procedures, systems, and methods in support of the corporate strategy. Empowerment denotes a strong feeling of authority, power, and ownership that motivates people to take initiative and to accept responsibilities and risks. With alignment and empowerment, people have a clear picture of the strategic direction and a sense of ownership in the success of the business. Empowerment means creating a sense of ownership by providing clear expectations, control of resources, responsibility and coaching, and by offering help without removing responsibility. The leader helps people retain ownership of a problem or idea while they work out a solution or implementation plan together.

One Taproot, Three Fruits

Empowerment, notes Rosabeth Moss Kanter, former editor of the *Harvard Business Review,* "is giving people access to the three key power tools in any organization: information, support and resources." Companies that excel in empowerment "make more information available to more people at more levels through more devices; permit collaboration so that people can build supportive problem-solving coalitions; and decentralize resources to make them more available for local problem-solving."

Even though this is elementary, *Empowerment 101,* it is still counter-intuitive for many control-centered or power-based managers.

"That's why any manager who hopes to empower his people must be principle-centered," says Stephen R. Covey, author of *The 7 Habits of Highly Effective People.*

"The taproot of empowerment is trust. If you have no or low trust in the culture, if management lacks character or competence, then you have to control people and measure their performance. But if you have high trust, people will supervise themselves and evaluate their performance on the basis of win-win performance agreements. You then become a source of help to them."

Among the many benefits that grow from the roots of empowerment are the big three: quality, relationships, and results.

1. Quality Products and Services. Quality starts with high commitment. "The primary challenge of leadership," say John Naisbitt and Patricia Aburdene, coauthors of *Megatrends 2000*, "is to encourage people to work effectively in teams and to be more entrepreneurial, self-managing, autonomous. The dominant principle has shifted from management in order to control to leadership in order to bring out the best in people and to respond quickly to change. While capital and technology are important resources, people make or break a company. To harness their power, leaders inspire commitment. They empower people by sharing authority, thus enabling their firms to attract, reward and motivate the best people."

The Malcolm Baldrige National Quality Award won't be won without empowering both employees and customers, says its former director, Curt Reimann. "The leaders of the past delegated or relegated quality and its internal standards to a department within the company. The new manager must have a different focus: quality driven externally by customer requirements." Every employee must be empowered to deal effectively with internal and external customers.

When John Grettenberger, General Manager of Cadillac and a winner of the Baldrige Award, was asked, "How do you prepare 10,000 people for a Baldrige examination?" he replied, "You can't. People either accept ownership for the process or they don't."

Too many companies are working on the symptoms instead of the root causes of non-competitiveness, says Philip R. Thomas, CEO of The Thomas Group and an expert in speed and responsiveness. "They are trying to improve forecasts instead of reducing cycle time so they won't have to forecast so far in the future. They are trying to control customer changes instead of reducing cycle time so that they are responding to the changes on a real-time basis. They are trying to manipulate work-in-process to meet a given need instead of removing barriers that reduce cycle time and improve business process predictability."

And when these efforts fail, says Thomas, "executives of these ill-fated companies apply excess resources in the form of people, inventories, equipment and risk in a vain attempt to improve cost, quality and customer service. Excess resources only compound the problems. The only way to solve quality and competitiveness problems is to create a short-cycle-time, rapid-feedback culture."

2. *Meaningful Relationships.* What W. Edwards Deming first taught the Japanese 50 years ago were *people empowerment* principles, not *product quality* practices. His 14 points constitute basic human development principles, and his "deadly diseases" are descriptions of anti-empowerment crimes committed by well-intentioned management. "The wealth of a nation (or company)," says Deming, "depends on its people, management, and leadership more than on its natural resources. All must adopt a new (empowering) style of management and acknowledge that the aim of leadership is to help people and machines do a better job."

Deming says that the artificial barriers between people and departments must come down, along with all else in the systems that create adversarial relationships among people who need to cooperate. People will be more threatened than excited about a new vision unless there are empowered change agents who champion the vision at every level, bringing it down to the gut level of each person by showing them how the vision will help them solve the biggest job-related problem confronting them.

When empowered, everybody feels that they are a legitimate part of what is going on. Stanford professor Steven Brandt says, "The magic, the zest that produces ideas and then converts them into quality products and services comes from being a legitimate part of what is going on. All members pull their individual oars because they know that if they don't, the boat won't move. People exhibit immense creativity and motivated behavior without being prodded if they are getting growth-enhancing feedback and soul satisfaction from what they are doing."

Synergy results from valuing differences, from bringing different perspectives together in a spirit of mutual trust, says Stephen R.

Covey. "Mature people view differences as potential strengths. They not only respect those with different views, they actively seek them out. They also seek objective feedback from both internal and external sources on their performance, products and services and look for ways to build complementary teams where the strength of one compensates for the weakness of another." For example, at 3M managers act more like "sponsors" who express a strategic vision and then let people with different ideas and styles find creative ways to contribute.

Authentic leaders replace fear with feedback, order giving with decision making. Intensive self-examination and feedback make for better people and products, notes John Grettenberger. "One way we secure this feedback is through our assemblers, the people who actually build our cars. These talented people study prototype models, surface problems and make suggestions and decisions to correct or eliminate them. People aren't afraid any more to tell any member of our team what is right or what isn't."

Today, says John Naisbitt, "We are replacing the manager as order giver with the manager as teacher, facilitator and coach. Facilitators draw out answers from those who know them best—the people who do the job. Facilitators ask questions, guide a group to consensus, and use information to motivate action."

How can we make the most effective use of the talents represented in our pool of human resources? By maintaining relationships. By remembering, even in the middle of all the new realities, the old verities: Forgive and forget; plan and work together; share a common vision; make sincere deposits and investments in your clients and customers.

The law of life and love is irrevocable—acts of kindness, courtesy, sacrifice and love are not done in vain. Learn how to express your love in various ways. Express gratitude both in speech and writing. Your thank-you cards and notes can make the difference between keeping and losing a valued employee or prospective customer. Affirm the worth of people. In all your conversation, be positive and affirming. People don't doubt the worth of the work they are doing as much as they doubt themselves—their ability to measure up to the task. So use your ears and heart at least as much as your tongue and head. Share freely your feelings about what you know to be right with the company. Many other people may need these positive feelings to keep producing.

These powerful investments and means of influence can open minds, soften hearts, and close sales. Offer friendship, fellowship, membership, companionship. These great gifts are sorely needed and wanted—and they should be the natural consequences of teaming with your organization.

Frequent social and business contacts and exchanges with key people will help you to win and to keep valued accounts. All work and no play with clients often means losing them. Keep in touch using all available resources. Invite marketing and sales reps, among the most mobile members of the organization, to spend some time with key contacts in areas they visit.

Encourage employees to convey positive messages and thereby contribute to the marketing efforts. Promote attendance and participation at the meetings and events you hold. Drop people a line to let them know you appreciate them. Quick memos and personal calls can mean a lot. Make creative use of audio and video media and materials. Create effective literature: a well conceived and crafted brochure may have the power to sell people independent of any other contact. Be resourceful in getting your key messages and images into people's minds and hearts. Find new ways to give your clients a positive message each day you work with them.

Challenge people to move on when you perceive they are ready to do more. Don't let people rust out, or burn out. Keep a balance. Make the challenge to change very personal and specific.

By working well with other people, you become a manager of additional resources. Know what resources are available to you. You likely have more resources than you suppose. Family, friends, neighbors, and other associates will share much with you, including encouragement and counsel. Your corporation has libraries of materials, other people with special talents and assignments, training programs, meetings, conferences, and gifted leaders. You may also have access to area reps, centers, programs, meetings, social activities, special events, and other facilities. Make creative use of these many and varied resources. Of course, your relationships are your most valuable resources because they can make unlimited resources available to you. As you invest wisely in these relationships—by telling the truth, keeping promises, treating others fairly and respecting the individual—you will receive many returns and create momentum.

3. Bottom-Line Results

More results accrue to the bottom line when more people are making meaningful contributions. That implies self-leadership. Charles Manz, author of the *Art of Self-Leadership*, says that empowerment efforts often fail and people fall far short of the dreams and goals they set because of short-comings in self-leadership. "To enhance self-leadership," he says, "build more naturally rewarding features into your activities and focus your thoughts on the naturally rewarding aspects of your work."

Authentic leaders often achieve a level of performance that is three times (300 percent or 3X) better than the industry standard. They do it by observing the prerequisites. They increase their understanding of company products, processes, systems, and services—through work experience, study of relevant literature, participation in meetings, team activity, and by keeping close to customers. They work with vision and a sense of mission, believing that they can make a difference. They work strictly within industry and company codes and rules, unless in a particular case, the "spirit of the law" overrules the letter. They practice "whole systems thinking"and see the "big picture" by adding daily to their knowledge of the industry, corporate culture, customs, beliefs, needs, and interests of people you work with and serve. They seek alignment between their personal values and goals and those of the organization. Their desire to contribute and their belief in their ability to contribute increase daily because of their expanding understanding of the importance of the work they are doing. By observing these conditions, they achieve 3X performance—and the increase in quantity and results does not come at the expense of quality or relationships.

To be a results-oriented self-leader, realize that you, in a very real sense, *are* the company—that you and your colleagues *are* the business, and that the two bottom lines of your business *are* the quality of your relationships and quantity of results.

With every new assignment, do some assessment. Get a quick overview of your area. Get information on the political leaders, transportation and information systems, special events, traditions, interests and needs of your customers. Learn all you can from your new colleagues, and seek other sources of information and insight. Within a month, you should be an expert on your area of assignment.

During this fact-finding and orientation period, develop your own personal vision of the strategy, plan, and process to pursue in order to get desired results. Create partnerships with your team members and with all the stake-holders (people who would benefit from the success of the operation). Ask: "Given the conditions and resources that face us here, how should we go about the work? Given our strategy, what plan makes the most sense for the near-term and long-term? Given our strategy and plans, what is the best process for getting results? How can we apply the lessons we learn daily and weekly to improve the process to assure quality?"

Expand your vision and pick up your stride. Seemingly small efforts in your life and leadership could do much to move your work forward. Your personal and professional growth in character and skills is the key to growth in your organization. So put your readiness to work. Take the next steps in your development, working under the watchful eye of a trusted team leader, coach, mentor, or tutor who will measure what you are ready for. Don't tarry long when you are ready to move on.

Remember: *Vision + Faith + Work = Fruit.* Much fruit requires much faith. Start your career fresh each month, each week and each day. Instead of having one career of 40 years, you can have a career a month, and a mission a week. Each week makes one cycle of learning. Review the past week with a degree of finality, as if your old career ends with that assessment and a new career begins. Learn from each passing week. Carry over all the insights and intelligence gained from weekly experience.

By having 52 *cycles of learning* a year, you will have 52 mini-careers and will accelerate results, be more responsive to the conditions and opportunities before you, and use resources more effectively. Ask the following questions once a week: "As this week (mini-career) ends, what have we learned that we can apply in our work this week to be more fruitful? What should be continued, stopped or started in our relationships and in our work?"

Sail progressively in five "ships" to become interdependent with others in leading the organization. Progress through five stages of maturity and seniority: 1) scholarship (the initial learning and training period); 2) apprenticeship (performing tasks under senior supervision); 3) stewardship (accepting a certain role and responsibility); 4) seniorship (the prime years of productivity); and 5) leadership (time to lead and mentor others). The timing of your assignments will vary, depending upon several factors. Understand the system, and don't try to manipulate it or seek particular positions.

Counterfeit leaders may contend that one's personal and professional development has little to do with one's effectiveness in managing organizations and leading people. But authentic leaders would counter that character and skill development form the foundation—the cornerstone of success—that private victories precede public victories, that style without substance is pretence, and that in spite of our egos and ambitions we must all start at the beginning to develop a new skill, trait or talent.

The manager's job is more demanding than ever before. For starters, the manager is often in the middle—sandwiched between top executives and subordinates—with staff on the side. On his or her plate is a tossed salad of concerns: quality, productivity, profitability, diversity, among others. Mangers deal with everything from theories to emergencies. Their desks are typically piled high with papers (in spite of computers); they face tight deadlines and heavy demands on their time, conflicting expectations, ethical dilemmas, and a myriad of details. Irony and paradox are standard menu items, as are politics; in fact, the manager's world is often polarized into camps. Employees may be in low states of motivation, living in a state of fear. And to survive, let alone succeed in this milieu, managers must be both effective and efficient. Of course, that's easier said than done.

Although many aspire to the corner office, the few who get the big promotions and top positions find that life in the fast lane is not all perks and privileges. A whole new set of challenges emerge. And once on top, the next step can be a long way down. Even with golden parachutes, life can seem more precarious than ever. Senior executives deal with difficult issues, big stakes, and people's economic lives. The identity and image of the corporation become mixed with their own. It can be lonely, even depressing; loyalty is hard to find and rather easily lost; competition can be hot, markets cool. Missions and causes can be blown off course. And to achieve quality in such climate and conditions requires four-season leaders. Leadership, after all, is the real issue here, and if the quest for authentic leadership fizzles, if quality fails, the career of the leader may well crash and burn.

But most leaders survive. And as a natural result of their progression, they evolve from being rather dependent on senior managers and company systems to being an independent producer to being very interdependent with colleagues and business partners.

You and your colleagues can make any management or marketing method effective or ineffective by how you approach it. Have eyes for opportunity, and hands and feet that follow up on each one. Your natural eyes will be almost useless to you unless they are trained to see some things that your intuition and insight see best. You will need discernment to sense the degree of preparedness of people to receive challenge and accept change.

Effective empowerment efforts result in more co-mission, co-ordination, co-operation. As the interests and activities of individuals are more closely aligned with those of organizations, people act more as responsible agents who are empowered at their level to make decisions.

Empowerment grows from the roots of trust, character, and competence—and without the roots, we simply won't get the fruits, season after season.

Abundant is the harvest for those who plant seeds with faith, and then work like souls inspired to pick the fruit. And once you taste of the fruit of your love, loins, and labor, you will desire to share it widely with all the people you know and love. And ultimately it is love, or charity, that leads and lifts people.

Step Six

Environment: Beauty All Around

Who doesn't want to live in a safe, secure, clean, beautiful environment? Only those who grow accustomed to mess, filth, and squalor, I suppose; in fact, these people may be uncomfortable, at least for a while, with order and cleanliness.

But transformations both begin and end with improvements to one's immediate environment. And authentic leaders extend their influence to make major improvements to an ever-wider and broader swath of land, sea, and society.

• Those who work in a political maze, in hierarchy and bureaucracy, live in a daze, a world of gray; their environment is a pecking order, a sort of welfare state for wounded souls. These mazes are the masterful work of counterfeit leaders who suppose that misery loves company.

• Whole systems change is often needed to reform bureaucracy; but who inside the company will perform the needed surgery to align the cultural systems behind the new vision and mission? Enter the internal leader and external consultant; their "rodeo" jobs require bucking tradition—even killing several sacred, if not MAD, cows.

• New environments of beauty safety and security come not so magically but with planning, preparation, foundation, finishing, and landscaping—one lot at a time. And so, over time, one's proverbial "lot in life" can be vastly improved, even if one never moves away from the hometown.

The crowing achievement of authentic leadership is the creation of safe, secure, beautiful environments for children, teens and adults— tidy places (not necessarily palaces) where love and enlightenment abound.

—— Chapter *16* ——

Hierarchy and Bureaucracy: The Political Maze

"Successful leaders fight bureaucracy aggressively on every front—preventing it when they can, attacking it when they find that it has crept in. They are obsessively dedicated to keeping their systems and structures simple."

—Richard Cavanagh

The eagle that eats too many rodents, so the tale goes, becomes bloated and grounded, unable to take off and use all its weaponry to full advantage.

Imagine the majestic eagle, America's national symbol, weighed down and unable to take off because of overeating on rodents. That image aptly characterizes many individuals and companies that have lost the competitive edge. Government and private consumers are burdened with debt. Companies and countries are heavy with hierarchy, bloated with bureaucracy, and hampered with counterfeit cultures; and so they are unable to soar, to fly, to win their way in markets, either because they are mesmerized by the management maze or they are fat and bureaucratic—hardly the symbolic eagle, more like an overstuffed turkey.

"Hold fast to dreams," wrote Langston Hughes, "for if dreams die, life is a broken-winged bird that cannot fly."

We need vision and dreams. We also must be fit to fly. The eagle within each of us, and within our corporations, will never soar to new heights or reach any point near its potential if it is gluttonous, greedy, out of shape, noncompetitive. The eagle becomes yet another victim if it's not fit to fly.

Fat Cats, Bloated Bureaucrats

When I first met UCLA professor Bill Ouchi, I asked him about the future of hierarchies and bureaucracies. His response was right on: "The miracle of bureaucracy," he said, "is that it can take thousands of people, each a complete stranger with no intention of staying very long, and out of that collection, coordinate efforts and actually produce a product!"

And now the bad news. "In order to prepare for a smooth transition, bureaucracies must make jobs sterile and boring, thereby encouraging the very mobility that necessitates its implementation in the first place."

In bureaucracies, information is virtually classified. In the military and defense-related industries, if you have no "need to know," you likely won't know; if you aren't cleared to see confidential information, you won't see it. All information is classified, and access carefully guarded. Similarly, in other organizations, information is more or less classified and guarded to keep some people in the dark. Counterfeit leaders fear that "these folks would be dangerous" if armed with this vital information, and yet the opposite is more common: Lacking this information makes them even more dangerous.

In hierarchies, a high degree of ignorance is built into formal and informal systems. People jealously guard the knowledge and information they have, knowing that's the only advantage they have on the people under them. They rarely share such information, even at gun point, because they feel it will jeopardize their job. So they keep subordinates in a state of ignorance. One sad fact of history is that many businesses, governments, and religions have intentionally kept people in ignorance.

Ignorance refers not only to an imposed condition, resulting in a lack of knowledge, but also to a chosen condition based on a belief that it is better to be ignorant and carefree than knowledgeable and accountable—that one can be saved or excused in ignorance. This notion serves as a cop-out, a withdrawal from life and the cause of a lot of counterfeiting. Ignorance is more miss than bliss. There is no joy in ignorance. People who "don't want to know" don't want to progress.

Ignorance loves the company of economic stagnation and social superstition, whereas enlightenment leads to self-direction and self-correction.

Intellectualism, the common curse of academic institutions, is another cause of much counterfeiting, as people who have never had real jobs, who have never had to make anything more than an argument, talk and think about concepts and theories all life long, victims of the paralysis of analysis. Worse, over time, the erudites, free from toil and strife, become the intellectual aristocracy of a nation, and a seed bed of pride, pomp, and ceremony. And for all their mental acuity and energy, they are the sources of impotency.

We are more likely to be counterfeit in the roles of consumer, spectator, and critic than we are in the roles of creator, player, and live performer. In the former roles, life is something that we observe as opposed to live. We no longer create and contribute; we consume, watch, criticize, and comment. Some days I think 80 percent of the people on the planet fall into these passive categories; I wonder, "Who is out there actually making something? Who is actually doing something? Who is contributing? Who is creating?" It seems that only 20 percent of the society is contributing—the rest are criticizing, commenting, discussing, processing, servicing, playing Monday-morning quarterback, watching, observing, buying, purchasing. What is the source of their income? Who is creating something real?

In hierarchies, such questions may seem irrelevant. There, high priests and sacred cows find a home, if not a seat in the inner sanctum. The environment, though undulated, is at least manageable, the lies at least playable. For example, one chief executive hopes to achieve desired results by "tweaking" people in front of their peers and whitewashing the competition in view of the world. Working under him is not for the fainthearted, as he can be charming one moment and take you apart the next. He ridicules the company's performance in front of its managers and calls the corporate university "combat training," a chance to personally "imprint" 4,000 people a year as they enter the system and attend sessions on such subjects as "The Art of Competitive Defense" and "Developing People Who Produce."

This is only typical of the salt-and-pepper ways and means of hierarchies, full of bluster and dichotomous thinking: hard and soft, white and black, art and war, college and combat. It's the old divide-and-conquer tactic, where you keep the various special interest groups that constitute your competition aware of their differences with each other while you stress how your interests and theirs are the same. You risk being Machiavellian, but if it works, it works. Crafty leaders now offer explicit details on ready-to-implement management tactics that make Attila the Hun look anemic.

So where is our foresight? Why can't we see certain things coming? Few people have the dreams of a biblical pharaoh—where they see the

seven lean cows eating the seven fat cows—and have a Joseph to inter-
pret that in seven years there will be a famine in the land (or a bear in
the market) unless they take measures now to prevent it. Still, there are
many signs and forecasts. But counterfeit leaders tend to ignore them,
as long as the sun is shining. They don't have the wisdom to abide by
good counsel or the weather vane to tune into forecasts. Their vane
points to vanity, and their rational dial is set on rock and roll.

Once I worked with a man who took over as president of an
organization. His predecessor was a living legend who had been there
for several years. The new president was an inside man who had
grown up as a favored son within the system. Many doors had been
opened for him throughout his life. When he became president, he
struggled to find his own voice and identity. Meanwhile, all the
desires and demands of the board and the hierarchy flooded in
through him and spilled over into every department and division.

The previous leader had been strong enough to stop those
demands at his desk. Until he left, we never realized what a strong
leader he was. When the "company man" came in, all directives and
demands of the board came flooding through the organization, causing
great consternation, even panic among some, as they searched for
lifeboats. Floods are terrifying. When you see a wall of water coming
at you, you sense that it is sink-or-swim time.

The person who gets hooked on command-and-control management
starts to clone people. "The major transformation," says management
professor Kirk Hart, "has been the consolidation of power into modern
organizations, led by a managerial elite and maintained by a cadre of
professional managers. The transition has been in values—from indi-
viduality to organizational obedience, from spontaneity to planning,
from volunteerism to paternalism, and from indispensability to dis-
pensability. People are being mechanized and depersonalized to more
perfectly fit the needs of organizations."

In a clearly defined hierarchy, where the word comes down from the
top, discussion is seen as rebellion. Most corporations need fewer speeches and more informal get-togethers where one can do as much talking as
listening. Unfortunately, the climate in most companies is hostile to informal discussion. In a more mature culture, you can find plenty of helpful
people to test opinions on. Authentic leaders aggressively resist pressures
that would turn their community into a plantation for ideology.

Without a succession of new leadership and enlightened management, any society, culture, or organization has a hard time avoiding the inevitable life cycle of a corporation, as described by Larry Miller in his book, *Barbarians to Bureaucrats*. We go from the prophet stage, to a builder stage, to an administrative stage, to a bureaucratic stage—from birth to death. Without new prophets who rise from the ashes of bureaucracy and, like the phoenix, start new enterprises and give new life to old organizations, we won't see much regeneration.

One troubling note, heard all too frequently today, is that prophets who are worthy of leadership roles see themselves as unworthy, unable, or unwilling to assume them. They are not comfortable with the role, title, office, and position of chief executive. They feel like impostors or actors who play a role and ride on the sheer momentum of the organization.

Because of deep-seated psychological problems, many never become themselves in those positions. They are intimidated by the legacy of the past or by those who currently surround them. They don't want to make the tough decisions and choices because of the awareness that they create enemies and divisiveness and that they won't be loved by everyone.

When counterfeit leadership goes unchecked, it gradually becomes accepted. Thus, a counterfeit culture is created. Counterfeit leaders create ever higher degrees of counterfeit in the culture and operations. The counterfeit culture is the legacy of the counterfeit leader. Followers will curse the counterfeit leader for generations because of what he or she left behind. Once ingrained in a culture, counterfeit is hard to ferret out. It is rooted in the soil of the land, in the ways and means of the people, in customs, traditions, mores, beliefs, holidays, and celebrations.

• *Sting operations.* Some counterfeit operations are sting operations. In the movie *The Sting,* Paul Newman and Robert Redford set up temporary barracks to serve as a betting house. The "sting" office has all the appearances of a real operation. Those inside know the procedures and policies, how the game is played, how people dress, talk and act. They set up a facade, like a movie set, and go through the motions to dupe the patrons of this operation.

At some point in time, many corporations function as sting operations. We see them in the papers every day. They are nothing more than movie sets. Behind the facades, managers are actors who are playing roles and parts. They learn the script and set up sting operations, either as independent business or as part of another legitimate business. Part of the role of authentic leaders is to detect and defrock these pirates and reveal them for what they are, and to take away their bark, bite, and sting.

Reverse discrimination adds an interesting twist: women and minorities are finding that NOW is better than never; and with admission policies and hiring quotas, even the WASPs are getting stung. The scorpions, wasps, vipers, and bees inside organizations set up sting operations to hurt groups of people or to sting them individually. When they inject their venom, the area swells and becomes sore and red. Once the venom then gets into the systems of the organization, we may need to apply a tourniquet to stop its spread and to get the venom out before it kills the body.

• *Pecking orders.* The colloquialism "pecking order" comes from the farm. In the animal world, there are many vivid examples of real pecking orders. If you get out of line, you're going to get pecked, literally hen-pecked by some beak—and those beaks are very sharp. If you've ever been pecked by a mad bird or a wet hen, you know how painful that can be.

In organizations, pecking orders refer to chains of command, lines of authority, and communication networks. Some pecking orders are part of the formal system, others part of the informal system. Often the formal system rewards position and authority; the informal rewards talent and ability to get things done. And so there may be two different pecking orders: one that deals with formal authority and position power, and one that deals with the ability to get things done.

The pecking order in a hierarchy can be reversed where the informal system takes over the formal system. Some executives are virtually confined to their corporate offices because they cower and cater to the talent of the organization, afraid of the working force because of their power and potential to get things done. They also realize how dependent they are on those people for their livelihood and success. That, too, can be a counterfeit culture—where the pecking order is reversed, and the top executive is getting pecked by everyone.

When the pecking order is top down, as it usually is, life at the lower levels can be hell, as the few who do the real work get hen-pecked constantly. And pecking becomes an acceptable style in the culture. All employees peck at the chicks in their charge whenever they get out of line or cross over onto their turf.

The company develops its own pecking order around whatever is most prized in the culture: The strongest, the loudest, the most articulate, most beautiful, or most powerful can start the pecking from any position in the company. Reversals in the direction of the pecking order can be very discombobulating and discomforting for people at the top or bottom, depending on which direction it's running that day.

In the small business of marriage, pecking orders persist, and the male is not always the aggressor. Arguably, this may be the worst time in history to be a man, according to the 30-somethings, because the man is getting pecked more and more. He used to rule the roost, and now he's subject to the roast. Since pecking orders in marriages, teams, corporations, and societies differ, when you get a clear idea of who's doing the pecking, you get a good sense of what constitutes real authority in that organization.

In healthy cultures, men are men, and women are women. They are valued and respected for who they are and for what they contribute, separate and apart from sex. The question is not one of power, position, and authority, but rather one of contribution.

Should the role distinctions between men and women be so blurred? Should the roles of male and female be different? Should one sex and role fit all? Authentic leaders understand differences in role, sex, ability, talent, and they value those differences to achieve a synergy. Real leaders don't try to homogenize. They don't confuse oneness with sameness or unity with uniformity. They understand differences and unique capabilities. They help people gain a clear sense of their roles and responsibilities, and they allow them a high degree of freedom and creativity in deciding how things are done.

Every house has its rules and odds to protect and safeguard its membership and maintain order. In Anatefka (*Fiddler on the Roof*), for example, everyone knows his place. Every family, club, association, and organization likewise must have its rules. But often the "real rules" are never made explicit. You learn these by trial and error and by the things you suffer.

Promises, Promises

The ultimate test of leaders is this: Do they keep their promises? Counterfeit leaders make big promises, but they either can't or simply don't deliver on them.

The big lie, of course, is the promise of the welfare state—the idea that "the company or the government will take care of you." The welfare mentality is an indictment against any enlightened society. And yet "welfare states," or at least pockets of welfare, are now found to some degree in virtually every country of the world, regardless of the form of government.

Some 20 years ago, after my wife and I both finished teaching a year of school, we packed our baby-blue Toyota and headed for Mexico City to enroll in the summer term at the National University of Mexico. Two classes there were most memorable: one on Cervantes and his novel, *Don Quixote,* taught by a Spanish priest who looked the part; and one on the political and economic problems of Latin America, taught by a Harvard-educated political scientist, who taught Fidel Castro all he knew about reform and consulted with several presidents of Mexico and other Latin countries.

The two men should have switched roles for the summer. The former could have inculcated the leaders of Latin America with the tenets and rewards of "practical idealism," and the latter could have injected "political realism" into the Quixotic classroom discussion.

To my way of thinking, both men had dangerous ideas. But I took issue most often with my political science professor; in fact, for the final, I wrote a paper that challenged his basic beliefs. He contended that the problems of Mexico and Latin America had nothing to do with moral principles and ethical practices—because the economic performance of a country was unrelated to these considerations. He was a moral relativist. He argued that what we perceive to be counterfeit in one culture may be very legitimate in another, given how those people see and experience the world. Besides, he would say, third-world countries are playing catch-up. Like the smaller kids in a street game, they have to live by their wits and do a little begging, borrowing, stealing, and imitating and get by on a boast, brag, and bluff.

I argued that he and his friends would forever be hacking at leaves, never striking at the root of their economic problems, unless and until they reformed corrupt government systems, policies, and practices.

My ideas haven't changed over the years. I still believe that economy and morality have much in common, and that without moral bedrock principles, it is very difficult for a country or culture to sustain economic growth. The gradual erosion of those principles in North America accounts for many of our current political and economic problems, and the growing acceptance of those principles in Latin America accounts for much of their progress. We are moving in opposite directions along the counterfeit continuum.

Historically, we see cycles of dictators, followed by military strong men, followed by consensus builders. We go from control to overthrow to consolidation—from benevolent authoritarian to barbarian to bureaucrat. All the while, the men and women on the street go through periods of terrible ambivalence and ambiguity where there is no real progress, only ploys and plots and empty promises. The voices and faces change, but the results are the same.

The question on the minds of those who live inside the counterfeit regime is, "Will we ever have any real leaders?" They wonder and wait. They long to be led by enlightened leadership. But they are confused; they aren't sure if they would recognize a real leader if they saw one. They don't know what tests to apply. On one extreme, they wonder whether to expect a miracle—some instant cure, some quick turn-around, some icon or Iacocca who can save a company or country from doom; who can improve the profit picture, balance trade, decrease the national debt; and increase the GNP.

In election or revolution years, people must often resign themselves to their fate and resort to economic expediency, on both a personal and national level. Then it becomes a real free-for-all: every man, woman and child for himself. And everyone is suspect. "How can I know if you are a real party member?" is the next question. "How can I know if you can be trusted?"

They want to see some sure identification—some paper, stamp, sign, seal, logo—some way of knowing, because it is so hard to tell by appearance who's real and who's counterfeit.

Counterfeit kingdoms, palaces, courts, constitutions, and governments may all have the look of authenticity. From a brick-and-mortar point of view, one capital is much like another. The seat of government in any country is but a seat, and those who occupy it are temporary residents. Mrs. Thatcher had her day in Parliament, but only the queen has her life in the palace—or so thought hotel owner Leona Helmsley when she posed as a queen at the entrance of her palace, now a prison.

America is no place for kings and queens. Royalty has its place, in history. The founders of America decided that it had no place in democracy. *To king or not to king* is still a question being asked in political chess in some countries today. A good king is not a bad thing, but it is hard to be good, even harder to stay good, once in power. Power and corruption have long been kissing cousins, and royalty—much more often than not in history—becomes a burdensome bureaucracy on the backs of working people.

Silent Majority, Vocal Minority

No wonder we, the people, are confused about candidates, credentials, courts, and jesters. We see so many counterfeit signs, symbols, and tokens; we assume with confidence that many are ministers of their own saved-by-grace faith. To them, of course, what they have is real, if not sacred. Upon examination, however, it turns out to be bogus. The innocents among the hopefuls of "unconscious incompetence" are to be pitied, their good intentions admired, but their candidacy for office dismissed. They do more harm than good by confusing intent with content on vital issues, or by passing tradition off as truth.

In counterfeit candidacies, the premium is on the grade, the style, the cut, the look, the cloth, the sound byte—elements that can be imitated by shrewd politicians. Pure and simple, the incentive to go counterfeit in political systems is to get ahead, be rewarded and recognized and ultimately to win election. When the race comes down to the wire, politicians are going head to head, jockeying for position, trying to get the vote and appealing to special interest groups and being all things to all people. Many of them don't know who they are or what they think, making it tough to have a legitimate platform or take stands on meaningful issues. Fortunately, that's not necessary to win.

Ah, but when it's show time, they know how to deliver the sound bytes. They are masters at manipulating people. The great con artists are tremendously proactive. They become counterfeit leaders by taking control, by seizing the day. They are quick to see that the sheep are in the pasture, and by picking up the staff, putting on the robe, and saying the right words, those sheep will follow them. They get on TV, in magazines and newspapers, and presto, they have a following—people who will fork over money to fund and sustain them, vote for them, buy into their promises, attend their rallies, and build their properties.

Counterfeit leaders may not cross the Delaware, but they will dutifully wear the cross. They know how to get their names in history books by taking charge in times of chaos and confusion, upheaval and change, decay or debilitation. These times are ripe for revolution, an invitation to warm up the tanks. When political opportunists see a social need, they see a chance to win votes by making promises of reform. Of course, the promises are empty, hollow as the monuments of waste and deception that dot the landscape, whether in the form of unfinished government-subsidized buildings and abandoned projects, or of shattered dreams or dead bodies.

Authentic leaders who sit back, who don't blow the whistle, are part of the problem. A high degree of passivity and resignation in a culture makes counterfeiting popular. By being assertive and aggressive, counterfeits can take over the world: they can get elected, get the positions, and win the seats, the voices and the votes that they need. It's never been easier. Meanwhile, people who have the traits of true leaders, but who are more passive, who stay in the closet rather than get on the ballot, are then led by demagogues.

Minorities and special-interest groups are vocal recording artists who cry and scream to make themselves audible and visible. The ears of legislators are pounded by these sound waves. Appointed agents, lawyers, lobbyists, and action committees keep these voices, faces, issues and impressions in front of elected officials day and night, to the point that they have a hard time hearing the often soft or silent voice of the majority.

This paradox comes in a box labeled "freedom," but it's counterfeit: It's really a pox. No illusionist, not even David Copperfield, could make this one disappear. Like King Lear, we lose our senses as power to flattery and filibuster bows. As the courts and Congress start reading copies of letters from their special interest constituency more than the original founder's version of the Constitution and selling out to the pressures of the day, they sell us down river, in chains.

Cultural Alignment	Shocks & Fresh Starts
Life & Body Balance	Improved Models
More Work Less Waste	Moral Education

Chapter 17

Cultural Alignment: Correcting System Errors

"In 94 percent of the cases, when a product is defective, it's not the workers who are responsible; it's the imperfect system in which they are forced to operate."

—W. Edwards Deming

Once on a flight into New York City on an airline that had filed for bankruptcy protection, I entered the aircraft carrying three small items: a briefcase, a suit bag, and a small suit case. A young stewardess stopped me, even as I was hanging my suit in the closet, and said, "I'm sorry, sir. You're only allowed to bring two items on board the aircraft."

"Yes, I know," I said. "And I now only have two items."

"That won't do," she said, removing the suit from the closet.

"Fine, then I'll put it inside the suitcase," I said.

"No, I must check one bag," she said, citing regulations.

"But why?" I asked. "After I put this inside my case, I will only have two carry-ons. Besides, this flight is only half full."

She couldn't understand. Her eyes could see three items. One had to be checked. That was the law, even when it made no sense under the circumstance.

But such is the power of programs, policies, and systems: people usually take a back seat to them.

On the return flight, the plane stopped in Denver late in the evening. The stop was scheduled for 50 minutes, but the board showed a delay of one hour in the departure of the connecting flight. Tired and anxious to get home, I scanned the board for an alternate flight and airline. It showed a flight leaving from another terminal in five minutes. I decided to run for it.

When I arrived, out of breath, at the gate, the door was closing, the jetway was moving away, and the plane was about to pull away. The attendant at the counter radioed the pilot and asked if he could accommodate one more passenger. The pilot said, "Sure," and the

211

attendant opened the door, repositioned the jetway and escorted me onto the flight. She said she would handle the paperwork. "Don't worry about a thing—enjoy your flight."

It occurred to me that the airline that was oriented toward meeting people's needs was financially healthy, while the airline that adhered to senseless policies and systems was bankrupt.

Signals of System Errors

Counterfeit systems will override all good intentions and stated missions. If not corrected, these systems will also overtake the culture.

Why are systems that run counter to stated missions found in most organizations? It seems that most everyone can see the discrepancies except the executives, who miss the signals because they are usually flashed in some code, as opposed to complete sentences. Cultural signals are flashed in discrete messages bits: who gets hired, rewarded, promoted, recognized; who gets resources; what gets celebrated; what gets punished; who and what gets attention; who and what gets forgotten or ignored. Employees attend to such signals, and when they point to counterfeit, there is a lot of posturing, positioning, politicking, parading, patronizing, pleasing, appeasing, and pandering.

Authentic corporate cultures recognize good work, team effort, origins, originals, significant contributions. They are based on the agricultural principles: faith, seed, plant, cultivate, weed, water, harvest and on natural processes, correct principles, constitutional and participative forms of government.

Once you become a native inside of a culture, you become part of the problem and less part of the solution. Typically, you no longer encounter the culture; you either run counter to it, or you go with the status-quo, missing all the signals sent by people in pain—signals that could help you correct what is counterfeit about the culture.

The longer I worked at a major aerospace company, the more I felt that the culture was counterfeit, from the top down, especially in the areas of marketing and public relations, where people were playing make-believe, using mirrors, lasers, lights and sounds to create images to make others believe in a quality, credibility, and capability that just wasn't there. When I was interviewed for a position at the corporate level in advertising and public relations, I couldn't take it seriously because of what I had experienced at the division level about the culture.

I had been sending and receiving signals for four years in the form of memos and suggestions. Most of these, of course, were written in code because I felt that being too candid would jeopardize my job. Communicating in plain English on company letterhead is the ultimate risk in a counterfeit culture. Heads do roll; messengers get shot. But I kept trying to tell senior management what signals we (in the trenches) were getting from their decisions on who gets hired, rewarded, promoted, recognized; who gets resources; what gets celebrated; what gets punished; who and what gets attention; who and what gets forgotten or ignored.

In every organization, these signals are criss-crossing in the culture and finding their way into the stories, tales, myths, and talk—the signs on the wall, the cartoons on the desks, the jokes in the restrooms, the questions in the minds of people. If top management misses or ignores such signals coming from all levels in the organization, they decorate the executive suites with denial and listen only to people who will tell them what they want to hear.

People then start retiring early on the job, parking their initiative and creativity at the door, and coasting through the day. Their life really begins when they get off work. The job is merely a means to an end, a ticket to a climate, or something to endure.

In some cultures, the ratio of real workers to freeloaders is 1 to 6, putting a tremendous burden on working talent to get the coal out of the mine, the points on the score board, or the missiles made and launched. With all of this game playing going on around them, real workers gain a deep and abiding resentment for their so-called "leaders."

In counterfeit cultures, "leaders" are people you despise. The real workers especially mock the newly minted MBAs who are hired at salaries that are at least double their worth and who spend their first year oozing their way around the executive corridors, washrooms, and lunchrooms. They attend religiously to the three cardinal rules for fast-track promotions: visibility, mobility, and assumed (or borrowed) credibility. These "high potentials" are seen following executives around, learning how to model, mimic, and mime their every gesture. They quickly build walls of resentment between themselves and the real workers over inequities in the systems. These barriers lead to union-management struggles and other conflicts. Workers, too, see the tremendous wastes within the systems, and since they bear the burden of these wastes when asked to forfeit wage increases and benefits, and then to do more with less, they are not happy campers.

So, why care about systems alignment? If you are in a counterfeit culture—a company, club, culture, guild, fraternity, sorority, or team led by counterfeit leadership—why worry about alignment of systems and of mission, motives, and means? Because when you're out of alignment, you're in for a bumpy ride. When your wheels are out of alignment on your car, your tires wear very fast; instead of 50,000 miles, you may only get 5,000. Likewise, when you are in a misaligned culture, the ride is characterized by dissension, division, divisiveness, turf battles, nonsense, and pretense. The ride is chaotic and bumpy. Disorder and discord are the twin offspring of misaligned systems.

How to Correct Systems Errors

I have high confidence in people's abilities to compensate for what is wrong with systems and to correct them.

• *Have checks and balances.* In the best organizations, I see checks and balances that detect and correct distortions in leadership, impurities in motives, uncertainty in missions. Checks consist of financial audits, personal and organizational assessments, periodic reviews, internal probes or investigations into alleged misconduct. Balances consist of competent councils and counselors, active boards, work teams, family, friends, family-oriented traditions, professional associations and affiliations, neighborhood support, community service, church activity, and continuing education.

• *Reward heroic behaviors.* The unsung heroes are workers who compensate for the deficiencies in company systems. These proactive people who serve as examples of dutiful, loyal, followers in spite of being subject to counterfeit leadership and "mushroom management," where they are kept in the dark, fed a lot of manure, and when they are fully ripe, their heads are cut off and canned. But they are not victims. From day-to-day, eight to five, and often on nights and weekends, they continue dutifully to do the work of the organization. Because of their pride and craftsmanship, they compensate in heroic ways for uncertainty and incompetence, sin and selfishness at the top. They make the organization and its products and services right for the customer, especially when they are stationed at the point of contact.

Because of the good works of the worker bees, the products and services may pass for quality for some time, even though mission, motives and means become tainted. But over time, they too tend to break down. Over time people start to say, "Why should we sacrifice to make it right, when we receive so little support?" Lack of confidence in the leadership, systems, or products of the organization will eventually wound, if not kill, the desire and confidence of individual workers.

Heroic behavior becomes rare when management and its systems are a large part of the problem. Managers who move around often have difficult adjustments. They may become, in fact, barriers to productivity in the new system, especially if they do not concentrate on the most critical aspects of their jobs. General Electric's George Kuper says, "People are not equipped to improve productivity simply by going to college—mostly because they concentrate on the wrong things while in school. The graduates we hire often need to be updated if not retrained. And virtually every graduate needs a sort of corporate initiation before being very useful to the company." If managers are not also performers, they tend to loose touch with the tools of the trade, and their key tools are the workers. If managers haven't experienced the frustrations and joys of working and performing, they can't understand their workers. Part of the curriculum ought to be aligning systems to create a supportive climate in which to work. If we ever want to achieve zero-defects, we need to create an environment where perfection is possible.

We can't have systems of quality without having leaders of integrity. Integrity means your mission, motives and means are aligned; you walk your talk; you practice what you preach; your beliefs and behaviors are congruent. Violations of integrity destroy relationships, and when these are destroyed people tend to loose pride in their work. They begin to think, "Maybe it's okay to lie, cheat, and steal a little." Manifestations of that attitude affect the quality of products and services. An organization is an ecosystem, a total environment, and the achievement and the maintenance of quality in products and services are intertwined with the integrity of the people from the top down.

The best arena for quality is a pay-for-performance system—a "rodeo" where there is shared risk. At the rodeo, we see cowboys who must pay an entry fee with no guarantee of return for the privilege of riding a one-ton bull or a bucking horse bareback. How dangerous is it? One cowboy was killed when a bull dislodged his rib, and the rib punctured his heart. The cowboy actually got up and walked away before he then fell down and died. No corporate boy or girl is going to risk that much without a pay-for-performance clause in the contract.

At one rodeo, in the bareback competition, I saw a horse go down on its side, and yet the cowboy stayed with the horse! The horse got up, and the cowboy finished the event, placing second in the competition. No corporate boy or girl is going to stay with such a tough assignment unless *sticking with it* means placing in the money. With no guarantees and a lot of uncertainty in rodeo, we still see entrants clamoring to get in because they have a chance to prove themselves against the challenge in the arena.

Having ridden a few bucking broncos in my life, I have a sense of the courage and toughness required in bull riding, steer wrestling, bareback riding. Contestants face hard rules and a hard life. If they fail to spur the animal or keep one hand free, they are either penalized or disqualified. They finish out of the money. These are the tough realities that cowboys have to live with. But those clear realities lead to authenticity in the culture inside the ring.

If the compensation system is based on pay-for-performance criteria, everyone, including CEOs, will have to ride out tough situations, rather than bail out in golden parachutes. They may learn to spur the bull for more points, and they certainly must learn that leadership requires exceptional balance and body control to maintain position regardless of what moves the market (bull or bear) makes.

Spectacular recoveries may delight spectators and the press, but the best executives try to avoid being so bent out of shape that they must recover. Often we reward the spectacular recovery when actually it was a bad decision that got us into the rough to begin with. We reward people who come back; we recognize those who lose weight once they are 100 pounds overweight. Recoveries and reformations are laudable, but what about the people (often the true leaders), who never get out of shape, never sin, never lie, never cheat, who are dependable and reliable? Often they are never mentioned, never get the spotlight, and yet over time, they become the winners. The choicest rewards are predicated on obedience to natural laws and principles, especially in legitimate corporate cultures.

In an age of specialization, we have lost the incentive and reward for the all-round champions who compete well in several events.

Their excellence in one area of specialty often spills over into other areas of excellence in work and life. The leader who is a specialist, who does just one event well, who somehow rises to the top from a narrow specialty, has two strikes against him coming in. He tends to be a prima donna in his event and woefully ignorant in other areas of life and leadership.

Of course, we need a few corporate clowns. In the rodeo, the clowns play an important role. They may even save the life of the most prized talent. The clowns themselves are often exceptionally gifted performers who mock raging bulls and assist at-risk colleagues, often by risking their own lives. Indeed, they can get thrown, gored, bumped, stomped, kicked, killed. True leaders are among the best "clowns" of the corporation. Behind the mask and the face of humor, they often hide deep hurts, feelings of inadequacy, insecurity or inferiority—all the more reason to reward loyalty.

All competent people get notice of greener pastures, higher wages, and better cultures from time to time. They hear reports of the good life in another department, division, company, or country. Professional workers are also predisposed to be more loyal to their professions than they are to their companies. Their affiliations and associations with professional groups give them a sense of belonging that they don't find within their own company. They may move from company to company in search of Camelot cultures or better climes and times. Recognizing and rewarding loyalty is the best insurance against high-cost turnover among the professional elite of the organization.

In authentic cultures, counterfeits are not made to feel comfortable. In genuine cultures, there is less chance for spectacular overnight promotions, short-cut performances, windfall profits, and manipulative management practices. One may have to sit the bench and wait one's turn because of what's in place: an all-world first team, capable substitutes, and refined systems in such areas as recruiting, hiring, communicating, and evaluating. Refined systems and genuine cultures tend to repel fast-track careerists and corporate politicians. However, these gamesmen will try to find or create pockets within the culture where they can create their own counterfeit sideshow.

If people have grown up in counterfeit social and scholastic systems, they are fish out of water in authentic systems. They may be challenged to find a place where they can operate. They typically seek get-rich-quick marketing schemes, companies where they can advance fast, make a mark, collect commissions, and buy nice things.

Some people are hunters. Not everybody is meant to be a farmer. And I am not saying that you have to be Farmer John to be authentic. But you do have to respect natural processes and systems based on agricultural principles and on natural laws and cycles. In counterfeit cultures, blessings and rewards are predicated not so much on obedience to natural laws and principles, but on one's ability to work the system, to wrench results, to rig machines, and to hot wire engines. There is a lot of latitude in counterfeit systems, and the bottom line is getting results, making money, bringing in the bucks.

All it takes is a poor substitution to signal a turn in the culture. The moment you hire someone who is not qualified for the job; the day you start practicing nepotism or favoritism; or the moment you create a double standard within your admissions program, you create a degree of counterfeit. You give signals to people that the old rules no longer apply, that the laws can be broken, or that there is a new standard. The moment you promote a manager who uses and abuses people, you send the strong signal that these behaviors are approved and rewarded. The moment you punish or banish a person for taking risks; for being creative; or for daring to address issues, daring to criticize the boss, daring to supply feedback, daring to deliver hard messages, you send a strong signal to those who remain. The moment you celebrate and recognize an artificial achievement or an inconsequential act and pass over real contributions, you show a lack of judgment and wisdom on what the real contributions are and who the real workers are. Cynicism creeps in the culture when good work, hard work, and creative work aren't recognized and rewarded.

In the *MADness* of Mergers, Acquisitions, and Down-sizing, many authentic babies are tossed out with the bath water. Few mergers are done for the general welfare of all stakeholders. The payoffs at the top are obscene. And how can you maintain a culture of authenticity in a climate of obscenity? When there are gross inequities at the expense of other shareholders and stakeholders, a sense of futility grows in the community or culture—a sense that "it doesn't really matter anymore." Visiting the corporate office of some organizations can be like visiting the Emerald City. These palaces, and all the trappings and trimmings, conspire against the chief executive who wants to understand people and promote fairness in the culture.

We need an alignment test that serves as a corporate litmus test of the degree of counterfeit in the organization. Beyond that, we need to know what to do about it, how to correct it, how to transform systems when people are addicted to quick fixes and one of several drugs, everything from caffeine to cocaine, from power to politics. The cure for malignant culture is to align mission, motives and means. That may require surgery or the equivalent of chemotherapy to keep counterfeits from spreading and ulcerating.

Genuine leaders and authentic cultures will pass the test of time. Authentic cultures have real people, products and services—an openness and honesty that comes from having something original, something good that helps people, even blesses their lives. What matters is not so much the nature of the product or service as the purpose: it is designed to improve the quality of life for people. Quality products and services are the natural fruits of healthy systems that are aligned with well conceived missions, motives and means.

When the systems are clean, the structure simple, the service personal, and the style open and honest, employees will feel like owners, assume personal responsibility for results, and ensure that the products they put out set new standards of quality.

One final caveat: enforce the house rules. Every house (family, club, association, organization) must have its rules to protect and safeguard its membership and maintain order. Make sure the rules make sense. And make sure the "real rules" are made explicit. Otherwise, you invite people to learn these by trial and error and by the things they suffer. They then begin to feel that the house odds are against them. The house odds will be in favor of all stakeholders if all have a clear sense of roles and rules.

——— *Chapter 18* ———

New Environments: Beauty, Safety, and Security

"All our research so far has not enabled us to produce one pleasure. Hence, we always try to work away from the natural condition of any pleasure."

—Screwtape to Wormwood
C. S. Lewis, *The Screwtape Letters*

Back in 1977, I bought an old home on a half acre in a tough Southeast San Diego neighborhood for $37,500. It was one of the few homes I could afford to buy in San Diego where inflation was record-setting. Because of the danger of gangs, the police didn't dare patrol our neighborhood, except by helicopter. Trucks making deliveries at the nearby supermarket had been running over the back part of my lot, compacting the soil and making it hard as cement. But over a period of 18 months, we transformed that property from an eyesore into a showplace.

At first, everybody thought I was wasting my time. But as the transformation neared completion, people gazed in amazement. Many neighbors started similar improvement projects with their properties. As the home values skyrocketed in the area, the whole neighborhood got into the act. People started helping their neighbors—some of whom they had never even met before.

Beautify Your Lot in Life

A lot of garbage may be dumped onto one's "lot in life," but those lots can be upgraded; they can be exchanged; they can be bought and sold; they can be improved.

For example, when my wife and I were searching for a building site for our third home, we looked at many lots—some were already improved, others were not. The lot that we selected was typical of vacant city lots: trash, weeds, cement, and rocks had been dumped on it. There was nothing inviting about it. But because it was in a good neighborhood, we bought it, designed a nice home and yard, and went to work.

To look now at the immaculately landscaped grounds, you'd have to say that the lot has been improved. These improvements have added value. All the weeds and junk items were cleared away. There is no more evidence of that element, just a beautiful living environment. So, we can own title to our individual and collective lots in life, and we can improve them.

Authentic leaders have an uncanny ability to do with lots what is best for that time, space, and place. They make real improvements that bless people's lives and add value. In building, they seek quality and productivity—natural outcomes of their leadership.

Whatever your "lot in life," you can improve it. The lot or field you are assigned to cultivate may, at first, be weedy, hard, dry; it may, in fact, be a dump. But with vision and smart work, you can transform that lot into a picture-perfect garden, complete with fruit and produce, in a matter of a few months.

In my life, I have seen some "worst-case" scenarios—truly tough assignments—become showcases. I have seen beautiful children come from "barren wombs." I have seen delicious fruit come from "cement." I have seen record sales come (in a period of six months) from "hopeless" territories.

Visionary founders have always faced skeptical associates and bankers; somehow, they still manage to build companies, buildings, and products. Are a few sales too much to expect if you are working faithfully in your assigned area? Not if you are working daily to improve "your lot" in natural ways: by adding organic nutrient, living examples, and sweat equity, and by protecting new prospects from all forms of deadly opposition—surrounding them with support; nurturing the health and welfare of customers; and picking the fruit when it is ripe and ready to be harvested.

To transform and beautify any environment, first survey the lot to define borders and boundaries—what's yours and what's not; many folks spend their entire lives building their dream castle, only to find that someone else has title to the lot. Second, fence it off. Lay claim and secure the area against vandalism; you can then work within the borders. Plan to landscape and interior decorate. Invest some money and "sweat equity" in improving appearances to make the property more inviting and to increase the market value considerably. Peel away the old cracked surface, the old facade or face, including overgrown foliage. Put on a fresh coat of paint to lighten and brighten the exterior. Prepare the ground by tilling and composting. Put in an irrigation and sprinkling system. Plant grass, trees, and a garden. Manage the progress of the project and dedicate it upon completion to serve worthwhile purposes.

Authentic leaders improve their immediate environment. Each city, county, and country has its own culture, and these cultures have their heros and models memorialized in the plazas and parks, museums and academic institutions.

Authentic leaders do much to combat pollutants, using the pound of cure when necessary and the ounce of prevention when possible. In our immediate environments, we tolerate various pollutants such as noise, smoke, profanity, vulgarity, obscenity, dumping, depletion, waste, contamination, and particulate.

I once worked in the immediate proximity of four smokers. Although I liked the people, I could not tolerate the smoke. And so I became a pioneer in getting some policies and attitudes changed. The attitudes prevalent in the work environment are more damaging than second-hand smoke. They, too, can give you headaches and heartaches. Attitudes of apathy, irresponsibility, complacency, mediocrity, and exploitation can ruin a healthy body. Environment matters. Biological-ly, if you put a healthy specimen in a harmful environment, over time that healthy specimen is going to become sick, and suffer some side effects. In the second and third generations, those side effects might even be passed on as birth defects. And the species, so says Darwin, may even be subject to extinction.

Counterfeit cultures are cultures of resignation, resentment, and remorse; in them, we see a great waste of human life and potential. We see people who are walking and working in their sleep, as if in a dream, who are living in a twilight zone, never seeing things clearly. We see people who waste their lives in coming and going, dressing and undressing, showering and brushing, eating and doing dishes— all the peripheral stuff—instead of doing real work, making lasting contributions, perfecting a craft, and improving the quality of their lives day by day.

Corrective Action in Companies

What action can be taken on a personal and corporate level to correct the counterfeit culture in organizations? One is to blow up the company and start over. That is to dismantle what is in place, to fire some key people, to lay off, to scale down. Short of that extreme, you might try the following.

• *Retain good people.* The book, *The 100 Best Companies to Work For,* indicates that companies that are good to work for are usually profitable because they retain good people. Some have no lay-off policies; all avoid lay-offs. They will do miraculous things to keep people, shuffling them among divisions, sending them overseas, creating new projects. They have a family-oriented culture. They send messages: "We love you; we want you to stay; we will do everything in our power to keep you."

• *Reduce turnover.* Great mischief is caused by job hopping. Few people count the total cost of turnover, estimated to be $100,000 per person at the management level. Imagine an apple turnover with a price tag of $100,000. One such "apple" a day keeps the profits away. When you count the total cost of losing a person, retraining, and getting back up to speed, then you begin to see the real worth of the people who are in place.

• *Maintain a quality environment.* Life is largely maintenance. Authentic leaders and cultures reward maintenance and recognize people who keep things in good working condition, who do the oil and lube jobs within the system, who keep the competitive edge sharp, who maintain order, who see that the water gets to the end of the row and that the weeding gets done. They reward the people who work through the heat of the day and the darkness of the night doing the real work of the company. They recognize and reward them as true heroes within the culture.

• *Grow a garden.* In most organizations, gardening is at best a metaphor for growth and development, but at one major university, groups of married students were given small plots of ground and invited to grow a garden. Most of them did so as a means of getting food to eat and keeping in touch with natural processes. In school, one can easily succumb to a pattern of cramming and short-cutting, especially when grades, not learning, are emphasized. By growing gardens, the students could see that in natural environments, weeds flourish, results don't happen overnight, erosion takes place, nutrients must be replenished, and the thin layer of top soil that supports all life is easily washed away without the right support systems. Such open-air lessons may mean more to them than closed-door classroom lessons in organizational behavior.

• *Train people in the basics of neat and clean.* To change a culture, start by getting the graffiti off the walls, the dope and drugs out, the gangs off the playgrounds. People must come to work and school in something more than beach wear and take pride in their appearance and their potential. Turnarounds start with basic training disciplines. Once the ground rules of "neat and clean, order and respect" are set, people have a chance to grow. Insist that people keep their areas clean, their noses clean, and their mouths clean. Authentic leaders ensure that their people are cleaning up and fixing up. Dramatic turn-arounds in schools and in corporate environments start with a clean-up effort, a discipline program that creates a fresh environment.

When I visited Chrysler, Dick Dauch, then vice-president of manufacturing, was proud of the transformation he'd brought about in the manufacturing area. What was once a dirty environment had become a spotless high tech haven. Manufacturing was now seen as the place to be in the company because he had bright people and a neat and clean workplace. He imposed martial law at the beginning and put everybody through basic training. Dramatic transformation often requires boot camp measures, as leadership puts emphasis on new learning and new growth in a clean environment.

• *Tune in to "Mission Possible."* Authentic leaders make missions possible. They don't try to be popular, only prudent and patient. They call for discipline and sacrifice.

During the dark days at Chrysler, Lee Iacocca called for "equity of sacrifice." He basically said that Chrysler had two choices: 1) death through bankruptcy, or 2) borrow and rebuild. He knew that rebuilding would require an equity of sacrifice on all parts. He promised rewards and kept most of his promises. When he later resorted to double standards, an "inequity of sacrifice," he became known as "Teflon Iacocca."

At Western Airlines (acquired by Delta), Chairman Larry Lee achieved a dramatic turnaround by first building immense credibility over a 40-year career, and then when the company needed its employees to sacrifice, he called for a 30 percent pay cut across the board. During the same period, he took a 100 percent pay cut, and he wasn't a wealthy man.

The chairman is like the physician who gives a prescription. The employees are like the patients who must believe in it, and take it as directed; otherwise, there is no promise. We forfeit the possibility of recovery when we dismiss the doctor's prescription and write our own based on a diagnosis of wishful thinking. Authentic leaders often prescribe a new belief system, a new faith in possibilities, and with work over time, they see the fruits in new products, new processes, new people.

    • *Believe in transformations.* Authentic leaders transform cultures by ensuring that they are grounded, rooted, and founded on enduring principles. When dramatic transformations are needed, they may declare the corporation bankrupt because of counterfeit behaviors, confess those transgressions, and commit to a change of mind and heart and a reparation of damages. They may speak with a voice that trembles with emotion as they ask for forgiveness and forbearance and faith, and then ask for redoubled efforts to rebuild on a new foundation.

Move to a Better Environment

    Creating or improving the enviornment is one option; moving to a new and better environment is another viable option.

    Counterfeit cultures make it hard for good people to be loyal because there is no reciprocation. In some industries, people are laid off in mass if the proposal isn't accepted. Legions of professionals become transitory and migratory as geese, moving with the winners of the contract, with the political winds of the corporation, or with marketing seasons and sales cycles.

    Competent people are attracted to genuine cultures and programs that have stable, winning programs, strong teams. The best and the brightest want to be part of genuine cultures where people return to the culture what they take out of it. There are park rules: you bring in your own firewood, take out your own garbage, and leave the camp better than you found it. These basic camp principles are needed to maintain a genuine culture. Otherwise, people begin to take more than they give, leaving the company without profit, margin, or mission.

    Of course, if people are not sharing in the profits, over the long run they become cynical and start moonlighting or job hunting and hopping. If there is equity building and profit sharing—where people are sharing in the profits—people will stay with the enterprise. Authentic cultures earn and reward loyalty.

    • *Look for greener pastures.* As people see greener pastures, they want to change from one division to another or from one department to another or from one desk to another to get out from under a certain boss or a certain constraint. They see a brighter future somewhere else. This movement and moonlighting runs rampant in a system with high degrees of counterfeit. Good people get out from under a tyrannical boss, a bad system, a heavy structure if they feel that they can't do their jobs. Good people seek and join good organizations. Good people are attracted to good things. When they see a chance to improve themselves and get in a better system, they make the change.

These judgments are happening here and now. People are already separating themselves into camps and kingdoms where they feel most comfortable. It would be unkind to put someone who is not prepared for paradise in that environment. They would not fit or belong; they could not tolerate the light. It would be like putting someone who has been living in a cave into bright sunlight suddenly. People are deciding here and now what degree of intelligence, light, truth, and knowledge they are most comfortable with. By obedience to law and submission to standards, people can achieve a high degree of quality, approaching perfection—the grand gift bestowed upon those who work at weaknesses a day at a time from the inside out.

• *Seek new frontiers.* You might move the corporate headquarters to a new area and start over. Moving has a way of unsettling people. When you have to pull up stakes, whether you are talking about a circus tent or a corporate headquarters, you are forced to decide what to take with you and what to leave behind. You make those decisions on every article and every person. The best way to venerate the pioneers of the culture is to emulate them. Authentic leaders challenge people who are rusting out to pull up stakes and settle in a new area.

The great anti-growth tendency in life is to "settle down." That often means to accelerate the degeneration process, in both corporate and personal life cycles where we tend to go from prophetic and promising beginnings, through the growth stages, to the bureaucratic stages, and finally into the grave. There is a constant need to reinvent, reform, and renew organizations. These 3 Rs are consistantly explored by the best consultants and executives. They see a constant need for movement, reformation, renaissance, renewal, restitution, resurrection, restoration, with new beginnings, new cycles, entrepreneurism and intrapreneurism, new research, and an emphasis on product development and new patents and new ideas.

Sometimes these new beginnings must take place in teams of people who are separated from the general culture because they don't want to be contaminated by the virus of the general culture. Often these people are hired into these teams from other cultures. They have never been in the counterfeit or contaminated cultures. That strategy works in human bodies and in corporate bodies.

Natural processes, cycles, seasons, and principles constitute universal law. Violations bring natural consequences. In systems and organizations that approximate nature, the same rule applies. We become counterfeit as we attempt to shortcut the natural flow of any cycle—production, manufacturing, research and development, marketing, distribution, sales—to achieve short-term results.

In nature we don't go from winter into summer overnight. We pass through spring. To go from summer to winter, we pass through fall. These seasons and cycles and processes are part and parcel of nature—they can't be cheated, short-cutted or short-circuited. You can't wire around them. It's so tempting to take a shortcut if it saves you a step, as it often does in counterfeit societies.

Genuine leaders understand the process of planting, cultivating, weeding, watering, hoeing, fertilizing, sacrificing, and doing what it takes to bring in the harvest. They understand that it all starts with seed. Many lessons come from gardening and farming—lessons on order, cleanliness, early to bed, early to rise, and the exercise of faith. Farmers understand how important these virtues are, because without them they have no harvest. The more we are divorced from the soil and from nature, the more likely we will develop counterfeit traits and counterfeit cultures.

Authentic leaders keep close to the soil. They grow something from seed. *Seed* may refer to sperm-and-egg conception, family generations, or germination. In nature, seed germinates under the right conditions and bears fruit unto its own kind. Seeds of apples will not bear apricots. That simple truth is lost on counterfeit leaders, who are always trying to cross-pollinate.

Genuine leaders keep a hand and an eye on natural processes. They are at ease in nature. They feel a oneness, a harmony with nature. They love to work the "soil" to raise fruit and produce, to develop people, and to grow companies. They work as agriculturalists who understand, respect, and observe natural processes in all cultures.

Counterfeit leaders look at land as a commodity to sell for quick profit. In *The Good Earth* by Pearl S. Buck, near the end of Wang Lung's life—a simple life linked closely to his land, his soil and toil— his two sons came to visit him. They had now become part of the new generation of professionals. They walked out on the land and talked: "The field we will sell and divide the money between us evenly."

The old man overheard these words, "Sell the land?" He could not keep his voice from breaking and trembling with his anger: "Now, evil, idle sons—sell the land?" He choked.

Then they soothed him, "No, we will never sell the land." *But over the old man's head, they looked at each other and smiled.*

New Concept of Corporate Safety

The old industrial concept of safety calls for hard hats and steel-toed shoes, special eye wear and gloves, to protect one from physical harm in tough jobs having an element of danger.

Regulations and rules designed to protect the safety of people in such jobs are more than justified. Working in factories, farms, plants, shops, ranches, mines, and mills with machinery, heat, light, cold, dark, chemicals, fire, water, steam, or dangerous animals, workers need protection from physical accidents and injuries. So the old concept is still appropriate—management must be concerned with the physical welfare of people.

But increasingly, a new concept is needed—one that protects people from damaging, even career-ending injuries to the mind and emotions. When working in climate-controlled and security-guarded offices and when working with ideas and concepts, numbers and names, paper and computers, the danger is not from the fang, the sharp edge of the blade, the heat of the furnace, the smoke and flame of the fire, the deafening noise of the engine—rather, it's more subtle, centered in relationships.

When a wet mop leaves a slick spot on the floor, we post a sign, warning people to watch their step. We post signs in public zoos and private yards to warn visitors of wild animals and turf-protective pets. We post signs in streets to caution drivers against road hazards. Why not post such signs on the desks of people who can't be trusted, who rape and run, who win all they can at the expense of others?

At DuPont, you can't lean back in a chair or walk the halls without holding a hand rail without receiving a citation. While I applaud such concern for physical safety, I wonder if it's then okay if a heavy-handed boss leans or rails on someone for next-to-nothing.

Safety from Head to Toe
I ask you. In your job . . .
- *Are your toes more in danger of being smashed by heavy objects or stepped on by an authoritarian boss?*
- *Are your ankles more in danger of being sprained in sport or in the madness of hostile take-overs and fast turn-arounds?*
- *Are your knees more in danger of being strained from deep bends or from blind-side hits?*
- *Is your stomach more in danger of being upset by what you eat or by how you're treated?*
- *Are your lungs more in danger of being polluted by poisonous gas or by second-hand smoke?*
- *Is your heart more in danger of being broken by demanding work and exercise or by cruel words and prejudicial labels?*
- *Is your back more in danger of being burdened by big boxes or by dead wood in the work force?*
- *Are your eyes more in danger of being blinded by lasers and sunlight or impaired by limiting systems and social mirrors?*
- *Are your ears more in danger of being damaged by loud and piercing sounds or by profanity, vulgarity, obscenity, egocentricity, and sheer babble?*
- *Are your teeth more in danger of being knocked out by a fist or by fraud?*
- *Is your head more in danger of being severed by falling trees or by a falling corporate ax?*

The answers may depend on where you work, but I dare say that even in the most physically demanding jobs, your chances of serious injury are as great or greater in relationships than in hardships.

Five Things to Protect
The new concept of corporate safety tries specifically to protect the following five things.
- *The mind.* Two of the most creative, intelligent people I know are currently out of work—their inquisitive minds, sharp wit and self-confidence shattered from on-the-job abuse.
- *The emotions.* There's still much fear in the work force. Edwards Deming said, "Drive out fear," for years, but the turf wars and mind

games continue. We've all seen many once-promising workers, young and old, so emotionally damaged and drained they are hardly fit for any meaningful work.

- *The signature* (your original work). Fresh ideas and insights, finished works and experimental research are often pirated with impunity—as if anything printed or otherwise in circulation could be considered "in the public domain." The Academy's use of *Snow White* at Oscar night is just one indication of lost regard for copyright. We see more cheap imitation than real innovation because it's easier to steal than create. The competition's next "original" brilliant idea may well be only a copy (of your material) away.

- *Career paths.* Two friends, both capable "30-something" careerists—one working in films in Hollywood and the other in finance on Wall Street—now want out of their professions. They are where they thought they wanted to be, but rather than fulfillment they find frustration and premature dead-ends.

Some organizations will rush you to the infirmary for a hang-nail—and give you a week off with pay—but not think twice about hanging you at high noon in the corporate lobby or about stabbing you in the back behind closed doors in the executive office on account of something as simple as being tired of seeing your face.

- *Self-esteem and self-worth.* In some organizations, it seems that everyone needs an agent to avoid being negotiated down to nothing. Why are so many companies (and individuals) so bent on depreciating self-esteem when it ties so directly to their bottom line performance and profit?

Three Things Are Banned

The new concept of safety bans the following three things.

- *The dirty deal.* In the movie, *The End*, Burt Reynolds, playing the role of a man who wants to die, swims far out into the ocean to drown himself. Once out, he decides that he wants to live. Realizing that he is far from shore and lacking strength, he strikes a deal with God: if God will grant him strength to reach shore, he will give Him 100 percent of his time and money for the rest of his life.

The man starts swimming for shore and, indeed, is blessed with strength. After swimming a while, he pauses to assess his progress and changes the deal to 50 percent. And the closer he gets to shore, the more he comes down, until finally upon reaching shore, he wonders aloud what God will do with the 1 percent he promised Him.

So often we make such deals in the extremity of our need. We employ people, and in good faith they begin work; but then as we receive the benefit of their labor, we change the deal—negotiating them down to next to nothing or out of it altogether.

• *The greasy meal.* I refer here to the fares and the fates we are served as a result of our ill-advised attempts to please everyone or, on the other hand, to cheat everyone. And not all greasy meals can be neutralized by a night's sleep and a couple of Alka Seltzer—they may burn as fires in the pits of stomachs for generations.

But management is not always to blame. Workers often flock to the greasy spoon, selling themselves short and never getting what they want from life because what they really want is not even on the menus of the places they work, eat and sleep.

• *All other forms of lie, cheat and steal.* An executive called me recently to ask if I would represent his company and help "improve its image." After visiting the man and his company, I declined. I found poor relationships and products no more substantive than cotton candy, spun sugar on a cone—a mere taste on the tip of the tongue—but sold at high prices in the circus he called a business.

Four of the six front-page stories of a recent issue of the *New York Times* featured versions of lie, cheat and steal. The headlines and story lines are all too common.

Metaphors of Safety

The new concept of corporate safety is best communicated by metaphor.

• *The clean room.* Before entering the number 10 clean room at National Semiconductor, you must first take off your shoes, put on all-white attire, and pass through three air vacuums. That would be a marvelous way to enter the office each morning—a system for leaving some dirt and baggage at the door.

• *Monthly milk production.* At DHI Computing Services, the progress and production of each cow in dozens of dairy herds are closely monitored by computers. Managers are given monthly reports on each cow and on the herd—they know each cow intimately. Sadly, many people managers know next to nothing from month to month of the individuals in their organizations.

• *Eagle's nest.* Plateau Mining Company near Price, Utah, has invested many thousands of dollars to protect two bald eagles nesting in the cliffs above their coal mines. The birds have become symbols of the care the company has for every miner—bald or full beard—who enters the tunnels each day.

Nuts and Bolts of the New Concept

The new concept calls for individuals and companies to share responsibility for total safety.

Individual Responsibility. Every person assumes responsibility for his or her own personal safety and pledges to protect the safety of others.

Management consultant Bill Oncken, an experienced sky diver, notes that veterans are almost casual about jumping from airplanes, while first-timers are bug-eyed and tentative. The difference, he says, is that the pro is prepared—he made the decision to jump and visualized the jump the day before.

Entering or starting a new company is sky diving. Among your personal safety responsibilities are the following:

• Make sure the parachute is properly packed.

• Go in with your eyes and ears open. You'll still miss much, both because your eyes are not trained to see some things and because you won't be shown other things.

• Carry your security in your back pocket; cultivate internal sources of personal security.

• Make sure your boss has "confidence in your competence," as Bill Oncken says.

• Show some mental-emotional competitive toughness on the outside and yet remain soft, sensitive and trusting on the inside.

• Suit up for the game. It's folly to enter the field in any competitive endeavor without first "suiting up."

• Play to get results, contribute, and make a difference.

That may mean coming to work each day willing to take appropriate risks. Spectators sit as many risks as competitors run on the field; in fact, the more one tries to safeguard every step of his life, the more risk he runs. Life means risk; every decision or action carries some degree of uncertainty and danger; every new relationship—personal or professional—has the potential to damage or to bless. We are free to choose, and in a free and open society, we trespass, and we are trespassed upon.

Corporate Responsibility. No society or organization can promise and deliver cradle-to-grave safety. Nor can safety be achieved through legislation or OSHA regulation. Business, particularly entrepreneurial activity, is risky.

If we seek cradle-to-grave security, trying avoid all risks, we run the greatest risk of all—that of losing our freedom. Freedom from all risk taking eventually leads to bondage. The facts of life are these: you must take measured risks. You must make decisions and implement them without a perfect knowledge and without guaranteed outcomes. In some instances, if you do not move swiftly and decisively, if you wait to get all the facts or wait to be proven right, someone else will seize your golden opportunity. Business will simply not allow you the luxury of avoiding decisions. And in making them, intuitive hunches and gut feelings (in addition to facts and experience) come into play.

Nonetheless, corporate executives can greatly reduce the risk of serious injuries, physical and nonphysical, if they create a company bill of rights and safety responsibilities:

• *Hiring*: Clarify expectations, define roles and goals, create and commit to a win-win performance agreement.

• *Firing*: Clearly state the grounds; provide an appeal process; and when a drunk captain pollutes a thousand miles of pristine water, fire him fast.

• *Training*: Expect all kinds of damaging "accidents" and injuries without proper training. When my 16-year-old son, Andy, was taking drivers' training, I told him: "There are rules of the road; they are printed in the handbook. Learn them. Observe them. Also, there are the realities of the road; they are not printed anywhere. Learn and observe them, too."

I then took him to a junk yard where hundreds of wreaked cars were heaped in piles in callous disregard for make and model, symbol and status. Each car had a sad story to tell. We walked along the rows in silence, but I sensed that he too heard the voices:

I thought that it could never happen to me: That accidents only happened to other people, distant and unrelated. I was supposed to be exempt from injury and harm. But it can happen to anybody, anytime. It's an imperfect world. There are people driving with extremely limited vision, faulty engines, no brakes, impaired by alcohol, drugs and stressed emotions. No buckles, no belts, no air bags, no helmets, no help. Worse, many drive under some distracting or debilitating influences: from alcohol to drugs to daydreams. There are people driving without insurance, without licenses, without training. There are people driving mad, driving bad, driving drunk, driving tired, driving to music, engaging in telephone conversations, eating meals and closing business deals. You never know who or what is on the road. So, take precautions. You are mortal. You can be killed at any moment. Be wise and beware.

On my way to work the next day, I drove behind student drivers. I noticed how they tended to overcompensate, exaggerate, or be tentative with their movements, a little out of sync with the ebb and flow of traffic.

There is a "bump and run" style in the business world, and people get their training from many different institutions. Not everybody is playing by the same rules. No one should assume that if they see a stop signal that everyone else sees "stop." One man's *stop* is another man's *go*.

• *Evaluating Performance*: Add "safe conduct" to the list of performance criteria; assassins should not be promoted, even in the name of high performance.

• *Career Pathing*: We see too many sad cases—dropouts, detours, dead ends, dead in tracks, dead on arrivals—without proper career recruitment, placement, paths, and promotion.

• *Outplacement*: When things don't work out, create safe landings whenever possible.

The new concept of corporate safety recognizes the risks inherent in human interaction and work-related activity, but seeks to minimize and eliminate flagrant violations of human rights, and prevent irreparable damage to people's minds, emotions, and careers. In the end, perhaps the best insurance against a corporate demagogue is a corporate decalogue.

New Concept of Corporate Security

Counterfeit leaders promise things they can't deliver. One such undeliverable is cradle-to-grave security. Counterfeits themselves are typically insecure, and insecurity loves company. And so the theme song of the campaign is, "Promise them anything."

• *Chronic insecurity*. Counterfeit leaders are often haunted by a sense of vulnerability or insecurity. They have guards at every gate, install intense and immense security systems (alarms, gates, sirens, wires, walls) to keep people in or out, because they live in fear, the force of counterfeit leadership. And they have low trust in the culture. And with fear and low trust, you need security systems.

We learn from *King Lear* that it's often difficult for a strong leader to create a strong successor, since an overbearing leader tends to demand loyalty that precludes an individual's own development.

The purpose of leadership is not to guarantee all consumers total satisfaction and safety. Nor is it to provide cradle-to-grave security for workers. Counterfeit leaders have always promised security. "You come with me," they say. "Trust me, believe in me, follow me, and your life will be safe and secure. I will provide for you. I will make sure that you are fully insured; and that come what may, the government will pay. You will be blessed with this blanket of security, enveloped, and wrapped in it." That is all part of the counterfeit plan—that all will be saved, that all will be secure.

We live in an age of warranties, guarantees, securities, safeties, and subsidies. Most of them aren't worth the paper they're written on. And yet, they are very important to people. Those things become so important that if the leader can even suggest that he can provide them, no matter what kind of track record he's got, people will vote him into office and follow him to their grave.

Security is a hollow promise—something that no one person can guarantee another. If you look at life as a test and a probation where there are many insecurities and inequities, no system, no organization, no government, no leader, no individual can guarantee security. Those who promise it are promising something that they cannot deliver. No employer, no boss, no parent can guarantee security.

The sources of security in a genuine leader are knowledge, confidence, discipline, temperance, integrity, character, love, mission, purity, chastity. Those are the only true forms of security, all other forms are counterfeit. One must literally carry it internally. You can't even put it in your purse or wallet. Money is not security. Possessions are not security. Even social friendships are not security. They may add to life, but they are not security.

The purpose of business is not to provide security—it is to provide "insecurity" in the form of incentive and opportunity.

Government is famous for promises of security, protection, and welfare. That's what all counterfeit leaders and dictators have promised. But, do they deliver? What are the proofs? What do we find when we visit? We see unfinished buildings and unfulfilled promises.

"Come one and all. Come what may, the government will pay." Citizens of every city and country want to believe that promise, and politicians in every city and country will make that promise, but they can't deliver on it.

Job one is to provide for the basic needs, the common welfare. You can't have enrichment without basic sustenance. You have to provide the basic needs first. Starving people don't go to the opera. Starving people are seeking bread and water, not education and enlightenment.

Any society is ripe for destruction when indulgence and an attitude of entitlement set in. The antidote is expressed by a noble anonymous writer:

I do not choose to be a common man. It is my right to be uncommon, if I can. I seek opportunity—not security. I don't wish to be a kept citizen, humbled and dulled by having the State look after me. I want to take the calculated risk: to dream and to build, to fail and to succeed. I refuse to barter incentive for a dole. I prefer the challenge of life to the guaranteed existence; the thrill of fulfillment to the stale calm of Utopia. I will not trade freedom for beneficence, nor my dignity for a handout. I will never cower before any master nor bend to any threat. It is my heritage to stand erect and unafraid; to think and act for myself; to enjoy the benefit of my creation; to face the world boldly and say, "This I have done."

Postscript

20-20 Hindsight:
Who's the Leader of the Band?

Among my earliest memories are two new arrivals: In 1950, when I was three years old, my mother brought home my baby sister from the hospital and allowed me to hold the dear infant; and soon thereafter, my father brought home our first television and allowed me to watch a program.

In hindsight, I can understand why these two events would be so indelibly etched in the emulsion of my memory. I would grow close to my sister and would grow up with television.

I sang the song of the Mickey Mouse Club: "Who's the leader of the club that's made for you and me?" And the answer:

"M-I-C-K-E-Y M-O-U-S-E." I aspired to be the leader of the club.

During the 50s, my parents played on the old hi-fi the music of the big band era. And so I aspired to be the leader of the band.

In the late 50s and early 60s, my heros were athletes, entertainers, and politicians. And so I aspired to be captain, star, and king.

But I noted in the 60s that leaders get killed, and during the 70s that many leaders were hated. So, in the 80s and for most of this decade, I've stayed home, on the sidelines, watching the big show on the big screen in Dolby "surround sound" stereo.

During this time, Mickey Mouse and my dream of leadership were kept alive only through the joyous childhoods of my three sons, with credits to Michael Eisner and the Disney cast of characters. Cartoons provided a convenient escape.

But all the while, I've been close to many leaders. As a magazine writer and editor, I've observed and interviewed hundreds of leaders and written and edited dozens of articles and books on leadership. Still, I suppose this book for me is a "coming out" of sorts. Many leaders, like me, have been hiding in closets. Many silent voices need to be heard. And some of our most vocal "countefeit leaders" need to be silenced, or at least challenged.

In hindsight, many things become clear and focused. We see the reality, the truth, of what in real time was unclear. We see people for who and what they are—their worth and warts. And we see with an amazing clarity who the real leaders of the club, band, class, team, gang, group, party, family, or company are, or were. On occasion, the recognition of authentic leadership comes late, too late to save the precious baby or band.

I sincerely hope that this book might inspire you to speak, write, and work for what you hold near and dear—your babies—so that every worthy band might play on and on and on.

ABOUT THE AUTHOR

Ken Shelton is chairman and editor-in-chief of Executive Excellence Publishing, publishers of newsletters, magazines, books, audio books, and CD-ROMs on personal and organizational development. The mission of Executive Excellence is to "help you find a wiser, better way to live your life and lead your organization."

Since 1984, Ken has served as editor of *Executive Excellence*, the world's leading executive advisory newsletter, and more recently *Personal Excellence*, a digest of the best thinking on personal and professional development. He is the editor of several books, including *In Search of Quality, A New Paradigm of Leadership*, and *The Best of Personal Excellence*.

For many years, he has enjoyed a close association with Stephen R. Covey, primarily as a writer and editor on various projects, including *The 7 Habits of Highly Effective People, Principle-Centered Leadership*, and *First Things First*. He is a former editor of *Utah Business* and *BYU Today* and a contributing writer to several other magazines.

Ken has a master's degree in mass and organizational communications from Brigham Young University and San Diego State University. In San Diego, California, he worked four years as a marketing communications specialist for General Dynamics Aerospace. He now lives in Provo, Utah, with his wife, Pam, and their three sons.

Beyond Counterfeit Leadership represents a creative synopsis of his writing and teaching, based on 30 years of professional experience, observation, and global travel.